AINMANES *of* KODAGU

AINMANES *of* KODAGU

Ancestral Homes of Kodagu and their Socio-Cultural Significance

Chinnappa Boverianda
and Nanjamma

NIYOGI
BOOKS

Published by
NIYOGI BOOKS
Block D, Building No. 77
Okhla Industrial Area, Phase-I
New Delhi-110 020, India
Tel: 91-11-26816301, 26818960
Email: niyogibooks@gmail.com
Website: www.niyogibooksindia.com

Cover illustration courtesy: N.S. Ponnappa

Editor: Sucharita Ghosh
Design: Shashi Bhushan Prasad

ISBN: 978-93-83098-43-9
Publication: 2014
Reprint: 2021

Printed at: Niyogi Offset Pvt. Ltd., New Delhi, India

TO THE PEOPLE OF KODAGU

OF

YESTERDAY, TODAY AND TOMORROW

Pommale Kodavuna

Kannodane kandano

Notina kodi poga

Suthinakadiyaga

The golden land of Kodagu

I have seen with my own eyes,

The more I see it, the more I desire it,

I will never tire of going around it

Pattole Palame by Nadikerianda Chinnappa

CONTENTS

PREFACE

This book is about the *ainmanes* (ancestral homes) of the native communities of Kodagu and about their socio-cultural significance. *Ainmanes* are architectural symbols and expressions of the heritage and culture of the people living in this rather remote and distinctive district of Karnataka state in South India. Each *ainmane* belongs to an *okka* (patrilineal clan) identified by its *mane peda* (house name). *Ainmanes* are unique to Kodagu and are regarded as 'heritage buildings'. They bear testimony to the strength and vitality of the *okkas* of Kodagu and their culture. These *ainmanes* and the traditions associated with them continue to play a significant role in the lives of the people of Kodagu in this, the twenty-first century.

The focus of this book is the traditional *ainmanes* of Kodagu that are functional. A 'traditional' *ainmane* has a verandah in front with carved, square, wooden pillars and wooden seats between the pillars, carved windows and door frames, and specific areas within the *ainmane* for the performance of rituals. A 'functional' one is where all the members of the *okka* gather to celebrate important ceremonies.

The origin of the *ainmanes* dates back many centuries. While the earliest dwellings in Kodagu began as simple mud huts, the more elaborate traditional *ainmanes* that are unique to Kodagu evolved since about 500 years ago. In fact, just about all of these early traditional *ainmanes* except for a few are no longer there. Some were rebuilt in the same traditional style, some were rebuilt as simple houses, and some not at all. The *ainmanes* that are in the traditional style and are functional—the focus of this book—date from about 150 to 250 years ago.

We felt the need to preserve, at least in writing and in visuals, information on these *ainmanes* and on the customs and rituals that continue to be followed there, as a legacy for future generations and as a record of local history.

While planning this project to collect information on the *ainmanes* of Kodagu and present it in a book and in a website that complements the book, we decided to cover the *ainmanes* of all the communities in Kodagu. We knew that this would be a time-consuming effort and would need ample resources and help. We were fortunate on both counts.

We consider ourselves blessed to have experienced the beauty of our land and the generosity of its people during the fieldwork for this project which covered a period of five years, from April 2003 to May 2008.

The book starts with an introduction and moves on to describe the *ainmanes* of Kodagu, their history, evolution, and current status. The structures in the *ainmane* complex and the architectural features of the *ainmane* are given in detail, along with floor plans of typical *ainmanes*. The socio-cultural significance of the *ainmane*, the traditions associated with it and the ceremonies and festivals held in it are also described.

The appendices give some background information that sets the *ainmane* in its geographical, historical and social context. They include a note on how we went about the fieldwork for this project, and descriptions of the land, a historical account of the people of Kodagu, and the system of land tenure in Kodagu. Also included in the appendices is brief information on the communities living in Kodagu, the languages spoken by the native communities, their religious beliefs, some of their unique ceremonies and social conventions, their folk songs and folk dances—all of which provide a glimpse of the socio-cultural life of the native communities of Kodagu.

Sketch maps of Kodagu showing the location of each *ainmane* we visited are provided in the appendices. The *ainmanes* are identified by numbers on the maps, and an accompanying index for each map lists the corresponding *okka* names of the *ainmanes*. Sketches of floor plans of the two types of *ainmanes* are given in an appendix.

The appendices include summary tables showing the number of traditional *ainmanes* (visited), the number of non-traditional *ainmanes*, the number of *okkas* with no *ainmanes*, as well as the total number of *okkas*, by community.

A time sequence of some important events in history is given in an appendix.

The information collected on each *ainmane* and *okka*, and photographs of the *ainmane* and of some of its interesting features are available in the website www.ainmanes.com that complements this book. This information can be retrieved by *okka* name, community name or village name.

As an illustration of the contents of the website, the information and photographs relating to two *ainmanes* are presented in an appendix.

All non-English words in the book are given in italics and are transliterated, but with no diacritical marks so as not to clutter the text. Diacritical marks for the transliterated words are given in the glossary. (Please see the note on transliteration and key to the transliteration on page 258.) The exceptions to this are proper names of persons and places where we have retained the conventional spellings.

INTRODUCTION

The cultural heritage of a people is a priceless legacy passed down from generation to generation. It is experienced in the current generation in both tangible and intangible ways. The tangible aspects of a culture include the habitats of the people as well as the costumes and artifacts that they use in their daily lives and rituals. The intangible aspects include their traditions, customs, festivals, rituals, language, folklore, songs and dances. The tangible and intangible aspects of a culture are so closely knit together that neither of these aspects can be observed or experienced in isolation.

An important part of the tangible heritage of the native communities of Kodagu is their architectural heritage—their *ainmanes* or ancestral homes. Each *ainmane*[1] belongs to an *okka*[2] (an exogamous patrilineal clan whose members claim descent from a common ancestor) which is identified by its distinctive *mane peda* (house or *okka* name). The *mane peda* identifies both the members of an *okka* and their *ainmane*. More details on *mane pedas* are given in Appendix 9.

1. '*Ain*' is believed to have come from Arabic and Persian into Hindi, Kannada, Kodava *thakk* and other Indian languages. '*Ain*' has many different shades of meaning, but all basically mean 'original, principal, prime' or 'genuine, true, real'.
2. *Okka* comes from '*ok*' which means one, one bond, unanimity or harmony.

The traditions, customs, festivals and rituals that are associated with the *ainmanes* are some of the intangible aspects of their unique culture and are an inalienable part of their heritage.

The *ainmanes* of many *okkas* are no longer there: some are in a state of disrepair or are in a dilapidated condition; and a few have in fact been rebuilt as simple houses.[3] The traditional *ainmanes* that are still standing today account for only about forty per cent of the *ainmanes* that were built in Kodagu.

It was our decision to visit and document only those 'traditional' *ainmanes* that are 'functional'. A 'traditional' *ainmane* is characterised

3. We have heard of *ainmanes* that have been dismantled or rebuilt as simple modern structures after our visit.

Chillavanda *ainmane*

by a *kayyale* (verandah) in front with carved, square, tapered, wooden pillars, *aimaras* (wooden bench-seats) between the pillars, ornately carved wooden windows and door frames, and specific areas within the *ainmane* for the performance of rituals. A 'functional' one is where all the members of the *okka* gather to celebrate important festivals, ceremonies and rituals such as *Karanang Kodpa*[4] (ritual offerings to ancestors), *Puthari* (harvest festival) or *Hari Seve* (worship of God Venkataramana).

It is estimated that currently there are about 1500 (1750) *okkas* in Kodagu and the total number of traditional *ainmanes* that are still standing and are functional (as defined above) is around 680. Kodavas, the largest among the native communities of Kodagu, with nearly 900 (1050) *okkas* account for around 430 of these *ainmanes.* There are about 270 (320) Gouda *okkas* which account for around 130 of the 680 *ainmanes.* All the other native communities put together—about 330 (380) *okkas*—account for the remaining nearly 120 *ainmanes.* (The figures within brackets include branches within an *okka* that have separate *ainmanes.*)

In about eighty per cent of the *okkas*, the total number of members[5] in the *okka* ranges from about 15 to 150. A few *okkas* have many more members. While in the past all the members of an *okka* lived together in their *ainmane* under one roof, that is no longer so. Currently the number of members of an *okka* who live in their *ainmane* ranges from none to fifteen, except in a few cases.

4. Also called *Karanang meedi beppa.*
5. It is interesting to note that in the past, the size of an *okka* was colloquially referred to in terms of the number of *thott kunji* (infants in cradles) in the *okka.* This perhaps speaks of the importance of progeny for the prosperity of the *okka.* Today, the size of an *okka* is measured in terms of the number of *ole* (hearths)—a count of the nuclear families in the *okka*, each of which uses a separate hearth to cook.

If the original *ainmane* was renovated or rebuilt with its front exterior retaining the traditional design of the typical *kayyale*, and if the *ainmane* was functional, it has been included in this project.

It may be noted that some *ainmanes*, mainly those of the smaller communities, are small and simple compared to most of those of the larger communities.

In a few *okkas* a split[6] in the *okka* has resulted in the total separation of the *bhagas* (branches) within the *okka*, with the breakaway *bhagas* building their own *ainmanes* on their portion of the *jamma* (ancestral) land or on land bought in a new location. Such an *okka* therefore has more than one *ainmane*, each belonging to a *bhaga* of the *okka*. If one of these *ainmanes*, invariably the original or the oldest among them, is considered the primary *ainmane* or *arvad*[7] of the *okka* (where all the *bhagas* meet at least once a year for *Karanang Kodpa*, *Puthari* or *Hari Seve*), we have visited and documented only the *arvad*. However, if a breakaway *bhaga* has an *ainmane* built in the traditional style, conducts all the important ceremonies in its own *ainmane* and does not join the other *bhagas* in their *arvad*, its *ainmane* is considered as functional and has been included in this project. Thus where there are two or more functional *ainmanes* built in the traditional style belonging to *bhagas* within the same *okka*, we have included all of them.[8]

In a few cases, *bhagas* that broke away from the original *okka* do not have *ainmanes* of their own and do not go to the original *ainmane* of that

6. The practice in the past was that when there was a bitter rift, the members who walked away from the *ainmane* would tear a piece of cloth into two (*muri keethuva*) and leave, saying, 'Just as these two pieces of cloth can never be made one again, we will never get back together with you!'

7. Also called *aroda*, from the Malayalam *arutam*, which means ancestral home.

8. Of late, in a few cases, there appears to be a patching up of relationships between *bhagas* of *okkas* who now get together in their *arvad* to celebrate festivals and ceremonies. This was often initiated and encouraged by the need to field a strong team from the *okka* for the very popular annual inter-*okka* hockey tournament among Kodava *okkas* that was started in 1997. Since then there have been similar festivals for cricket as well, among Kodavas, Goudas and other communities.

okka. In many of these cases there is not even 'familial' contact between the *bhagas*. However, it may be noted that in nearly all these cases, all the *bhagas* within the *okka* continue to use the original *thutengala* (cremation ground) or *kekola* (burial ground) of the *okka*.

In recent years, many old *ainmanes* that were in a state of disrepair have been rebuilt in brick and stone like simple modern houses. Although these houses might serve as the *ainmanes* of their *okkas*, they have not been included in this project because they are not in the traditional style. We hope that, at a later date, the second phase of this project will be undertaken—to collect information on *okkas* that have either rebuilt their *ainmanes* in a non-traditional style or do not have *ainmanes* now.

The description of the *ainmanes* of Kodagu, their evolution and their socio-cultural significance presented in this book is based on the picture that emerged when we analysed the information collected from the nearly 700 *ainmanes* that we visited. While there were individual divergences from the picture presented here (these divergences have been pointed out in the text), the overall impression is of a broad similarity in the physical features of the *ainmanes* all over Kodagu, and in the traditions, customs and rituals followed in them.

AINMANES OF KODAGU

The following is an extract from the English translation of the *Batte Pat*, a folk song that describes the *ainmane*. This song is sung during weddings and festivals to this day.[1]

Behold the lane leading to the house of this *okka*,
The lane is paved with *pandava*[2] slabs;
Behold the beauty of the boundary wall,
The wall built with stones from the jungle;
Behold the shed[3] at the gateway to the house,
The shed built with cut laterite[4] stones.
On crossing the gateway we are in the courtyard,
The courtyard where the oxen are tethered,

1. *Pattole Palame,* Nadikerianda Chinnappa, trans., Chinnappa, Boverianda M. and Nanjamma (New Delhi: Rupa & Co., 2003), pp. 88–89.
2. Rough granite stone slabs similar to the slabs used in dolmens of antiquity that are called *pandava pares* in Kodagu.
3. The *bakka pore* for the sentinel or guard.
4. Laterite is a clay and pebble substance, found as a natural deposit, which oxidises into a hard block when cut and left to dry.

Mookachanda *ainmane*

The courtyard paved with polished stones.
Behold the work on the steps to the house,
The steps built with ruby-like stones;
On climbing the steps we see the verandah,
The decorated verandah we walk across.
On crossing the verandah we see the doorway,
The carved doorway we pass through.
Behold the beauty of the house of this *okka*!
Five hundred carpenters worked on it for five years;
The golden wall plates, the silver beams,
The four *aimara* slabs, and carved pillars.
What are the figures carved on the pillars?
Figures of birds, figures of snakes,
The figure of God Vamana is carved,

The figure of a tiger, lord of the rocky cave,
The figure of a wild bison in the forest,
The figure of a barking deer is carved,
The figure of a crowing cock is carved,
The figure of a mewing cat is carved,
The figure of God Nadatha[5] is carved.
The thatch of the house is like a silken cover.
Its walls are plastered with four kinds of mud—
White mud that is white as milk,
Yellow mud, the colour of saffron,
Black mud, dark as eye-black,
And red mud, the colour of drops of blood,
With these four kinds of mud the walls are plastered,
The walls of the central hall, the walls of the verandah,
The walls of the verandah and the wall in front.
On these walls are painted pictures,
A picture of the Sun god is drawn,
A picture of a lotus flower in water,
A picture of a sword that cuts is drawn,
A picture of a *kembathi*[6] flower is drawn,
A picture of a white tortoise in water,
A picture of a creeping snake is drawn,
A picture of a beehive in a red pot,
A picture of the Nandi[7] bull is drawn,
And a picture of her own husband,

5. The snake deity, also known as Natha.
6. Hibiscus.
7. Name of the bull that is Shiva's *vahana* (mount).

Along with it, a picture of herself,
These, the lady of the house has drawn.

Ainmanes are the ancestral homes of the native communities of Kodagu. They are found all over Kodagu and are an integral part of their architectural and cultural heritage. The *ainmane* is the house that an ancestor built on land that belonged to the *okka*. *Ain* means 'original' and *mane* means 'house'. It is also called a *balya mane* (big house) since it is a large house with many rooms which, in the past, accommodated all the nuclear families of the *okka* who lived together in their *ainmane* like a large joint family.

The native communities of Kodagu include the *mula nivasis* (earliest inhabitants)—the Kurubas, Kudiyas, Kembattis, Kodavas and Ammas; the very early immigrants to Kodagu—Jains and Goudas; later immigrants such as Okkaligas, Koleyas, Koyavas, Hajamas, Airis, Madivalas, Gollas, Heggades, Kaniyas, Jagir Thurkas and Bunts; as well as the converted Jamma Mapilles. (Appendix 5 has brief notes on the communities in Kodagu.)

The focal centre of each *okka* belonging to the native communities of Kodagu is its *ainmane*. In many ways the *ainmane* serves as a repository of the early history and collective memories of the *okka* as well as of the customs and traditions of the community to which it belongs. While these customs and traditions have evolved (and continue to evolve), influenced by time and events that have shaped the history of the region, the noticeably distinct culture of these communities of Kodagu has to a large extent been preserved in their *ainmanes*.

Kodavas and most of the other native communities of Kodagu deify their ancestors. They pay obeisance and make ritual food offerings to them periodically. The *ainmane* that their ancestors built and lived in, is revered as a hallowed precinct. The founder or the earliest-remembered ancestor of the *okka* is worshipped as the *karanava.*[8] In some *okkas*, a female ancestor, the *karanachi*, is worshipped if she is the earliest-remembered ancestor or is renowned for something important that she had done for the *okka* (for example, getting the *ainmane* built).

Some *okkas* have more than one *karanava*. If the earliest-remembered *karanava* had no children and the members of the *okka* are descendants of his brother/patrilineal cousin, the latter is also considered a *karanava.* There are instances where the ancestor who built the first *ainmane*[9] or a famous hero is regarded as a *karanava.*

EVOLUTION OF THE *AINMANE*

As early as the eighth century AD, probably even earlier, the *mula nivasis* lived in simple mud huts, with sloping bamboo and reed roofs thatched with wild grass, in *ur guppes* (village settlements, *ur* meaning 'village' and *guppe* 'cluster'). It is very likely that the earliest of these used very little wood, if at all. Simple openings in the walls perhaps served as entrance doors and windows. Even today, many cowsheds and attics in some *ainmanes* have such simple openings in their mud walls that serve as doors and windows.

All the members of an *ur guppe* shared the natural resources of the area and lived together in harmony. Each *okka* cultivated its own piece of land and grazed its cattle on common pastures. The *okkas* helped each other with manual labour while sowing, harvesting and thatching roofs—a practice called *pache pani* (barter of labour), which continues to

8. Also referred to as *karana* (literally 'cause', meaning 'origin'), *guru karana*, ('preceptor/guide' who is the origin), or *karana purusha* (the original person).

9. He is also called the *mann mane thangnava*—which means 'the one who built the mud-house-shelter'.

be prevalent in some areas of Kodagu. Members of an *ur guppe* also shared a common *thutengala/kekola* (cremation/burial ground).

It is believed that since about 600 years ago, the *paleyagaras* (local chieftains) broke up the *ur guppes* and gave each *okka* 'rights' over large tracts of land nearby so that more land could be brought under cultivation and more produce could be collected as revenue. This included wetland for cultivation of rice, land for grazing cattle and forest land.

Over time, each *okka* built a bigger, isolated house on its land and all the members of the *okka* lived together under one roof in this house. These houses were simple ones, with mud walls and sturdy tree trunks for pillars. Horizontal rough-cut wooden cross-beams laid over the pillars supported the triangular roof trusses built with rafters and reapers of bamboo and reed. The sloping roof was thatched with wild grass or rice straw. Wood that was available in abundance was used for doors and windows. This house, called a *balya mane* (large house), was probably the origin of the *ainmane* of the *okka*.[10] These early *ainmanes* are believed to have been built after people moved out of the *ur guppes*.

All the *okkas* who had lived together in an *ur guppe* continued to maintain close and friendly ties with each other. Some even continued to share the same *thutengala/kekola* that they had shared when they were members of the same *ur guppe*. The earliest settlers in a village proudly call themselves '*ninda kula*' or '*thangi ninda kula*' (clans who settled) and refer to those who came later as '*banda kula*' (clans who came). They are recognised by the temporal order in which they settled in the village as '*ondane kula*' (the first *okka* to settle in that village), '*dandane kula*' (the second *okka* to settle), etc.

FACING PAGE: Roof with rough-cut wooden beams and bamboo rafters found in old *ainmanes*

10. Some *okkas* continue to refer to their *ainmanes* as *balya manes*.

When an *okka* moved away from an *ur guppe* to an isolated *ainmane*, there was a need felt for a friendly and caring *okka* to call upon for help during good and bad times. This *okka*, usually a neighbouring one that had originally lived in the same *ur guppe*, was called its *aruva*[11] *okka*. A few *okkas* have more than one *aruva okka*. The *aruva okka* could be from any community, although it was most often from the same community. This mutually agreed upon arrangement to help each other, called '*aruvame*', is permanent and usually reciprocal. Even today the *aruva okka* plays an important, if ceremonial, role during the wedding and death ceremonies in the *okka* for which it is the *aruva*.

All the members of an *okka* lived together in their *ainmane* and shared the work on the land attached to it. Income from a portion of the ancestral property was often set apart for the maintenance of the *ainmane*, for expenses related to the ceremonies conducted there and for maintenance of destitute members of the *okka* who lived in the *ainmane*. This practice continues to this day.

When an *okka* grew and more living space was required, some of the nuclear families of the *okka* built *ale pores*[12] (dwelling huts) also called *pora manes* (outhouses) for themselves, around their *ainmane* and close to it. Some built houses on land belonging to the *okka* in *koppas* (hamlets) further away, and these were called *koppath mane* or *koppa*. Originally these were probably shelters built by the *okka* for temporary stay when grazing cattle and looking after their land in those areas.

Later, as the *okkas* grew even larger and the need for privacy and independence became stronger, some of the wealthier nuclear families

11. *Aruva* stands for *ariyuvava*, which means 'one who knows'.

12. *Ale* appears to be the Malayalam *thadbhava* (form derived from Sanskrit) of *alaya*, which means 'dwelling', and *pore* means 'hut'.

acquired land in locations that were quite dispersed and not adjacent to the land belonging to the *okka*, and built their own individual houses there. However, members of all these families who lived away from their *ainmane* assembled in their *ainmane* for ceremonies and festivals.

The *ainmane* of an *okka* was built on its *jamma*[13] land, with its front facing east towards the rising sun, with a few exceptions.

When they could afford it, the *okkas* rebuilt their *ainmanes*. The rebuilt *ainmanes* were large imposing structures of mud and wood. They had wooden ceilings with sloping roof trusses made of wooden beams, rafters and reapers, and were thatched with rice straw. The woodwork in many of them was finely crafted with doorways and windows displaying beautiful carvings by skilled artisans from neighbouring Malabar (in north Kerala), some of whom had migrated to Kodagu even before the advent of the Kodagu rajas (kings of the Haleri dynasty) in the 1600s.

The rebuilt *ainmane* was usually built on the base of the older *ainmane* or close to it. There are instances where the *okka* rebuilt its *ainmane* a little away from its former site because the original location was considered to be unlucky for the *okka*. In a few cases, an *okka* was forced to move its *ainmane* to another village, because the raja found the *okka* becoming too powerful in the area where its *ainmane* was originally situated and, fearing that power, gave the *okka* alternative *jamma* land in a far-away village. In one case it was because the raja wanted to build a palace at the site of the *ainmane*. There are rare cases where an *okka* exchanged its *jamma* land and *ainmane* with that of another *okka*.

13. Ancestral property of the *okka* that is hereditary for the *okka*, jointly owned by its members and nominally taxed. From the Sanskrit *janma* which means 'a life-time'. See Appendix 4, Land Tenure.

The architecture of the *ainmane* evolved to include the characteristic features of what is now considered a 'traditional' *ainmane*—a typical *kayyale* (verandah) in front with solid, square, carved, wooden pillars tapering upwards, often with beautifully crafted carvings on the capitals on top of the pillars; *aimaras* (bench-seats) of solid, polished slabs of wood laid over low parapets of mud built between the pillars; a sturdily built wooden *machi*[14] (ceiling of wooden planks plastered with mud on top to form the floor of the attic) resting on horizontal joists supported by the pillars; and a sloped roof thatched with rice straw. The *kayyale* invariably has a window with a beautifully carved wooden frame, inset with an intricately carved wooden screen and a carved wooden panel on top. The main door in the *kayyale* that leads to the *nellakki nadu bade* (central hall) has an ornate, carved door frame with a carved wooden panel above it. Doors from the central hall lead to the rooms of the *ainmane*. The mud floor of the *ainmane* is stamped down and washed with a mixture of cow-dung and water. This type of traditional *ainmane* with a single roof is called an *othe pore*, a one-winged house (*othe* literally means 'single' and *pore* is a 'hut' or 'thatched roof'). See Appendix 16 for a sketch of the floor plan of a typical *othe pore*.

The other type of traditional *ainmane*, which is not as common as the *othe pore* is a *mund mane*,[15] at the centre of which is a *mund*, a square,

14. In the folk songs of Kodagu, a *machi mane* (house with a wooden ceiling and attic) is attributed to a well-to-do *okka*.

15. Of the 683 traditional *ainmanes* we have seen, 85 are *mund manes*. These are somewhat similar to the 'courtyard houses' found in many parts of India, especially the *nal kett* (*nal* means 'four' and *kett* means 'structure' in Malayalam) *tharavads*, the ancestral houses of the Nairs and Namboodris in Kerala; the *malla illu* (*malla* means 'large' and *illu* means 'house' in Tulu) ancestral homes of Tulunad; and the *thotti mane* or *dodda mane* (*thotti* means 'trough', *dodda* means 'large' and *mane* means 'house' in Kannada) houses of Karnataka. The main difference is that the *mund mane* in Kodagu has *aimaras* around the *mund* and in the *kayyale*—a feature not found in the other houses. Besides, square pillars tapering upwards are unique to the houses in Kodagu.

Machimada *ainmane*

sunken inner courtyard open to the sky, with a hallway, the *nellakki nadu bade*, on all four sides around it. The carved pillars at the four corners of the *mund* are similar to the ones in the front *kayyale*, with carved capitals and *aimaras* between the pillars along the edges of the *mund*. The rooms of the *ainmane* are situated around this inner hallway with doors leading into them. It is said that in the past, a *mund mane* was a symbol of a *thakkame* (hereditary leadership role, see Appendix 10 on *Thakkame*) held by the *okka* or of a special honour granted to it by the raja, and could only be built with his permission. See Appendix 16 for a sketch of the floor plan of a typical *mund mane*.

Thus the architecture of the *ainmanes* evolved from (a) simple mud huts clustered in *ur guppes*, with crude openings in the walls for doors and windows and sloping bamboo and reed roofs thatched with wild grass, to (b) isolated houses with mud walls, mud floors, sturdy tree trunks for pillars, wooden doors and windows and sloping bamboo and reed roofs thatched with wild grass or rice straw, to (c) what are now called 'traditional' *ainmanes*, with mud walls; *kayyales* with square, carved, wooden pillars tapering upwards supporting the attic, *aimaras* between the pillars, beautifully carved wooden door frames and windows; mud floors washed with a mixture of cow-dung and water; wooden ceilings of cross-beams; and sloping roofs with wood rafters and reapers, thatched with rice straw.

Many of these traditional *ainmanes* burnt down over time due to accidental fires (caused by sparks from the open wood stoves in the kitchen hearth igniting the thatched roofs) or when they were set on fire by enemies. In the distant past, when *nads* (administrative units, each of which consists of a group of villages) in Kodagu were under the control of local chieftains called *paleyagaras/nayakas* who fought amongst themselves over territory and power, it was common practice to set *ainmanes* of enemies on fire. Later, some *ainmanes* were burnt down by Tippu Sultan's soldiers.[16]

With the passage of time, some of these traditional *ainmanes* collapsed due to incessant heavy rains. Some were dismantled because they had deteriorated, either due to lack of resources to maintain them (often because very few members were left in the *okka*), or because of neglect by members, many of whom no longer lived in their *ainmanes*. By tradition, an *ainmane* was never allowed to collapse or fall in ruins. If it was in a state of disrepair it had to be dismantled, after which it was rebuilt, often on the same base and in the same style.

16. Informants in eleven *ainmanes* that we visited told us that their original *ainmanes* along with the inmates were burnt down by Tippu Sultan's soldiers. Tippu Sultan, the ruler of the neighbouring province of Mysore, led many armed campaigns against Kodagu in the late 1700s, in an attempt to subdue the people of the region.

Ammeyanda *ainmane.* (This ainmane was dismantled around 2008)

When the size of the *okka* was large enough and sufficient resources were available, some of the *ainmanes* that got burnt, fell down or were dismantled, were either rebuilt in the traditional style, exactly as they were earlier or even more sturdily, on the base of the old *ainmane* or near it. In some cases the original *mund mane* was rebuilt as an *othe pore.* The thatched roof of the *ainmane* has in most cases been replaced by clay tiles (introduced in Kodagu in the late 1800s) and the flooring in many *ainmanes* has now been partly or wholly cemented.

The impression one now gets is that where an *ainmane* is not well maintained, it could be due to any number of reasons—neglect by the younger generation that has moved away for economic reasons; disagreements between members on the use of the common resources of the *okka*; lack of resources; or simply because its members do not appreciate the social, cultural and historical importance of their *ainmane.*

In recent years, however, many old *ainmanes* that were in a bad state have been replaced by simple houses that are smaller in size and are made of brick and mortar to make maintenance easier, so that the *okka* still has a common place where its members can assemble and conduct the traditional ceremonies and rituals associated with the *ainmane.* Some *ainmanes* that have fallen or were dismantled have not been rebuilt at all.

STRUCTURES AND AREAS IN THE *AINMANE* COMPLEX

The *ainmane* is the hub of a composite cluster of structures and designated areas, all of which are located on the *jamma* land of the *okka* and many of which are still found in the vicinity of the *ainmane.* They include the following—listed roughly in the order in which one comes across them when one visits an *ainmane.* (Detailed descriptions of most of these are given in the text that follows.)

Kalloni - Stone-paved lane that leads to the *ainmane.*
Ubba - Gate made of a pair of stone posts and bamboo poles.
Bale bakka - Clearing by the side of the path leading to the *ainmane.*
Bakka pore - Guard's lookout hut at the top of the lane leading to the *ainmane.*
Patti - Forecourt or yard in front of the *ainmane.*
Kall boti - Stone post in the centre of the *patti* and/or in the *kala.*
Kala - Threshing yard, usually located to the south of the *ainmane.*
Kanathare - Circular well, usually located to the north-east of the *ainmane.*

Gudda - Bathing shed located outside the main house in a separate roofed structure.

Ale pore - Outhouse, a structure close to the *ainmane* built for additional living space.

Pathaya - Large wooden structure for storing harvested paddy.

Atha kott - Cattle shed, located near the *ainmane.*

Koundi kott - Shed where *koundi* (quilts placed on the back of pack-oxen) are stored.

Ora kott/Meypa kott - Shed where harvested paddy is pounded manually to make rice.

Karana thare - Ancestor platform, a precursor to the *kaimada.*

Kaimada - Shrine to ancestors, near the *ainmane.*

Beera/Veera kall - Carved hero stone commemorating a hero.

Gudi - Small shrine dedicated to a god/goddess or to a spirit-deity.

Nele/Sthana of a spirit-deity - Sacred platform dedicated to a spirit-deity.

Thutengala - Cremation ground of the *okka.*

Kekola - Burial ground of the *okka.*

***Kalloni*:** A narrow, steep *kalloni* (stone-paved lane) with angular bends[17] and high stone walls leads up from the paddy fields below to the stone-paved *patti* (yard) in front of the *ainmane*. The *ainmane* was strategically located, usually on an elevated area, and was built like a fortress with a steep, winding lane leading to it for good reasons—to overlook the surrounding area and keep a lookout for foes and marauders. Even if the *ainmane* has another approach, it is the *kalloni* that is used during traditional ceremonies.

17. Folk songs refer to this as a '*mummadakandoni*', which literally means *oni* (lane) with *moond* (three) *madak* (folds or bends).

***Ubba*:** A gate or stile with a pair of tall, flat, granite posts (one on each side of the path) with a set of three or four matching holes through which long bamboo poles are slid in and out. It is located at the top of the lane to the *ainmane* at the entrance to the *bakka pore* or to the *patti* and, in the past, served as a gate or barrier to control the passage to the *ainmane*. *Ubbas* are seen in a few *ainmanes* even today.

***Bale bakka*:** Clearing by the side of the path leading to the *ainmane*, where *bale* (banana) stems are staked to the ground for the *bale birudu* (honour) ceremony during weddings (when a member of the groom's or bride's party is given the honour of cutting the banana stems).

***Bakka pore*:** In the past, the entrance to some *ainmanes* was through a *bakka pore* (guard's lookout hut, *bakka* means 'guarded passage' and *pore*

FACING PAGE: *Kalloni*—Pongera *ainmane*

Ubba—Thumbera *ainmane*

means 'hut') located at the top of the lane leading to the *ainmane*. Only a few of these *bakka pores* have survived the ravages of time. The *bakka pore* is a fortified structure with an arched or rectangular entrance to the yard in front of the *ainmane*, and rooms on either side of the entrance. These rooms, that originally served as guards' rooms, were later used as outhouses, cattle sheds or stables.

***Patti*:** Passing through the *bakka pore* one steps on to the stone-paved *patti* or yard in front of the *ainmane*, paved with dressed laterite or rough granite stone slabs. In some *ainmanes* this yard is enclosed by the *bakka pore* in front and by stables, storerooms and servants' quarters on the other two sides. If the yard is not paved, a narrow path paved with flat stones leads from the *ubba* to the steps in front of the *ainmane* for people to walk on when the ground is wet and slushy during the rainy season.

FACING PAGE: *Patti*—Pattacheravanda *ainmane*

Bakka pore—Chendrimada *ainmane*

Occasionally, instead of the stone-paved path, flat-topped circular stones called *batte kall* (*batte* means 'path' and *kall* means 'stone') are placed in a line across the yard.

***Kall boti*:** Many *ainmanes* have a *kall boti* (stone post) in the centre of the *patti*. This post is about one-and-a-half to two-and-a-half metres high and its top is often carved with figures of a lotus, crescent moon, seated bull, etc. A *kall boti* may also be planted in the *kala* (threshing yard) adjoining the *ainmane*. The *kall boti* is used to tether oxen and, during the threshing season, as a post around which cattle are driven to stamp on and thresh harvested sheaves of paddy spread on the ground. It is also used for rituals during *Puthari*, the harvest festival. The *kall boti* is a focal point of the *patti* and is considered an adornment for the

Kall boti—Charamanda *ainmane*

yard, as in the saying, '*Pattik chingara kallra boti*' (the stone post is an adornment for the yard).[18] Instead of a *kall boti*, some *ainmanes* have a *marathra boti* (wooden post) which needs replacement whenever it breaks.

There are no *kall botis* in some areas of Kodagu because their presence is considered to be disrespectful to the deities in the temples nearby. Such is the case, for example, in Nalnad where the Igguthappa temple is located, in Beth near the Makki Sarthavu shrine and in Beckesodlur near the Mandathavva temple.

***Kanathare*:** Circular well, usually located to the north-east of the *ainmane*. It is lined on the inside with cut laterite stones and has a wall built of stones along its rim. Two pillars on the stone wall support a wooden cross-bar, from which hangs a pulley that is used to draw water in a *bindige*—a bronze or copper pot. The Ganga *puje* (Ganga stands for 'water' and *puje* means 'ritual worship') is performed here by the new bride and by the mother of a newborn baby.

***Gudda*:** Bathing shed located outside the main house in a separate roofed structure. The bathing area is paved with rough granite slabs. A large vessel in the shed holds water that is heated using firewood. The *gudda* is also used for bathing rituals during weddings.

***Ale pore*:** Outhouse, a structure close to the *ainmane* built for additional living space. In the past, persons under ritual pollution (for example, a woman during her monthly periods) stayed here for the duration of the

18. There is another saying, '*Boti illatha kalathrannake*' (like a yard with no *boti*), to describe a person or task with no focus.

pollution. Sections of the *ale pore* were sometimes used to house servants of the household, or as a cowshed or stable.

***Pathaya*:** The *pathaya* used for storing harvested paddy is located by the side of the *ainmane*. It is a wooden structure with a sloped roof, built on stilts made of mud and stone to keep the stored paddy dry during the rains. In some cases, the *pathaya* is a room with wood-panelled walls located inside the *ainmane*, either on the main floor or in the *atta* (attic). In rare cases it is built of mud and is called a *mambathaya* (*mann pathaya*, a mud *pathaya*).

***Atha kott*:** Cattle shed located near the *ainmane*. Cattle were important assets of the *okka*. Cows provided milk for consumption. Oxen were used to plough the paddy fields of the *okka* and as pack animals to carry loads to

FACING PAGE: *Karana thare*—Thumbera *ainmane*

Pathaya—Kalimada *ainmane*

distant markets and to carry votive rice offerings to temples. Cattle dung was used as manure in the paddy fields of the *okka* and to periodically smear the mud floors of the *ainmane*.

***Karana thare*:** The *karana thare*, also called the *karana kala*, is the sacred ancestor platform near the *ainmane*, located at the foot of a sap-exuding tree.[19] It is a simple raised earthen structure on which a rough-hewn stone, symbolic of the *karanava*, is embedded. Rituals associated with paying obeisance to ancestors are conducted here. In most *okkas* the *karana thare* has been replaced by the *kaimada*.

***Kaimada*:** The *kaimada* is the sacred shrine to ancestors. It is generally located near the *ainmane*, often next to the grave of the *karanava*.

19. Since milk is equated to *amritha*, the nectar of immortality, a tree that exudes milk-like sap is considered to be sacred.

FACING PAGE: Ancestor images in wood—Kanganda *kaimada*.

Kaimada—Nadikerianda *ainmane*

Sometimes it is located close to the paddy fields of the *okka*. It is a small, square (about 3 m x 3 m), four-pillared, east-facing, roofed structure built on a raised plinth and enclosed by a low wall. Inside it is a small, raised, covered altar within which is placed a lamp made of clay, stone or bell-metal that is lit with wicks dipped in oil. Space is provided around the altar for ritual circumambulation. During festivals and ancestor propitiation ceremonies food offerings to the ancestors are placed in the *kaimada*.

In some *kaimadas*, small crude figurines of clay, stone, wood, or metal, are placed in the altar. These figurines represent the *karanava*—the first male ancestor of the *okka* or the one who built the *ainmane*, the *karanachi*—the first female ancestor, and any other famous ancestor—usually a *pade beera* (war hero). In a few *ainmanes*, the *kaimada* is also a shrine to the *kula devathe* (deity of the *okka*).

In some areas there are no *kaimadas*. We were told that this is because of the proximity of the *ainmane* to a shrine.[20]

Gouda *okkas* do not have *kaimadas*. Some of them have a *devara gudi* (shrine to the *kula devaru*—deity of the *okka)* or *devva kottadi* (shrine to spirits) near the *ainmane*.

Beera/Veera kall: These are large, carved stone tablets, commemorating heroes of the *okka* who won fame in ancient battles or hunts. They are generally erected in or near the *kaimada*. Most often the tablets have carvings showing the hero in a battle scene or fighting a tiger. These carved stones are more common in the northern areas of Kodagu.[21]

20. It would appear that when there is a shrine to a god/deity nearby, the *kaimada* is not needed, probably because ancestors are worshipped as intermediaries between humans and gods/deities.

21. In Surlabhi we saw numerous *beera kall* in the *ur mand* by the roadside, placed there in honour of the men of that area who had died in battles with intruders—one stone per *okka* that had lost one or more members. These stones are worshipped during *Kail Polud*. Once in twenty-one years there is a big festival when the spirits symbolised by the stones are worshipped.

Beera kall—near Porimanda *ainmane*

***Nele/Sthana/Gudi* of spirit-deities**: Not far from the *ainmane*, on the *jamma* land of the *okka*, are simple unhewn stones that symbolise spirit-deities such as Puda, Kuliya, Natha, etc., planted on earthen platforms, each under a sap-exuding tree. The platform, called the *nele* or *sthana* of the deity, denotes the spot where the deity was established. Sometimes there is a small *gudi* (shrine) to the deity. Natha, the snake god of fertility is represented by a stone with serpents or a hooded cobra carved on it. The spirit-deities are propitiated annually and on special occasions.

Thutengala/Kekola: Every *okka*, barring a few exceptions, has its own separate *thutengala/kekola* (cremation/burial ground) which is usually located in a wooded area on the *jamma* land of the *okka*, some distance away from the *ainmane*. It is here that all adult members of the *okka* are cremated or buried when they die and some of the funeral rites are performed. However, if a person desires to be cremated or buried

Mandana-murthi's *nele/sthana*—Chandangada *ainmane*

on private land owned by his/her family when he/she dies, that wish is respected.

While cremation is more common, burial is adopted in some *okkas* and areas of Kodagu. If a person is famous he/she is buried, and a tomb is erected for him/her, usually near the *kaimada*. During the time of the Kodagu rajas, high officials in the court or those who had shown bravery in wars were honoured by permitting erection of the image of a large *basava*[22] on their tombs. Even where cremation is the norm, if there is a shrine close to the *ainmane*, or if a temple festival is in progress, the dead are buried in the *thutengala* to prevent smoke from the funeral pyre to desecrate the deity.

22. The bull Nandi, mount of God Shiva, worshipped by the Kodagu rajas who were Lingayaths.

Koravanda graveyard

Infants and unmarried youth are not cremated and there are separate areas in the *thutengala* for their burial.

In some *okkas*, an area called *masni*[23] *kad* is set apart in the *thutengala/kekola* for the cremation/burial[24] of a married 'daughter' of the *okka* if she dies in her natal home and her body cannot be taken to her conjugal *okka* (where she should be cremated/buried by right), either because of distance or due to heavy rains and floods that make crossing of streams or rivers difficult. It was (and still is) customary for a married girl to visit the *ainmane* of her natal *okka* during festive occasions and for childbirth (especially that of her first child) if her parents live in the *ainmane*. Maternal death during childbirth was not

23. From the Kannada word *masana* derived from the Sanskrit *smashana*, meaning 'cemetery'.

24. A woman who dies in an advanced stage of pregnancy is buried along with the foetus.

uncommon in the past. This practice of cremation/burial in the *masni kad* is prevalent to this day.

In certain parts of Kodagu, neighbouring *okkas* share a *thutengala/kekola*. This is a carry-over from the time when the *okkas* lived close to each other in an *ur guppe* and shared a common cremation/burial ground.

Jamma Mapilles bury their dead in the burial ground attached to their mosques.

ARCHITECTURAL FEATURES OF *AINMANES*

There are three kinds of *ainmanes*:

1. *Othe pore* - the most common kind—a rectangular, one-winged structure;
2. *Mund mane/nal kett mane/thotti mane* - a square structure built around a *mund* (a square, sunken, inner courtyard open to the sky); and
3. *Madak mane* - L-shaped structure (rarely found these days).

All traditional *ainmanes* are somewhat similar in external appearance, the characteristic feature being the typical *kayyale* in front with square, wooden pillars tapering upwards and *aimara* seats between the pillars. Despite this broad similarity, most *ainmanes* have their own distinguishing features. With a few exceptions, all of them face the east towards the rising sun. Some *ainmanes* face the west or north[25] because a shrine (whose presiding deity is worshipped by the *okka*), or the paddy fields of the *okka* (which they wish to oversee) are in that direction, or because the raja required

25. No *ainmane* faces the south, since it is believed that the abode of Yama, the god of death, is in the south, a direction that is therefore considered inauspicious. For the same reason there is no entrance door to the *ainmane* on its south side.

the *okka* (whose *ainmane* was located near the border of the kingdom) to keep a lookout for invaders from that direction.

Traditional *ainmanes* are generally large. The larger among them range in size from about 10 m to 20 m both in length and width. *Mund manes* are usually square, while *othe pores* are rectangular in shape. Sketches of the floor plans of a typical *othe pore* and a typical *mund mane* are given in Appendix 16.

The *ainmane* was built on a raised plinth (mud platform) and had no foundation below the ground level. Wood shavings from the bark of the *kulur mavu*[26] tree found in the forests of Kodagu were soaked in a vat of water for many days to ferment into a sticky resin. This resin was mixed with mud to form a wet mixture, which when dry became hard and strong like concrete. A large quantity of this wet mixture was applied in layers to build a rectangular platform, generally to a height of about one-and-a-quarter metres above ground level. This mud platform was allowed to settle and consolidate over a period of one summer and one rainy season to form the base on which the *ainmane* was built. Laterite blocks were sometimes used at the corners of the base to provide a firm support for the pillars above. Space was left for a narrow, open walking path called a *thethi* or *eriya* that extended all around the four outer walls of the house, along the top edge of the raised platform.

The walls of these *ainmanes* were built of mud.[27] The outer walls are more than 30 cm thick, and were built to be sturdy enough to withstand the ravages of time and the elements, especially the heavy monsoon rains.

26. Machilus tree (*Priscia macrantha*). This tree is fast disappearing because its bark, used as a binding agent in incense sticks, is highly valued and is costlier than sandalwood. Once the bark is removed, the tree dies.

27. We have come across one or two rare exceptions where the *ainmane* was rebuilt in stone and was called a *kall mane* (stone house).

Likeness of an old folk painting on wall: A tiger attacking a deer (Bacharaniyanda Annaiya's painting)

In one *ainmane* that we visited the walls are about 50 cm thick. Lumps of the same wet mixture of mud and resin (as was used for the base of the house) were slapped in a row to form the base of a wall. When one row of lumps dried, the next row was slapped on top of it to build the wall up in layers. Alternately, the walls were built with a mixture of mud, paddy husk, resin and water. This mixture too has good binding properties that insulate the house from heat and cold and prevent the walls from cracking. These houses with thick, strong walls built on high platforms sheltered the inmates from the severe monsoon rains and provided them protection from the wild animals inhabiting the surrounding jungles.

In the early days, the walls were plastered with cow-dung mixed with *masi* (black soot from burnt hay). Later, chalk-like *bolle mann* (white mud) from riverbanks was used. The mud, moulded into balls, was brought once in two or three years and soaked in water to be used to whitewash

Likeness of an old folk painting on wall: *Puthari kol* dance (Bacharaniyanda Annaiya's painting)

the walls of the house every year before the *Puthari* festival. This mud was mixed with powdered eggshells to enhance the white tone of the wash. In the olden days, women painted pictures of flowers, birds and animals on the walls with vegetable colours—mainly red, black and yellow—mixed with the fine white mud. The brush for painting was made by pounding one end of a twig of the wild *munde*[28] plant or the stem of a *thora*[29] leaf. Unfortunately, there are no remains of these paintings that are described so beautifully in the *Batte Pat* song (Song for the Way).[30] Many elderly people whom we met during our fieldwork had heard of such paintings but few had seen them.[31]

28. *Pandanus odaratissimus.*

29. *Polygonum chinense.*

30. See pp. 21–24 for a translated extract from the *Batte Pat.*

31. The folk paintings of late Bacharaniyanda Annaiya (1924–2000) very likely resemble these old wall paintings.

Each of the four outer walls of the *ainmane* has a hole, about an inch in diameter, at eye level. These holes, called *thombe kann* (*thombe* means 'heart' and *kann* means 'small hole' or 'orifice'), are aligned in facing walls. It is believed that if evil spirits happen to enter the house they will be induced to flit out through the hole in the opposite wall and not remain in the house and cause harm to the residents.

The mud floor of the *ainmane* was laid over the raised platform that formed its base. A thick layer of the same wet mixture of mud and resin as was used for the platform was used for the floor. It was stamped down, hardened and washed with a mixture of cow-dung and water—a common practice in rural India. This mixture consolidates the floor, giving it a smooth finish. Cow-dung is considered to be a ritual purifier and is believed to act as a disinfectant. Over the course of time, the floors of at least some rooms in most of the *ainmanes* have been cemented to reduce the labour involved in periodically daubing cow-dung on the mud floors to maintain them—a chore for the women of the house. Cow-dung washed mud floors may still be seen in many *ainmanes*.

The *machi* (ceiling) of the *ainmane* was built to be very strong with long, heavy beams and cross-beams of wood to form a crisscross pattern, and wooden planks were laid over it to form the floor of the attic. The ceiling is supported by the solid wooden pillars in the *kayyale* (verandah) and in the *nellakki nadu bade* (central hall). Traditionally, the large leaves of the *bunakke*[32] tree, the *kuvale*[33] creeper or the *ote/kolli ote* (wild reeds) were spread over the planks in the attic before applying a thick layer of mud over it. These leaves are long lasting and

32. *Garcinia xanthochymus.*

33. *Schumannianthus virgatus.*

are believed to prevent moisture and insects affecting the wooden floor planks. The mud floor of the attic was levelled and washed with a mixture of cow-dung and water. In some *ainmanes* the thick layer of mud on the floor of the attic has been removed in recent years to reduce the weight of the ceiling and prevent it from sagging.

The *atta* (attic), generally a large hall, is reached by a steep, often narrow, wooden staircase (usually without handrails) from the central hall, kitchen or *kanni kombare* (sacred room). In the case of a *mund mane*, this hall in the attic extends on all four sides of the *mund* and overlooks it. The *atta* is used to store paddy, rice and other items such as salt, which are kept dry by the smoke directed to the *atta* from the kitchen hearth. Paddy is stored in *thuliyas* (or *thuyyas*; also called *kadikes* in Are-bhashe[34])—large, open, cylindrical standing structures of cane and reed, about 150 cm in diameter and 120 cm high, plastered with cow-dung. Rice is stored in large, pot-shaped cane containers called *kommes* or in large, wooden boxes called *akki potti, akki pathaya* or *pitari*. Some of these boxes have partitions to store different kinds of rice. In the past salt was stored in the *atta* in large wooden containers called *upp pathaya*. (That was when salt was a precious item, bartered for rice and brought from Malabar in caravans of oxen.) In much the same way as in any attic, old vessels and other household items that are not in current use, as well as dried tamarind and homemade pickles preserved in large *baranis* (earthenware jars), are stored in the *atta*.

If an *okka* has a *thakkame* related to a shrine, the *bhandara potti* (box in which money offerings, jewels, processional

34. A mix of Halegannada (old form of Kannada), Tulu and Kodava *thakk*, spoken by the Goudas of Kodagu.

Thuliyas with a *komme* on top—Bachira *ainmane* attic

images and other paraphernalia related to the deity are kept) and the *moga* (sacred mask) of the deity are stored in the *atta*, often in a room that is kept locked. In *ainmanes* of Goudas, the *mudipu*[35] for God Venkataramana is usually hung from the rafters in the *atta*. In *okkas* that have the *koyime* (customary right/honour) to perform the *kudre* (horse) or *ane* (elephant) dance at temple festivals, the horse or elephant-shaped cane frames that the dancers use are generally stored in the *atta*.

In the past, the *atta* was also used as a dining hall during weddings and other ceremonies and festivals celebrated in the *ainmane*. Seating was on long, wooden benches and food was served on banana leaves

35. Cloth bundle in which money promised to God Venkataramana in fulfilment of vows is kept. This money is sent to, or offered personally at, the Venkataramana temple in Thirupathi by members of the *okka* who undertake the pilgrimage. (*Mudipu* means a 'bundle' or 'money bag' in Kannada.)

Bhadrakali *moga*—
Machimada *ainmane*

placed on long wooden tables. This practice continues in a few *ainmanes* to this day.

Some *ainmanes* have rooms in the *atta* that are used as additional living space. Generally the *atta* has small windows to let in air and light. A few *attas* have one or more balconies. Some *atta* floors have openings with a hinged hatch to pour the paddy/rice stored in the *atta* down to the ground floor. If more than one family lives in the *ainmane*, the *atta* is often partitioned with thin mud walls or bamboo slats called *nerke*, to allow each family its own space to store things or use as a living area.

The roof of the *ainmane* slopes downwards on all four sides to let the rain water flow down. In the case of a *mund mane* the inner portion of the roof slopes inwards into the *mund* on all four sides, and the rain water that falls into the *mund* is drained off through an underground channel to the yard in front. The roof was built over a structure of cross-beams, roof trusses and rafters with reapers across them, all made of bamboo and reeds in the past and later replaced with wood. The sloping roof trusses were cleverly held together at two nodal points, each with a simple wooden bolt—no nails were used. It was so crafted, that if the bolts were pulled out, the whole roof structure would come apart. Often a decorative carved wooden *thombakke* (the bud of a banana plant), so called because of its shape, was hung at each of these nodal points.

Panjurli *moga*, Mootera *ainmane*

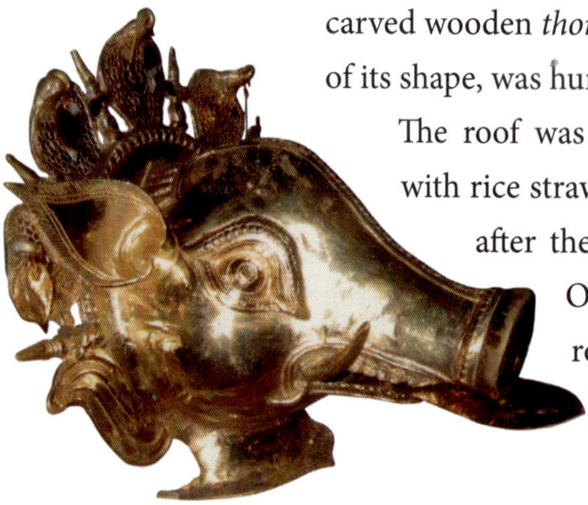

The roof was thatched with wild grass in the distant past, later with rice straw and increasingly since the late 1800s with clay tiles, after the bamboo roof structures were replaced with wood. Originally the tiles were the small, narrow, humped or rounded kind called *pathi anchi* or *pathi od*, sometimes called *chipp anchi* or *chipp od*, or *dabbe hanchu* in Kannada. (*Pathi* means 'conduit', *chipp* means 'shell',

Thatched *ainmane*—Meniyanda

referring to the rounded shape of the small tiles, *dabbe* means 'piece of bamboo split vertically to make it a conduit', and *anchi/od/hanchu* means 'tiles'). Some roofs had flat tiles that were made locally in Kodagu.[36] A few *ainmanes* had *marathra kupp* (wooden slats) for tiles. Later, most of these tiles were replaced by the broad Mangalore tiles with grooves, that are common in South India,[37] and the ridges of the roofs were covered with *mule anchi* (inverted V-shaped tiles; *mule* means 'corner'). Even today there are a few *ainmanes* whose roofs are thatched with rice straw.

Stone steps from the front *patti* lead to the *kayyale* of the *ainmane*. This flight of steps is located directly in front of the main entrance door of the

36. We were told that, in the past, Madikeri had a factory where flat tiles (with no grooves) were manufactured, and that rain water used to flow down like a sheet from those tiles.

37. The manufacture of Mangalore tiles started in 1866 with the opening of the Basel Mission tile factory near Mangalore. The Mission was founded in 1860 by the German missionary, Plebot.

WEL-COME

house, which is usually to the right of centre of the *kayyale*. Occasionally the steps are flanked by low stone walls carved with coiled elephant trunk and lotus motifs. Carvings like these are believed to have been permitted only in *ainmanes* of *okkas* whose members held high offices in the raja's court. A stone slab with a rough surface is laid flat near the bottom of the steps, for visitors (who, in the past, walked barefoot) to scrub and wash their feet before entering the *ainmane*. Traditionally, hosts in Kodagu offer their guests water in a *chemb* (small pot) to wash their hands and feet, and a towel to wipe them dry before entering the *ainmane*. This gesture is symbolic of a courteous welcome.

Wood that was available in abundance was used for the doors, windows, slabs on top of *aimaras*, pillars, roof trusses, planks on the attic floor, etc., of the *ainmane*. The wood used most commonly was that of the *ajini*[38] tree because it is strong and durable. In some *ainmanes*, the walls of the *kayyale* are built with pillars and panels made of wood with designs carved on them.

The solid wooden door frames, window frames and capital beams on top of the pillars, especially those in the *kayyale* and in the *mund* are often beautifully carved with figures of flowers, birds, animals, snakes, plants, creepers, etc., reflecting the love that the people of Kodagu have for nature. The panels on top of doors and windows are generally carved with themes from Indian epics/mythology, displaying the knowledge and skill of the Airis (artisans from Malabar, steeped in Hindu culture) who crafted the woodwork.

A few *ainmanes* have two *kayyales* in front. The second (outer) *kayyale*—a later addition—was built in front of the older (inner) *kayyale* to

FACING PAGE: Steps flanked by carvings of coiled elephant trunks—Chetrumada *ainmane*

38. *Artocarpus hirsutus*, wild jack tree.

Wood-panelled wall—
Puttichanda *ainmane*

protect it from the rain that beat relentlessly during the monsoon season. This outer *kayyale* is quite simple, with narrow *aimaras* and pillars with no carvings on their capitals, unlike the older inner one. Some *ainmanes* also have *kayyales* at the back and at the sides of the houses. But it is usually only the traditional older *kayyale*s in front that are richly decorated with wood carvings.

The western wall of the *kayyale* often has a niche to hold a stone or clay lamp lit with wicks soaked in oil. This lamp is lit on ceremonial occasions, during local temple festivals, or when a member of the *okka* dies outside the *ainmane* and the corpse is laid out in the *kayyale*.[39]

In some *ainmanes*, stag and bison horns or stuffed heads of wild animals from past hunts decorate the pillars and walls of the *kayyale* and many have

39. In such cases, custom requires that the corpse is not taken into the house to be laid out in the *nellakki nadu bade*, as is the common practice.

Details of carvings on wood-panelled wall—Puttichanda *ainmane*

family photographs displayed on the walls. In the *kayyale*, and occasionally in the central hall or kitchen, a *nele/bedake* is suspended from the ceiling. It consists of two pairs of wooden battens hung from the ceiling, with aligned holes near their lower ends, through which are slid two bamboo poles. The *nele* was used in the past to hang *koundis* (quilts placed on the back of pack-oxen), ploughs, yokes, guns, *kol* (canes) and *peeli* (peacock feathers) used in folk dances, or *mudi* (cane framework of the tall headdress worn by the person who gets possessed by a deity during a temple festival), to keep them safe and out of reach of young children. When used exclusively to hang guns, the *nele* was called a *thok mara* (*thok* means gun and *mara* means wood). In rare cases the *nele* was used to hang a swinging cot.

The square wooden pillars tapering upwards in the *kayyale* (at its outer edge) and in the *mund* (at its four corners) are called *chadara kamba* (square pillars). Occasionally, there are such pillars along the inner wall

Carved panel on top of door—Kadira *ainmane*

of the *kayyale* also. In rare instances where the *mund* is rectangular, there are pillars midway between the corner pillars. The two half columns that are embedded in the walls at the extreme ends of the *kayyale* are called *padi kamba* (*padi* or *hadi* means prop in Kannada). Generally each pillar has four finger-like protrusions pointing upwards, carved on each of two levels at its four corners—midway along its height and further up the pillar. These serve as pegs to hang various items. We were told that in the past, during times of war, the housewife hung bundles of *kupodi* (mixture of cooked rice and curds, along with pickle and dried meat/fish, packed in banana leaves) on these pegs every day, so that the menfolk, if called to war at short notice, could take them and leave quickly.

The first pillar to the left at the top of the steps from the yard to the front *kayyale* in an *othe pore*, and the pillar in the south-west corner of the *mund* in a *mund mane*, are both called the *kanni kamba*, or the *gode*

Carved panel on top of door—Machetira *ainmane*

kamba in Are-bhashe. This pillar has ritual significance and is venerated, since it is sacred to the memory of the *karanava* of the *okka*. In rare cases any one of the pillars in the *kayyale* may be designated as the *kanni kamba*. In some *ainmanes* it was the custom in the past to bury a piece of gold where the *kanni kamba* was erected.

Aimaras (bench-seats) are long, solid, polished, wooden slabs fixed on top of low parapets of mud between the pillars. They function as seats in the *kayyale* and in the *nellakki nadu bade*. *Aimaras* in the *kayyale* are traditionally located between the pillars on its outer (eastern) edge. Some *kayyales* also have *aimaras* on the western side and occasionally on the southern side. The *aimara* in the *nellakki nadu bade* of an *othe pore* is built along its eastern wall; while the four *aimaras* in the *nellakki nadu bade* of a *mund mane* are fixed along the outer edge of the *mund*, between the pillars located at its four corners.

In most *ainmanes*, the wooden slabs of the *aimaras* are generally between 5 cm to 15 cm thick and between 40 cm to 60 cm wide. A few *aimaras* have sloping, slatted backrests made of wood that extend over the whole length of the *aimara*.

The *aimara* between the first two pillars to the left at the top of the steps leading to the *kayyale*, the *aimara* along the eastern inner wall of the *nellakki nadu bade* in an *othe pore* and the one that extends from east to west on the north side of the *mund* in a *mund mane* have ritual significance.

The doors in the *ainmane* have no hinges. Each door has two leaves (vertically separated halves) made of solid wood with pegs at the top and bottom that act as pivots which swivel within sockets chiselled in the door frame. The pegs support the door and allow it to swing. The doors are sometimes fitted with decorative brass knobs.

The main entrance door to the *nellakki nadu bade* from the front *kayyale* is almost invariably to the right of centre of the *kayyale* (viewed from the front) and directly opposite the steps from the *patti* to the *ainmane*. This door has a wooden *kattole* (door frame) that is usually carved artistically with geometric patterns[40] intertwined with figures of creepers, flowers, birds and animals. The panel on top of the doorway, except in a few cases, has impressive carvings of gods and goddesses—Gajalakshmi along with musicians playing their instruments, Krishna with *gopis* (milkmaids), or scenes from the epics, *Ramayana* and *Mahabharatha*. It is believed that it was the custom in the past to bury a piece of gold where the *kattole* for the main entrance door was placed.

Occasionally there is one more door at the left of centre of the *kayyale*, leading to the *nellakki nadu bade*, and often this door too has an artistically

40. A common intricate pattern along the doorway is called '*katturup sal bott kuri*' which translates as 'design of a row of large black ants'.

FACING PAGE: Pillars and *aimaras*—Kalengada *ainmane*

carved door frame and panel on top. *Ainmanes* always have additional entrance doors at the back (western) and on the northern side. They have no entrance doors facing south since that direction is considered to be inauspicious (see footnote 25). If there are rooms on one or both sides of the *kayyale*, the entrance to these rooms is generally from the *kayyale*.

The doors to the rooms in the *ainmane* also often have carved door frames, but these carvings are not as elaborate as those on the main door frame at the entrance.

The inner wall of the *kayyale* (that separates it from the central hall) has a rectangular wooden window whose shutters open on the inside. This window is often inset with a wooden screen that is intricately carved with beautiful, circular, heart-shaped or geometrical, perforated patterns set in a carved frame. The perforated screen allows the householders to see strangers approaching the house, without being seen. Often, the panel on top of the window has impressive and elaborate carvings.

Some of the older *ainmanes* have long windows called *therangidike* (*therang* means 'slide' and *kidike* means 'window') on the inner wall of the *kayyale* or on the outer wall of the kitchen. The shutters fixed to these windows slide sideways to expose narrow vertical slits through which one can look out without being seen. Most of the other windows in the rooms of the *ainmane* are small, to keep the house warm and protect it from wind and rain.

In an *othe pore*, the *nellakki nadu bade* is a long one that often extends beyond the length of the *kayyale*.

In a *mund mane*, the *nellakki nadu bade*, also called the *ola kayyale* (inner verandah), is an open hallway around the central sunken *mund* from which one enters the rooms in the house. The *mund* is about 3 m to 4.5 m square and is paved with laterite stones. It is open to the

FACING PAGE:
Carved door frame—Moodera *ainmane*

sky and brings in light and air to the rooms around it, which would otherwise be dark since their windows tend to be small. The *mund* has four solid, carved, wooden pillars at its corners, with *aimaras* between the pillars.

The narrow passage from the *nellakki nadu bade* leading to the back of the *ainmane* is called a *muri bade* (a piece of the hall), *kunji bade* (tiny hall) or *adchi bade* (attachment to the hall). This is normally to the left of the *nellakki nadu bade* (viewed from the front).

A lamp called the *nellakki bolcha*, made of clay or stone and lit with wicks dipped in oil, is kept in a *gud* (a triangular or rectangular niche or recess) facing east in the western wall of the *nellakki nadu bade*. If, as is most common, the *ainmane* faces east, this lamp is visible from the front entrance. Occasionally, if a shrine is located near the house, the lamp is kept in a *gud* facing the shrine, even where the shrine is not to the east of the house.

ABOVE: *Mund*—Pattamada *ainmane*

FACING PAGE: Carved window—Nayakanda *ainmane*

Often there is also a *bhasma kutt*, a carved wooden container for *bhasma* (sacred ash), shaped like an inverted pyramid, which hangs in the *nellakki nadu bade*. In Gouda *ainmanes*, the Venkataramana *mudipu*, when not stored in the attic, is kept in a niche in the wall or hung from a rafter in the *nellakki nadu bade*.

Many *ainmanes* have one or more *thuk bolchas*—ornate brass lamps hanging from the ceiling in the *nellakki nadu bade*, instead of or in addition to the *nellakki bolcha*. Some of these hanging lamps are dedicated to a particular deity called the *mane devathe* (house deity), *ishta devathe* (chosen deity) or *kula devathe* (deity of the *okka*).

In some *ainmanes* there are hearths built on the floor of the *nellakki nadu bade* for individual families in the *okka* to use for cooking. This was more common in the olden days, if the nuclear families in the *okka* who lived together in the *ainmane* chose to cook separately. In these *ainmanes*, the kitchen is used primarily for cooking ritual meals during occasions such as *Karanang Kodpa* and *Puthari*. Some *ainmanes* have two or more kitchens (six in one case)—one for each *bhaga* (branch) of the *okka*. A few *ainmanes* have shallow 'fire-pits' in the floor of the verandah or the *nellakki nadu bade*, where fires are lit on cold and rainy days to keep the residents warm.

It is said that in the past, in order to be prepared to fight enemies, *thud* (flammable torches used to light the way in the dark) dipped in pork fat were kept handy and ready in a *thud gud*, a small hollow under an *aimara* in the *nellakki nadu bade*. Some *ainmanes* had a tunnel or an underground passage, leading from one of the rooms to a fairly distant point outside the house. These tunnels were wide enough to let people crawl through. It is believed that when the house was attacked, women and children would use the tunnel to escape, lighting their way with *thuds*, while menfolk would crawl out with their weapons and surround the enemies, taking them by surprise. We have seen one such tunnel.

Ainmanes are generally large with many rooms leading off the *nellakki nadu bade*. Some *ainmanes* have rooms on one or both sides of the verandah. The majority of *ainmanes* have between four to ten rooms each.[41] *Ainmanes* with more than ten rooms are usually two-storied, with rooms upstairs and downstairs. When *ainmanes* were rebuilt to make maintenance easier, the number of rooms was often reduced. One of the largest *ainmanes* we saw had twenty-four rooms; another is believed to have had sixty-four rooms at one time, now reduced to eighteen. In another large *ainmane* with broad verandahs on all four sides, the members of the *okka* claimed that it was large enough to celebrate four weddings simultaneously and that, in the past, its thatched roof needed more than a hundred villagers working together to help replace the thatch.

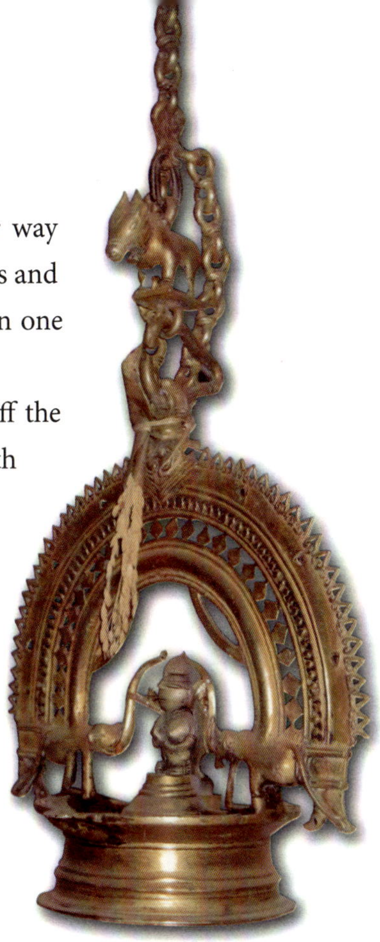

On entering the *nellakki nadu bade* from the verandah, the room to the right is a fairly large common kitchen called the *umbala mane/kombare* (dining house/room), since it was common practice in the olden days to eat in the kitchen itself. *Paleyas* (low wooden stools) were used for seating, and the plate/banana leaf on which the food was served, was placed either on the floor or on a slightly higher *paleya*. Also found in kitchens are *mukkalis* (low, three-legged, wooden stools) which, besides being used

ABOVE: *Thuk bolcha*—Karthamada *ainmane*

FACING PAGE: *Bhasma kutt*—Kuppanda *ainmane*

41. The count of rooms excludes the verandah(s) and the central hall, but includes kitchens and the *kanni kombare*. Also, only rooms in the traditional *ainmane* (referred to as the *thayi mane*, meaning 'mother house') are included, and rooms in later extensions (*vasara*) are excluded.

as stools, have ritual significance. The *mukkali* is used to seat the bride/bridegroom during wedding rituals. The sacred *thaliyathakki bolcha*[42] is placed on a *mukkali* during wedding, death and other ceremonies. The kitchen hearth is usually on a raised platform along the eastern wall of the kitchen. Firewood is used for cooking. Above the hearth hangs a *nele/bedake* (a wooden plank hung with ropes) on which salted meat and fish are kept to be smoked and cured.

ABOVE: Tunnel entrance (in a small room near the central hall)—Padeyanda *ainmane*

BELOW: Swords, spear and rod given by Veeraraja—Nerpanda *ainmane*

42. Oil lamp lit with wicks, placed on top of rice spread on a bell-metal plate.

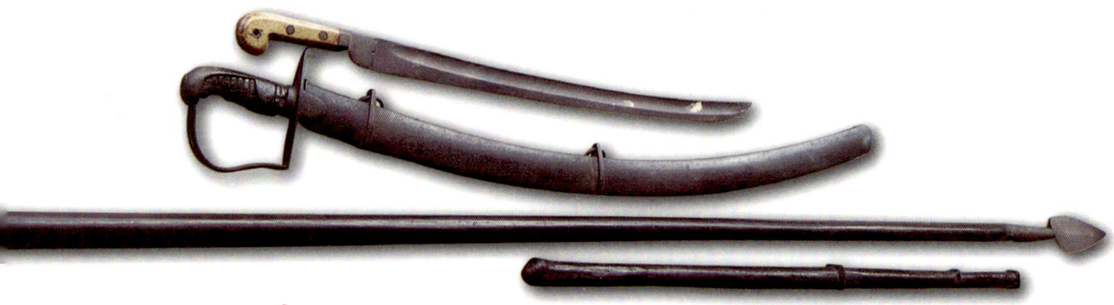

The sacred *kanni kombare* (also called the *kanni mule kombare* or the *meedi kombare*) is in the south-west corner of the *ainmane.*[43] It is a small room that is empty except for a shelf or niche, usually on its western wall, where a stone or earthen lamp is placed. The daily *meedi* (ritual offering of a small portion of the food prepared for the day) to the *karanava* is placed in front of this lamp. Often the *karanava's odi kathi* (war-knife), *thand* (staff) and sometimes old weapons belonging to ancestors (guns, war-knives, swords, spears and, in rare cases, bows and arrows) as well as *dudis* (Kodava drums) belonging to the *okka* are kept in the *kanni kombare.* In a few *ainmanes*, images or figurines of the *karanava* and *karanachi*, made of clay, stone, wood, or metal, are also kept in the *kanni kombare.* If the *okka* has the *thakkame* for a shrine, the locked *bhandara potti* and the *moga* of the deity are kept here, when not kept in the *atta.* Because it is a sacred space, the mud floor of this room is retained and periodically washed with cow-dung (a ritual purifier) even if the rest of the house has cemented floors.

Kodava drums *(dol* and *dudi)*—Karthamada *ainmane*

Except for the kitchen and the *kanni kombare*, the other rooms of the *ainmane* are bedrooms designated for the use of each nuclear family in the *okka.* Typically, a bedroom in the *ainmane* has a small window and is furnished with one or two simple wooden cots and wooden chairs. Matresses are stuffed with coir or cotton. In the past hay was also used. A feature common to all bedrooms is one or more *potti mara* (a horizontal wooden plank fixed to the wall) that serves as a shelf to keep chests and other belongings.

43. *Kanni* (literally, virgin) is planet Virgo, whose location is in the south-west corner of the zodiac chart. *Mule* means 'corner'.

SOCIO-CULTURAL SIGNIFICANCE OF *AINMANES*

The *ainmane* of an *okka* is considered to be sacred and holds a very special place in the hearts of its members. The *ainmane* and the *jamma* land attached to it is their birthright and they feel a special affinity towards them—evoking a deep sense of belonging. It symbolises their roots and provides a link to their ancestors whom they venerate as gods. Besides being hallowed by the memories of their ancestors, the *ainmane* is where the customs and traditions that embody the culture and way of life of the native communities of Kodagu are followed and preserved.

In the past, when all or most of the members of an *okka* lived together in their *ainmane* or around it, all the traditional ceremonies connected with births, marriages and deaths were conducted in the *ainmane*, which was large enough to also accommodate the limited number of guests who had to walk long distances to attend the ceremonies. In those days relatives, friends and neighbours who were invited to these ceremonies got to visit the *ainmanes* of other *okkas*. Nowadays, since few members, if any, live in their *ainmanes,* most of these ceremonies, except for funerals, are usually conducted in rented halls in towns and cities. Consequently many *ainmanes*, especially those located in remote areas with no proper approach roads, have become isolated and very few people, other than members of the *okkas* to whom these *ainmanes* belong, have seen them.

Among the other traditional ceremonies and festivals that were conducted in the *ainmane* in the past, *Karanang Kodpa* (ritual offerings to ancestors), *Karana There* (performance ritual in honour of ancestors) and *Puthari* (harvest festival), continue to be celebrated in the *ainmane* by most native communities. *Hari Seve* (worship of God Venkataramana) is celebrated in Gouda *ainmanes*. Members of the *okkas*, even if they do not live there, make the time and effort to go to their *ainmanes* on these occasions and pay their respects to their elders and ancestors. Ceremonies to propitiate spirit-deities are initiated in *ainmanes*, but only those living in or near the *ainmane* tend to attend them. While the festivals of *Kail Polud* (veneration of agricultural implements and weapons) and *Kaveri Sankramana* (celebration of the birth of river Kaveri) are generally celebrated in *ainmanes*, those who live far away from the *ainmane* celebrate them in their individual homes.[1]

Traditionally, the eldest male member of the *okka* is called the *pattedara* (headman) of the *okka* and the ancestral *jamma* property is registered in his name. *Pattedara* literally means one who holds the *patte* (title deed) to the *jamma* land of the *okka*. When a *pattedara* dies, the name in the land registry is changed to that of his successor, the next eldest member of the *okka*. In the past, the *pattedara* exercised considerable authority over the affairs of the *okka* and the *ainmane*, and

1. Outside Kodagu, in towns and cities with sizeable populations of people from Kodagu, the festivals of *Puthari, Kail Polud* and *Kaveri Sankramana* are celebrated jointly in community halls or in one of their private homes. Nowadays these celebrations are also conducted in countries abroad such as UK, USA, Canada, Australia and UAE, where a fair number of people from Kodagu live.

his word was law. These days his role is largely symbolic, although a respected one. The *pattedara*, also called the *koravukara* (one who takes responsibility), is consulted on the affairs of the *okka*. If the *pattedara* is not capable of attending to the affairs of the *okka*, the one next to him in age is named the *koravukara*, and performs that role under the guidance of the *pattedara*. Although rare, we have come across a Banna *okka* and a Jaina *okka* that have a *pattedarthi*, a female—the eldest member of the *okka*—as the head of the *okka*.

Jamma property was inalienable and all the members of the *okka* together cultivated the land and shared its produce. However, over time, male members of the *okka* were given occupancy rights over portions of the *jamma* land and each nuclear family in the *okka* began to cultivate its share of the *jamma* property. This however did not break up the *okka* or the *jamma* property of the *okka*.

Every member of an *okka* has rights and responsibilities related to the *ainmane*—including the right to live in it and to share the produce from the *jamma* land attached to it. A girl married out of the *okka* also enjoys the same rights and is entitled to live in the *ainmane* of her natal *okka* when she falls on bad times and has nowhere else to go.

If a *thakkame* (hereditary leadership role) for an *ur*, *nad*, temple or local shrine is held by an *okka*, the *ainmane* of the *okka* becomes a hub of activities during the *ur*, *nad*, or temple/shrine festivals. The *pattedara* of that *okka* is the *thakka* (headman) responsible for the conduct of these festivals. (See Appendix 10 on *Thakkame*).

As part of the *Puthari* celebration, villagers gather in the *ainmane* of the *ur thakka* (village headman), collect the *kols* (canes) that are stored there and go in procession to the *ur mand* (open space set apart for sports, dances and social gatherings in the *ur*) for the *kol* dance (traditional folk

Pudiyodi shrine

dance by men holding canes). After the dance they return to the *ainmane* of the *thakka* and sing the *mane pat* of his *okka* (song of the *okka*) before going to the other *ainmanes* in the village to sing their *mane pat*. (See Appendix 12 for the translation of an extract of a *mane pat*.) It is customary at that time for the villagers to be treated to a feast in the *ainmane* of the *ur thakka*.

During temple festivals, villagers go to the *ainmane* of the *bhandara thakka* of the shrine who is responsible for the safe-keeping of the *bhandara potti*—the box in which money offerings to the deity and other paraphernalia related to the festival, such as the *thadamb* (processional image of the deity), decorations for the image and *moga* (mask of the deity that is worn by the person possessed by the deity), are kept. The *bhandara potti* is taken in procession, first to the *ainmane* of the *deva thakka* (headman of the shrine) who is responsible for the administration

Kekmani shrines—from left to right, Bhadrakali, Ayyappa and Choundi shrines

of the village shrine, and then to the shrine. Villagers collect the *peeli* (peacock feathers) and *chouri* (yak-tail whisks) that are stored in the *ainmane* of the *deva thakka* and proceed to the shrine to participate in the temple dances (*peeliyat, chouriyat,* etc.) that are an important part of the festival.

If the *okka* has a *koyime* (customary right/honour) to perform the *kudre* (horse) or *ane* (elephant) dance at a temple festival, the horse and elephant-shaped cane frames that the dancers fix around their bodies are stored in the *ainmane* of the *okka*. These frames are decorated for the festival and the members of the *okka* wear them and dance at the temple.

The traditions, customs and rituals related to the ceremonies and festivals that continue to be held in *ainmanes* are described in brief in the following sections. They could vary somewhat between *okkas*, between communities and between the different regions in Kodagu.

Horse-frame made of reed—Mechamada *ainmane*

TRADITIONS ASSOCIATED WITH THE *AINMANE*

The *ainmane* is revered and footwear may be worn only up to its front steps[2]—as is the practice in any holy space or building.[3] It is customary to use the right foot first to cross the threshold to enter the *ainmane* without stepping on the threshold.

The south-west direction is considered sacred and the south-west corner of the *ainmane*, called the *kanni mule*, is venerated as a sacred space dedicated to ancestors. The sacred *kanni kombare* is the room located in the south-west corner of the *ainmane*, and the sacred *kanni kamba* is the pillar located in the south-west corner of the *mund* in a *mund mane*. The

2. These days, in many *ainmanes*, footwear may be worn in the *kayyale*, but not in the *nellakki nadu bade* or in any other room in the *ainmane*.

3. In many areas, during the days preceding the local temple festival, when traditional restrictions (*devada kett*) apply, those not belonging to the *okka* are prohibited from entering its *ainmane*.

naga sthana (a platform with a stone symbolising the snake god placed on it) is usually located in the south-west direction in the yard outside the *ainmane*. However, the *devara kone* (*puje* room) set apart for worshipping deities in many Gouda *ainmanes* is not necessarily in the south-west corner of the house.

The *aimara, nellakki nadu bade, nellakki bolcha, kanni kombare, kanni kamba* and *kaimada* have a place in many of the traditions and rituals of the native communities of Kodagu.

Members of an *okka* come to their *ainmane* before commencing any new venture or taking part in an important event. Before entering the *ainmane* they go to the *kaimada* to offer prayers and seek the blessings of their ancestors. Then they offer prayers to their ancestors at the *kanni kamba,* at the *nellakki bolcha* and at the *kanni kombare* in the *ainmane* before taking the blessings of the elders present in the *ainmane.* If there is a *thuk bolcha* dedicated to the deity of the *okka*, prayers to the deity are offered there. These are important rituals for a newly married couple visiting the groom's/bride's *ainmane* for the first time. In the past, men going to war followed the same ritual, seeking the blessings of their ancestors, deities and elders in the *ainmane.*

The doors of an *ainmane* are invariably kept wide open all day long and shut only at dusk, after the *nellakki bolcha* is lit. In rare instances, where there is no member living in or near the *ainmane*, hired help is used to maintain it and the front door of the *ainmane* is kept locked.

The main door in front that faces east is used to enter the *ainmane.* In exceptional cases where the *ainmane* faces west or north, it is the entrance door facing east that is used for all ceremonial occasions, even though it is not the main door. Early in the morning, the front door (or the door facing east) is opened and a simple prayer is offered to the rising sun. In the past in many Kodava *ainmanes*, women and non-Kodavas did not enter the *ainmane* through the main door but through the second entrance door to the left of the main door in the verandah, if there was one. Otherwise they used one of the other entrances—the door to the north of the house or the one at the back. (See footnote 25 on page 50.)

There are rituals and taboos associated with sitting on *aimaras*. On climbing up the steps to the verandah, the first *aimara* to the left (between the first two pillars to the left) is revered as the *karanavanda aimara* (*aimara* for the *karanava*). It is meant for the use of the *pattedara*, elders, honoured guests and the one possessed by the ancestor during *Karana There* (performance ritual in honour of the *karanava* of the *okka*). In the past, a fine reed mat was spread on it for guests to sit on.

The *aimara* running east to west on the north side of the *mund* in a *mund mane* and the one along the eastern inner wall of the *nellakki nadu bade* in an *othe pore* have special significance. As per custom, a newly married woman is made to sit on this *aimara* in her husband's *ainmane* on the day after her wedding. This is symbolic of her having become a member of her husband's *okka*. However, that is the only time when she may sit on it or on any other *aimara* in that *ainmane*.[4] When she dies, the corpse is laid in state on that *aimara* (as is that of any deceased member of the *okka*) if it is a *mund mane*.[5]

Except for these *aimaras*, all the other *aimaras* in an *ainmane* are used for general seating. Proper decorum has to be maintained while seated on an *aimara*. No one may ordinarily step on it or across it.

The *kanni kamba* is sacred to the memory of the *karanava* of the *okka* and is ritually saluted as in prayer during auspicious occasions.

4. She may however sit on *aimaras* in any other house.

5. If it is an *othe pore*, the corpse is laid on a cot placed in the east-west direction in the central hall.

Every day, at dawn and at dusk, a lady of the *okka,* dressed in the traditional style, sweeps the floor of the *nellakki nadu bade* and the *kayyale.* She sprinkles the area under the sacred *nellakki bolcha* in the *nellakki nadu bade* with a mixture of cow-dung and water to ritually purify the space, lights the sacred lamp and prays to the ancestors of the *okka.* Others in the *okka* also offer daily prayers to their ancestors at the *nellakki bolcha.* All important rituals, ceremonies (such as weddings), agreements, etc., are made in front of this sacred lamp which is considered a witness to the act. The flame in the sacred lamp is never allowed to go off on its own, because that is inauspicious; nor is it blown out, because exhaled breath would defile it. It is snuffed out with the fingers or the palm of the hand. The term used for 'putting out' the flame of the sacred lamp is '*dumbchiduva*', a euphemism which literally means 'filling it up'.

BELOW LEFT: *Gud* with sacred lamp and ancestor images—Naliyammanda *ainmane*

BELOW: *Gud* with sacred lamp and ancestor images—Bommanda *ainmane*

Where no one lives in the *ainmane*, members of the *okka* who live nearby take turns to sweep the floor and light the *nellakki bolcha*. If there is no member living near the *ainmane*, families of the *okka* who live far away agree to take turns to come to the *ainmane* and light the *nellakki bolcha* at least once a month on *Sankramana*[6] day and/or during festivals and ceremonies. There are also instances where a caretaker who lives in or near the *ainmane* lights the sacred lamp.

On all ceremonial occasions, members offer prayers to the *nellakki bolcha* and to the deities symbolised by the *thuk bolchas* hanging in the *nellakki nadu bade*. They also apply *bhasma* (sacred ash kept in the *bhasma kutt*) on their foreheads.[7]

In the past, when weddings were held in the *ainmane*, the *murtha* (ceremony where the bride/groom is blessed by all those assembled) was held in the *nellakki nadu bade*, with the sacred *nellakki bolcha* as witness to the ceremony. If it was a *mund mane*, the *murtha* of the groom (occasionally of the bride) was held inside the *mund*,[8] while the *murtha* of the bride and the joint *murtha* of the bride and groom were held near the sacred *nellakki bolcha* in the open hallway around the *mund*.

In Gouda *ainmanes*, in preparation for the wedding of a daughter/son of the house, a *hase* (decorative composition) is drawn by a male relative of the bride/groom or by a wellwisher from the village on a blackened part of the wall of the *nellakki nadu bade* near the sacred *nellakki bolcha*. The *hase* has sketches of a house, moon (for a bride), sun (for a groom), and flowers, etc., drawn in white chalk—symbols of a happy married life.

---

6. *Sankramana* is the first day of the month according to the traditional calendar in Kodagu—the day when the sun passes from one zodiac sign to the next.
7. This is probably a Lingayath tradition from the time of the Kodagu rajas who were Lingayaths.
8. Some *ainmanes* have steps to get down into the *mund* from the open hallway around it.

These days the drawing may be made on a black cloth which is fixed to the wall. We have even heard of a 'readymade' *hase* that is embroidered in white on a black cloth. The bride/groom sits on a mat in front of the *hase* for the preliminary wedding rituals.

Disputes within the *okka* are settled in the hallowed precincts of the *ainmane*. Vows are made in front of the *nellakki bolcha*, with its flame as witness. In the past, when there were no courts of justice, anyone in the *okka* accused of a crime such as stealing, cheating or lying was forced to swear his innocence in a ritual called '*sathya pramana*' (swearing to the truth of a statement) conducted in front of the *nellakki bolcha*. Eight days prior to the swearing, the *pattedara* or *koravukara* would pray in front of the *nellakki bolcha* holding a strip of white cloth about 4 cm wide and 15 cm long across his eyes, and hang the cloth from the *bhasma kutt*. The suspect was then given eight days to think over the accusation. On the eighth day, at the appointed hour, the piece of cloth was set on fire in

Hase—Nidyamale *ainmane*

the presence of all the people assembled in the *nellakki nadu bade*, and the accused was made to touch it and swear that he was not guilty. It is believed that those guilty would invariably admit to the guilt at that point and accept appropriate punishment. If the person swore innocence and was later proved to have been guilty, he was ostracised by the *okka* and that was considered to be very severe punishment.

The daily *meedi*—a ritual offering to the *karanava* of a small portion of the food cooked that day—is placed in the sacred *kanni kombare.*[9] This is indicative of the belief that the spirits of their ancestors, to whom the members of the *okka* feel very close, are present in the *ainmane*. Even if *meedi* is not offered every day, it is offered on special occasions and whenever there is a feast. Women are not allowed to enter the *kanni kombare* during their menstrual periods, when they are considered to be ritually 'impure'. Some of the rituals related to the *Karanang Kodpa* ceremony are also conducted in the *kanni kombare.*

People visit Thalakaveri on *Thula Sankramana,*[10] the day when Goddess Kaveri is believed to reveal herself in the water that bubbles up and gushes out of the Kundike (the small pond that is the source of the river Kaveri). They collect the fresh *theertha* (sacred water) from the Kundike and some of it is kept in the *kanni kombare* of their *ainmane*. This *theertha* is stored for use during purification and death ceremonies.

CEREMONIES HELD IN THE *AINMANE*

Most of the native communities of Kodagu are primarily ancestor worshippers. Their ancestors are their guiding spirits while their elders

---

9. In rare cases where there is no *kanni kombare*, the *meedi* is kept in the central hall in a niche on its southern wall or near the *nellakki bolcha* or in the kitchen.

10. The first day of Libra, when the sun transits from the zodiac sign of Virgo to Libra.

are their living guides. They pray to their *karanava* and seek his blessings and guidance in their daily lives. The daily *meedi* offering to the *karanava* is kept in the *kanni kombare*. During the *Karanang Kodpa* and *Karana There* ceremonies they pay obeisance to their ancestors and honour them with formal worship and ritual offerings in their *ainmanes* and *kaimadas*. During *Karana There* ceremonies they also invoke the spirits of their ancestors and honour them with ritual performances. The *Karanang Kodpa* ceremony is held annually. The *Karana There* ceremony is not common to all *okkas*. Those who have the tradition hold it annually or once in a few years. These ceremonies[11] are also held during special occasions to seek the blessings of the ancestors or in fulfilment of a vow made to the *karanava*.

In Gouda *ainmanes* the *Hari Seve* ceremony (ritual homage to God Venkataramana) is held annually, once every few years or in fulfilment of a vow.

In the past, birth, marriage and death ceremonies were conducted in the *ainmane*. Nowadays, for reasons of convenience, birth and marriage ceremonies are for the most part conducted in large community halls in towns and cities.[12] Funeral ceremonies, however, generally continue to be conducted in the *ainmane* by most *okkas*.

Propitiation of spirit-deities is initiated in the *ainmane* and is conducted at their *sthanas* near the *ainmane*.

---

11. The forthcoming book on aspects of Kodava culture will have more details on these ceremonies.

12. Details of customs and rituals related to birth and marriage ceremonies of Kodavas are given in the '*Pattole Palame*' by Nadikerianda Chinnappa (1924); of Kembattis in *Kembatti Holeyara Samskriti* by M.G. Nagaraj (1993), published by the Karnataka Sahitya Academy, Bangalore; of Poomale Kudiya in *Poomale Kudiya* by Iythichanda Ramesh Uthappa (2002), published by the Karnataka Kodava Sahithya Academy, Madikeri; and of Goudas in *Akshaya* by Bythadka Janaki Belliappa (2009), published by the Gouda Mahila Okkuta, Madikeri. Most of the native communities of Kodagu have customs that are very similar to those of the Kodavas.

While all members of the *okka* visit their *ainmane* to celebrate *Karanang Kodpa, Karana There* and *Hari Seve*, generally only those living in or near the *ainmane* participate in the ceremonies to propitiate spirit-deities.

Karanang Kodpa (ritual offerings to ancestors)

The *Karanang Kodpa* ceremony (ritual offerings to ancestors) is the most important of the ceremonies held in the *ainmanes* of the native communities of Kodagu. All the members of the *okka* and the *thamane mudiya* (daughters of the *okka* who are married out) along with their families are expected to join in this ceremony. It is generally held during *pathalodi*—the ten days following the *Kaveri Sankramana* festival—on a day fixed by each *okka*. In a few *okkas*, *Karanang Kodpa* is celebrated during *Bishu* (the first day of the new year according to the solar calendar). Some *okkas* celebrate it on a day close to one of the days mentioned above, when it is convenient for all the members and the *thamane mudiya* to attend the ceremony along with their families. *Thamane mudiya* have a special role in this ceremony.

Gouda *okkas* customarily celebrate *Karanang Kodpa* before an auspicious occasion such as a wedding, a practice that is followed by some Kodava *okkas* also. Some Jamma Mapille *okkas* too celebrate *Karanang Kodpa*.

During *Karanang Kodpa* rituals, food, liquor and animal blood offerings are made to the ancestors at the *karana thare* or in the *kaimada*. In some *okkas* the offerings are also made inside the *ainmane* and in the *thutengala*. These offerings are called *ede*[13] or *barani*.

13. Ritual offerings of food and liquor during special occasions. In rare cases, *ede* is also offered to a member of another *okka* (even if he is from a different community) who prevented this *okka* from becoming extinct by marrying a daughter of the *okka* (in accordance with *okka paraje* or *makka paraje* rites—see Appendix 9 on *Mane Pedas*) or by being adopted by the *okka*, or if he helped an ancestor of this *okka* at a difficult time. There are examples of Kodavas offering *ede* to Jamma Mapilles, to Ammas, to Heggades and to Kembattis; and of Heggades offering *ede* to Kodavas. There are examples of *ede* being offered to a lady from another *okka* who prevented this *okka* from becoming extinct by saving a child of the *okka*.

Early in the morning the *okka* gathers in the *nellakki nadu bade* and the officiating priest for the day (an elder member of the *okka* who keeps himself ritually pure for the occasion) lights the sacred *nellakki bolcha* and prays to the ancestors and the deities. They then proceed to the *karana thare* or *kaimada* where, after some rituals, chicken and occasionally pigs are sacrificed and offered to the ancestors, along with liquor. Selected portions of the sacrificed meat are cooked on a separate hearth by the *thamane mudiya* for the *ede* offerings to be placed in different parts of the *ainmane* and in the *thutengala*. The rest of the meat is cooked for the feast that day.

From the *karana thare* or *kaimada*, members of the *okka* go to the *thutengala* where, after more rituals, they offer food and liquor and pray to their ancestors.

Karana There (performance ritual in honour of ancestors)

Karana There or *Karana Kola* is a colourful and elaborate performance ritual that some *okkas* belonging to native communities conduct in their *ainmanes* in honour of their ancestors. It is held periodically (annually in some *okkas*), in honour of a deceased member, or in fulfilment of a vow to the *karanava*, and is well attended. The performance ritual may include *theres* of many ancestors and of animals or deities associated with them.

The *there* starts late in the evening and often continues through the night, until after daybreak. Songs extolling the greatness of the ancestors, or songs of the animal or deity whose *there* is being performed, are sung to the mesmerising beat of the *chande* (large drum). The central roles in these rituals are performed by Bannas, Panikas or Maleyas, who have their faces painted and wear elaborate, colourful costumes fashioned for the occasion from palm fronds, split bamboo and cloth—much like the

Theyyam dancers of Kerala. Dressing the performers for this ritual is an elaborate process that takes many hours. One of the performers invokes the spirit of a famous ancestor of the *okka* (sometimes a *karanachi*, a female ancestor, in a '*thayi there*'), gets into a trance and is possessed by the spirit of that ancestor. He dances in the *nellakki nadu bade* with graceful and vigorous steps, acting out well-remembered incidents from the ancestor's life (such as defeating enemies or killing a tiger). Other performers invoke and get possessed by the spirits of other ancestors, of deities or of animals associated with the *karanava*[14] and go through a similar ritual.

The last *there*, that of 'Ajjappa', the *karanava* or founder of the *okka*, is very special. After dancing, he goes to each room in the *ainmane*, blesses the room and the people there and stops in front of the sacred lamp where he acts as an oracle and foretells events concerning the *okka*. Members of the *okka* then seek his advice about their fears and concerns, believing that they are speaking directly to their *karanava*. They accept his *anuvada*—words of guidance and reprimand that transmit the commands and opinions of the ancestor—with utter faith.

At the end of the performance ritual, the Ajjappa *there* blesses the gathered people and goes to the *karana thare* or *kaimada* where the chicken and liquor brought by the families attending the event are offered to the ancestors.

The person possessed by the *karanava* speaks Kodava *thakk*, whereas the one possessed by a deity normally speaks in Malayalam, since most of the deities 'came' to Kodagu from Malabar.

Each performance ritual ends with the spirit being released from the body of the performer, who by then, having been possessed by an invisible force, is both physically and mentally exhausted.

14. The deity could be someone who had cursed the *karanava* or the *okka* and needs to be appeased by this ceremony. The animal is often a tiger that was killed by an ancestor, or an ox that helped an ancestor.

In the past, Jamma Mapille *okkas* also conducted *Karanang Kodpa* and *Karana There* ceremonies in their *ainmanes.*

While the practice of *Karana There* or *Karana Kola* is still prevalent, it is not as common as in the past, mainly because, with time, few of the youngsters in the families that traditionally performed the *theres* are continuing in the profession. Besides, a *Karana There* is time consuming and expensive; and there are those among the younger generation who no longer have the enthusiasm to organise it.

Hari Seve (worship of God Venkataramana)

Hari Seve is the most important ceremony held in Gouda *ainmanes.* In most Gouda *ainmanes* this ceremony is held annually, once every few years or in fulfilment of a vow made to God Venkataramana. All the members of the *okka* attend this ceremony.

A temporary *gunda* (*devara gudi* or altar) sculpted with mud is erected outside the *ainmane* and decorated with flowers. The *mudipu* (cloth bundle in which money offered to God Venkataramana is collected) is placed in front of the *gunda*. A *dasa* (singing mendicant belonging to the Telugu Banajiga community), or a Brahmin, is engaged to serve as the priest for the occasion and to perform *puje* (ritual worship) at the altar. One of the members of the *okka* or an invited devotee gets possessed by God Venkataramana, recites the *okkane*[15] and blesses the assembled people. Members approach him for advice regarding their troubles. He is offered milk, fruit and flowers. In some *ainmanes* another person gets possessed by Kenchiraya, a 'guard' of God Venkataramana, to whom chicken, goats or sheep are offered. He too gives advice on how members may overcome their problems.

15. A recital of the names of the ten *kutumbas* (founding families) and eighteen *gothras* (lineages traced back to ancient sages) of the Gouda community.

The money collected in the *mudipu* is sent to the temple at Thirupathi to be offered to God Venkataramana. If it is taken to Thirupathi in person by members of the *okka*, the *Hari Seve* is celebrated after their return from the pilgrimage.

Propitiation of village deities and spirit-deities

Village deities (to whom there are shrines in villages and platforms in *deva kads*—sacred forests dedicated to the deities) and spirit-deities[16] (represented by stones embedded in earthen platforms under sap-exuding trees, not far from the *ainmanes*) are important in the daily lives of the people of Kodagu. These deities are believed to have the power to protect cattle, land, or the *okka* from harm. People fear their power and seek their protection to ward off evil. They appease them periodically in their shrines or sacred platforms as well as in the *ainmanes*. The ritual propitiation ceremonies for some of these deities involve *there* performances somewhat similar to *Karana There*. Most of the deities are offered animal sacrifices and liquor. Only Natha, the snake god of fertility (represented by a stone with serpents or a hooded cobra carved on it) is propitiated with offerings of milk, fruit and flowers.

Many Gouda *okkas* have *there/kola* performances in their *ainmanes*, to propitiate deities and spirits during the *Hari Seve* ceremony. These ceremonies are officiated by *dasas*, not Brahmins. The *theres* are performed by members of the Paruva, Paleya and Ajala Paleya communities from Dakshina Kannada or by Panikas from Malabar.

16. See Appendix 7 on Religious Practices. Examples of spirit-deities are Bhumi Kuliya/Guliga who guards the land; Pashana murthi who guards against death and suffering; Kuttichatha, the spirit-deity of *thanthras* or mystic rites; Angara who cares for cattle; and Natha, the snake god of fertility. They are believed to have been adapted from the cultural traditions of the neighbouring regions of Tulunad and Malabar.

While in a trance during a *there* performance, the medium acts as a bridge between the spirit world and the people. It is believed that the spirits of deities 'possess' the medium and communicate through him. People have implicit faith in the medium and speak candidly with him, in the belief that they are speaking to the spirits of those with whom they have a personal bond. They accept his *anuvada* (words of guidance) with utmost respect.

More details on spirit-deities are given in Appendix 7 on Religious Practices.

Death ceremonies

As noted earlier, while in the past, birth, marriage and death ceremonies of members in the *okka* were conducted in the *ainmane*, nowadays in almost all *okkas* only death ceremonies are conducted there.[17]

A dying person or the corpse of one who has just died is laid on a mat on the floor of the *nellakki nadu bade* of the *ainmane*, with the head to the south, and sacred Kaveri *theertha* is trickled into the mouth. The corpse is later taken outside the house, bathed, dressed in traditional attire and laid in state in the *nellakki nadu bade* with the head to the west, on a special cot[18] if it is an *othe pore*, or on the *aimara* running east to west on the north side of the *mund* if it is a *mund mane*. The *chavu pat* (funeral song), a poignant song lamenting the dead, is sung and relatives come to mourn and pay their last respects. The body is then taken in a procession to the *thutengala/kekola* of the *okka* where the last rites are performed, before the body is cremated or buried.

17. The *Pattole Palame* gives detailed descriptions of birth, marriage and death ceremonies and the songs sung during these ceremonies.

18. This cot is made with two long planks of wood unlike the regular cots used for sleeping, which are made with three planks each.

The *okka* to which the deceased belonged is thereafter under ritual pollution until the *mada* (ceremony that ends the period of ritual mourning) is performed. The *mada* is usually held in the *ainmane*, even if the death had occurred elsewhere and the corpse could not be brought to the *ainmane*. On that day, a portion of the food prepared for the occasion is offered at the *thutengala/kekola* for the departed soul. The *polichi pat* (laudatory song) in praise of the dead person is sung on this occasion.

Al rupa (a unique part of death rituals)

An *al rupa* (*al* means person and *rupa* means image) is a small crude figurine (about 9 cm to 16 cm high) embossed on a beaten silver sheet, carved in wood (or moulded in clay in the olden days) to represent a recently deceased adult. *Al rupa* rituals are not observed in all *okkas* and many *okkas* that observed them in the past no longer follow them.

As part of the death rituals, an *al rupa* is ritually sanctified by a *puje* at the local shrine for one or more days. It is not brought inside the house, but is tied in a white cloth and hung from the branch of a sap-exuding tree (such as a jackfruit tree) near the *ainmane*, until it is taken for immersion in the sacred Kundike[19] at Thalakaveri. The tradition of immersing the *al rupa* in the Kundike is part of the *deekshe uthuva* (literally 'untying abstinence restrictions'—denoting the end of traditional restrictions observed during mourning) ritual that is performed by very close relatives of the deceased. This ritual ends the formal state of mourning for the close relatives, and the immersion of the *al rupa* symbolises the soul of the deceased flowing with the river of life to the sea and merging with the

19. These days it is immersed in the Sangama, the sacred confluence of the rivers Kaveri, Kanake and Sujyothi at Bhagamandla, so as not to congest the Kundike, the small pond that is the source of the river Kaveri.

Wooden *al rupas*—Thapanda *ainmane*

FACING PAGE: Silver *al rupas*—Machetira *ainmane*

God-head (universe) to attain eternal peace. A few *okkas* immerse the *al rupa* in the waters of the Kaveri without a *puje.*

Some *okkas* get a second *al rupa* made of silver or carved from the wood of a sap-exuding tree. After the first *al rupa* is immersed in the Kaveri, the second one is dipped in the Kundike to consecrate it and is brought to the *ainmane* ceremonially with much celebration and feasting. This symbolises the spirit of the dead person being united with the spirits of the ancestors of the *okka*[20] who are worshipped in the *ainmane.* If made of silver, this *al rupa* is stored in a small container along with the *al rupas* of the earlier ancestors and is usually kept in the *nellakki nadu bade.* In some *ainmanes* the *al rupas* are displayed in a niche in the western wall of the *nellakki nadu bade.* If made of wood, the *al rupa* is called an *ur kutt* or *urit kutt* (meaning a rounded piece of wood) and is stored on the rafters of the *kaimada.* A few *ainmanes* have *al rupas* numbering in the hundreds. During the *Karanang Kodpa* ceremony, these *al rupas* are taken out, cleaned and worshipped.

A few *okkas* observe *al rupa* rituals only if a vow is made, or if an astrologer or priest declares that there is some *dosha* (fault or blemish) pertaining to the deceased person and prescribes immersion of the *al rupa* in the waters of the Kaveri to absolve the soul of the deceased. This is more common among Gouda *okkas.*

In the Shirangalli and Muvathoklu villages, instead of *al rupas,* some *okkas* keep large, smooth, round stones in memory of their deceased, one for each dead person. On the eleventh day after a death, the day before the *mada,* a large round stone is brought from the riverbed, tied in a white cloth and hung from the branch of a sap-

20. This is referred to as *Pathanda kutk pannand*, which means 'uniting the eleventh' (spirit of the recently dead person) 'with the ten' (symbolic of the spirits of the ancestors who had died earlier).

exuding tree. On the day of the *mada* it is brought down and kept alongside the stones representing those who had died earlier, generally in a row according to seniority, in an area designated for the purpose under a fig or jackfruit tree near the *ainmane*. This ceremony is called *kall beppa*, and the stones are called *karana kall* or *ajjappa kall*. *Ede* is offered to these stones during *Karanang Kodpa* and on special occasions. Some of these stones have a crude figure of the dead person etched on them.[21]

FESTIVALS CELEBRATED IN THE *AINMANE*

The festivals of *Kail Polud* (veneration of agricultural implements and weapons), *Kaveri Sankramana* (celebrating the birth of the river Kaveri) and *Puthari* (harvest festival) are the three important traditional festivals that are unique to Kodagu.[22] *Puthari* and *Kail Polud* are associated with the changing of the seasons and with the main occupations of the native communities in the past—rice cultivation and hunting. *Kaveri Sankramana* celebrates the annual resurgence of the waters of the river Kaveri, worshipped as their mother goddess, because it is she who blesses their land and nourishes their crops. In the past all the native communities celebrated these three festivals in their *ainmanes*. These days only *Puthari* continues to be celebrated in the *ainmanes* by most *okkas* and all members of the *okka* join in the festivities. *Kail Polud* and *Kaveri Sankramana* are generally celebrated in the *ainmane* only by

21. We have seen a new stone erected for a man who had died recently. His figure was etched on the stone with eyes marked on them, and next to him was etched the figure of his wife, but with no eyes marked. We were told that as long as she was alive they would not mark her eyes so that she would not see her husband's spirit. Once she dies her eyes would be marked so that the spirits of the couple could thereafter see each other.

22. Other common Hindu festivals celebrated by the native communities include *Yugadi, Bishu, Shivarathri* and *Subrahmanya Shashti*.

those who live there, while other members of the *okka* celebrate them in their individual homes.

Kail Polud (festival venerating agricultural implements and weapons)
This festival, also known as *Kail Murtha*, falls around the third of September. It marks the end of the season of sowing and transplanting paddy and the start of the hunting season. Agricultural implements that are to be put away and arms that are taken out of storage for the hunting season are venerated as part of the celebrations.

Early that morning, all agricultural implements (ploughs, sickles, etc.,) and arms (swords, knives, guns, etc.,) are collected and cleaned thoroughly. In the past, around midday, the agricultural implements were stacked neatly in a corner of the cowshed or in the *patti* and the arms (including bows and arrows) were kept on a mat spread under the *nellakki bolcha* in the *nellakki nadu bade*. Dots of sandalwood paste were applied on all these items and incense sticks were waved over them in a ceremony called *ayudha puje* (*ayudha* means implements or weapons). Nowadays, in most *ainmanes*, only arms are kept in the *nellakki nadu bade* and worshipped in this ceremony. A small portion of each dish prepared for the feast that day is placed on a cut banana leaf and kept near the arms as a ritual offering. A grand meal follows.

In the evening, all the members of the *okka* assemble in front of the *nellakki bolcha*. The *pattedara* says a few words on the significance of the day and advises youngsters on the use and care of weapons. He then ritually hands over a gun that is passed from hand to hand among the younger male members of the *okka*.

Following that, members of the *okka* go to the *ur mand* where all the villagers assemble to participate in games of skill and strength. The first event is shooting at a distant target. Thereafter they proceed to the forest shrine of Ayyappa (god of the hunt) and offer prayers.

In the olden days, on a day following the festival, the villagers would assemble with guns in hand (with bows and arrows in an even earlier age) and proceed to a forest[23] nearby to hunt wild animals that destroyed the planted crops. Hunting is now forbidden by law.

Kaveri Sankramana (celebration of the birth of the river Kaveri)

This festival that celebrates the birth of the sacred river Kaveri is held on *Thula Sankramana* day—around mid October, when, at the auspicious time calculated by priests, water bubbles up and gushes forth from the spring at the Kundike, the small pond which is the source of the river Kaveri at Thalakaveri. This annual phenomenon, believed to be a covenant of Goddess Kaveri with the people of Kodagu, is hailed by the vast congregation of pilgrims who wait near the Kundike to collect the fresh *theertha*. Some of the *theertha* is taken to the *ainmane* and left in the *kanni kombare* and the rest is taken to their individual homes.

Very early that morning, after offering prayers to the *karanava* at the *ainmane*, householders plant *bothu* posts (made from branches of specific trees) in their paddy fields, and near their wells and cattle sheds to mark and reaffirm their custody of the land. The belief is that Goddess Kaveri bequeathed the land to the care of the people of Kodagu and that on this day she visits the areas where *bothu* posts are planted and blesses the land.

On the day after *Kaveri Sankramana*, *kani puje* (worship of Goddess Kaveri and mother earth) is celebrated according to tradition in every house. A coconut or cucumber (symbolically representing Goddess

23. Hunting has never been allowed in *deva kad* (sacred forests) on Wednesdays and Saturdays because it is believed that the gods hunt there on those days.

Kaveri as water) is covered with red silk, decorated with jewellery and placed on a *thaliyathakki bolcha* (see footnote 42 on page 74), and fresh flowers are arranged around it. Early in the morning all the members of the household pray in front of this lamp. The lady of the house draws fresh water from the well and uses it for cooking the festive meal. Only vegetarian food is prepared on this day, except in some parts of Kodagu. Before having their meal, small portions of the cooked food are placed on the *bothu* posts as offerings to Goddess Kaveri. Later that day, the flowers used for the *kani puje* are strewn on water flowing in a stream or river.

Even if they celebrate this festival in their individual houses, people generally visit their *ainmane* on this day for *akki iduva* (ritual sprinkling of rice on the lamps in the *kaimada* and in the *nellakki nadu bade*) and to seek the blessings of their elders.

Puthari (harvest festival)

Puthari is the most important of the festivals celebrated in Kodagu. It signifies the start of harvesting the rice crop, and is celebrated on the night of the full moon in late November or early December, three months after the *Onam* (harvest) festival in Malabar.

Puthari is celebrated over a period of many days. Members of the *okkas* of all the communities in the village celebrate *Puthari* in their respective *ainmanes* and then all the villagers join together in the *ur mand* (village green) for the *kol* folk dances.

On the evening of *Puthari* day, men collect leaves and creepers from specific plants and prepare *neres* (leaf rolls, each tied with a length of a creeper) in the yard in front of the *ainmane*. Meanwhile ladies make preparations in the kitchen for the ceremony to follow.

At dusk, at the auspicious time, under the light of the full moon, a male member of the *okka,* who is chosen as the sheaf-cutter for the occasion, carries the *polud kuthi* (a bamboo container with milk, honey and a few other items in it) and a sickle and goes in a procession from the *ainmane* to the rice fields of the *okka* to bring the *kad* (first ears of paddy). The procession is led by a girl carrying a *thaliyathakki bolcha* and a band playing traditional *volaga* music with horns, pipes and drums.

When they reach the designated plot in the rice fields, the sheaf-cutter prays facing east and ties one *nere* (leaf roll) around a few stalks of rice plants and pours the contents of the *kuthi* at the base of the stalks. All the assembled people shout, '*Poli Poli Deva*' (Shower, shower in plenty, O God), praying for a good harvest. A gun is fired in the air and the sheaf-cutter ceremoniously cuts the first sheaf of paddy (around which the *nere* was tied), symbolising the start of the harvest. He cuts more stalks and distributes bunches of stalks to those present, after which he places some in the *kuthi* and carries it back to the *ainmane* in a procession. A few of the stalks are placed in the hollow of each *nere.* These *neres* are then tied, one each, to a pillar in the *kaimada,* the *kall boti, kanni kamba* and *nellakki bolcha* as well as in other prominent places in the *ainmane.*

The sheaf-cutter keeps the *kuthi* in the kitchen and prepares '*elakki putt*', kneading together some rice flour with a few ripe bananas, milk, honey and other specified ingredients. Small balls of this mixture are placed on peepal[24] leaves and each member of the *okka* throws a peepal leaf with some '*elakki putt*' on it at the ceiling, calling out the name of an ancestor. It is believed that the ancestor is satisfied if the leaf sticks

24. *Ficus religiosa.*

to the ceiling. The rest of the mixture is then distributed to the gathered people to eat.

On this occasion special dishes—*thambuttu* (made with ripe bananas and rice flour) and *puthari kalanji* (a special kind of yam boiled and mashed with honey and ghee)—are prepared. A few grains of rice from the first sheaf of paddy cut that evening are added to the pot when the *payasa* (rice cooked with milk and sugar) is cooked for the feast that follows. After the feast, members of the *okka* dance to traditional *volaga* music.

Every evening during the week preceding *Puthari* day, all the men in the village gather in the *mand* by moonlight to practise the *kol* dances. They also sing songs and recite humorous stories (*nade kakuva*) that are part of *Puthari* traditions. On the day after *Puthari*, the *ur kol* dances are performed in the *ur mand*. Following that, villagers go first to the *ainmane*

Kuruli *ambala*, *mand* and *mad* around a *chithal* tree

of the village *thakka* and then to all the *ainmanes* and other houses in the village singing the *mane pat* of each *okka* and the *Puthari* songs. In many villages, boys dressed as *kunda* (dancing boy) and *kodichi* (dancing girl) go from house to house and dance to *kodichi* songs. On the following day, the *nad kol* dances are performed in the *nad mand*. (A note on the songs and dances is given in Appendix 11. The translation of an extract of a *mane pat* is given in Appendix 12.)

In the past these festivities ended with a hunt in which all male members of the *okkas* in the village participated, followed by an *urorme* when all the people of the village assembled in the village *mand* for a grand feast. The practice of *urorme* continues, but without the hunt, since it is now forbidden by law.

CONCLUSION

Nearly sixty per cent of the *ainmanes* of Kodagu are no longer there. The reasons for this are many. In the past, when *ainmanes* had thatched roofs, many of them burnt down accidentally or were set on fire by enemies. With the passage of time, many *ainmanes* collapsed due to heavy rains, neglect, or because of insufficient resources to maintain them, especially among *okkas* with very few members. Perhaps the most common reason for the neglect of *ainmanes* today is that with population growth and better education, nuclear families have left their *ainmanes* and migrated to urban areas in Kodagu and elsewhere in search of better economic opportunities. Hence, most (sometimes all) members of many *okkas* no longer live in or near their *ainmanes*. Members who live far away seldom visit their *ainmanes* and, over time, they appear to have lost their attachment to them and tend to show less and less interest in their maintenance.

Many of the *ainmanes* that burnt down or fell were rebuilt, often at the same site and usually in the traditional design. Recently, however, most of the ruined ones that have been rebuilt are not traditional in design. Some have not been rebuilt at all. A few of the *ainmanes* that we had visited during the fieldwork for this project have since been brought down and some are being dismantled even as we write.

As a result, many *okkas* no longer have traditional *ainmanes*. Some of them have built a simple hall or a two or three-roomed modern structure in brick and mortar, where their *ainmane* once stood. This is where the members of the *okka* now meet to conduct the *Karanang Kodpa* ceremony and to celebrate festivals. Some *okkas* have retained only the *kaimada* and use the open yard in front of it to conduct the *Karanang Kodpa* ceremony.

Some *okkas* became extinct because they no longer had male members and the lineage of the *okka* was broken, despite the provisions in the traditional customs (such as *okka paraje*, *makka paraje* and adoption—see Appendix 9 on *Mane Pedas*) which would have allowed the clans to continue their lineage. Their *ainmanes* were neglected and have invariably been reduced to ruins.

Ainmanes are buildings of historic value that are important both socially and culturally. They symbolise the identity and pride of the native communities of Kodagu and serve as physical repositories of their collective memories. Over the centuries, the *ainmanes* and the traditions and rituals associated with them have together ensured the preservation and continuity of the distinct culture of these communities of Kodagu. They are part of the precious architectural and cultural heritage of this region—a testimony to the diversity of cultures in India that needs to be preserved for future generations.

It is our hope that documentations such as this one will increase awareness of the cultural significance of the *ainmanes* of Kodagu and of their current condition. We believe that this study will also give outsiders a feel for the ethos of the people of Kodagu and allow them to understand these distinct traditions that have not yet vanished. In addition, this study could help future research on the communities in Kodagu—many of whose numbers are dwindling and whose cultures are being diluted or forgotten. Above all, we hope that documenting these heritage buildings will promote a better appreciation of the value of their *ainmanes* among the people of Kodagu and encourage *okkas* to maintain and preserve them.[1]

In the website that complements this book, besides information on each *ainmane* that we visited, we have also documented anecdotes and stories pertaining to the *okka* that were told to us. We suggest that efforts be made to collect anecdotes and historical information about every *okka* and its *ainmane*. We hope that youngsters will be fascinated by the snatches of the oral history of their *okka* presented in the website and will be enthused to build on and add to them by consulting their elders. We urge them to do so and record them for posterity before they are forgotten by the *okka* and the community, and are lost forever.

Ainmanes are bastions of the culture of the native communities of Kodagu and if they vanish, so will the heritage of a people, their way of life and their collective memories. It is our fervent hope that these architectural symbols of the heritage and culture of this region will be maintained and preserved for generations to come.

1. See 'Broad Guidelines for Maintaining Old Buildings', Appendix I in 'Silent Sentinels', 2005, The HECAR Foundation.

EPILOGUE

Current status of traditional *ainmanes* and their functioning

Most of the traditional *ainmanes* that are standing today have tiled roofs and many of them have floors that have been cemented for the most part. But their thick mud walls have rarely been replaced because they were built sturdily. Increasingly there is an appreciation of the value of the beautifully carved woodwork in these ancestral homes and efforts are being made to preserve them.

In order to make maintenance easier, some *okkas* have demolished many of the rooms in their *ainmanes*, while keeping intact the *kayyales* with the traditional *aimaras* and carved pillars that are characteristic of these distinctive ancestral homes.

With the spread of modern conveniences to the rural areas of Kodagu, many *ainmanes*, except those in remote locations, have electricity and a few have telephones. The advent of cell phones and television sets has made a big difference to the communication and entertainment facilities available in rural areas, and many families who live in or near their *ainmanes* possess them today. Such conveniences and facilities as well as better access to the *ainmanes* have in a few cases encouraged retirees to return and settle in their *ainmanes*.

Firewood (that is still available in plenty in the land attached to the *ainmane*) continues to be used for cooking and for heating water, although there are a few instances of gas being used in *ainmanes* that are close to urban areas. Plumbing is rare except in *ainmanes* close to urban areas where piped water is available. Underground sewage has not yet penetrated many of the rural areas of Kodagu, but where it has, *okkas* have built modern toilets.

Furniture in the *ainmane* is minimal and is usually restricted to long benches, long tables, a few simple chairs and cots, all made of wood. *Paleyas* (low wooden stools) and *mukkalis* (low, three-legged wooden stools) are used in kitchens. Some *ainmanes* have a *nalkali* (four-legged high wooden stool) that is used by the person possessed by an ancestor during the *Karana There* ceremony.

Over the past century, the functioning of *ainmanes* has changed perceptibly in many *okkas*. Although the nominal role of the *pattedara* as the head of the *okka* is respected, the decision-making on all common matters concerning the *ainmane* and the *okka* is done in a fairly democratic manner by a General Body that usually comprises of the adult male members of the *okka*. The General Body meetings are presided over by the President and minutes of the meetings are kept by the Secretary, both of whom are appointed for a fixed period by the General Body. In some *okkas* women too are members of the General Body or are invited to participate in its meetings.

Most of these *okkas* have annual or bi-annual General Body meetings where issues relating to the *okka* are debated and resolved by vote. These meetings are held in the *ainmane*, usually during the annual *Karanang*

Kodpa or *Puthari* celebrations when a large attendance is assured. Decisions are taken on the maintenance and upkeep of the *ainmane* and its land, on the conduct of festivals, and on financial matters relating to income from the common property of the *okka* and expenses related to the *ainmane*.

The General Body meeting is also an occasion when all the members of the *okka* meet to honour members who have distinguished themselves. The members are also given the opportunity to display their talents in sports, singing, dancing, etc.

Many *okkas* have set up funds to which nuclear families of the *okka* are required to contribute a specified amount every year. These funds are earmarked for the upkeep and maintenance of the *ainmane,* for the festivals and ceremonies conducted in the *ainmane*, and for various other common needs of the members such as sports, education of children, loans in times of difficulty, and expenses to cover emergencies (such as illness or death of a member). In large *okkas*, the responsibility for conducting an annual festival or ceremony in the *ainmane* is rotated between the *bhagas* (branches) of the *okka*, and the turn of each *bhaga* is called a *therige.*

Some *okkas* have a 'Ladies Fund' which is managed by ladies. This fund is used to make improvements in the kitchen and to buy necessities such as kitchen utensils. A few *okkas* have a Co-operative Grain Fund to which members contribute paddy (in kind) and from which they are entitled to draw when needed.

All these trends suggest that *ainmanes* continue to be the focal centre of the *okkas* of the native communities in Kodagu and continue to preserve their unique culture and age-old traditions, despite the inevitable influence of modernisation. Awareness of the value of the *ainmanes* will, we hope, help in their maintenance and preservation.

APPENDICES

These appendices complement the main text of this book with additional background information. In the appendices we have woven together the common threads of information that were repeated in the many *okkas* that we visited, and the information gathered over the years from various sources and through various means. These include books, articles in newspapers, magazines and souvenirs in Kodava *thakk* (language), Kannada and English, and conversations we have had with elders in and from Kodagu. When we got differing accounts from different sources, we have tried to verify the information and used our judgement to present a coherent picture.

The first appendix is a note on how we went about the fieldwork for this project. The following appendices give brief notes on the land, a historical account of the people and the system of land tenure in Kodagu, all of which set the *ainmane* in its geographical, social and historical context.

Short descriptions of the communities living in Kodagu are given in an appendix. Other appendices provide a brief glimpse of the socio-cultural life of the native communities of Kodagu, covering information on the languages they speak, their religious practices, some unique ceremonies (*nari mangala)*, some distinctive social conventions (*mane peda* and *thakkame*), their folk songs and folk dances.

An extract from a *mane pat* (song of the *okka)* of one of the *okkas* is given as an example of folk songs that are typically sung in *ainmanes.*

The appendices include sketch maps of Kodagu (in nine sections) showing the location of each *ainmane* we visited.

Summary tables by community of the number of traditional *ainmanes* (visited), the number of non-traditional *ainmanes*, the number of *okkas* with no *ainmanes*, and the total number of *okkas,* are given in the appendix.

An appendix which gives a time sequence of some important events in history provides a time perspective for the history given in the text.

Finally, as an illustration of the contents of the website www.ainmanes.com that complements this book, the information and photographs relating to two *ainmanes* are presented in an appendix.

Appendix 1

FIELDWORK

Our first task was to list the *mane pedas* of all the *okkas* in the communities currently found in Kodagu, to enquire whether each of these *okkas* has a traditional *ainmane* and, if so, the village where it is located. We started with the *mane pedas* we knew and added to the list by asking people whom we met for their *mane pedas* and the location of their *ainmanes.* We expanded on this by advertising in local Kodava language newspapers, seeking this information from the readers.[1] We also handed out a simple questionnaire at the Kodava Hockey Festival[2] in Napoklu in 2003, to elicit this information from the spectators. The list built up quickly with further additions of *mane pedas* referred to in news items in the local newspapers of Kodagu and in other media publications.

The information in the list was confirmed, or corrected and added to during our fieldwork. In each village we visited, we started a conversation with those at the local tea-stall (a common meeting place for men, especially the elderly) and asked for the names of all the *okkas* with *ainmanes* in that village and for

1. We received nearly sixty postcards and letters in response, some with detailed information on the history of the *okka* and, in one case, photographs of the *ainmane.*
2. Annual inter-*okka* hockey tournament among Kodava *okkas*, inaugurated in 1997.

directions to the *ainmanes*. Interestingly, in each *ainmane* that we visited we often learnt of *ainmanes* in other locales from the women married into the *okka*, who gave us the names of their natal *okkas* and the location of their *ainmanes*. We believe that the list of *okkas* that we have compiled is substantially complete. We hardly ever find a *mane peda* that is not on our list. This list includes the names of all the *okkas* of the native communities in Kodagu—with or without traditional *ainmanes*.

The fieldwork for this project extended over a period of five years—April 2003 to May 2008. It involved forty trips to Kodagu, visiting each and every traditional *ainmane* where important ceremonies and rituals relating to the *okka* continue to be conducted. This took us to about 800 *ainmanes* belonging to the different communities in Kodagu, among which we found 683 traditional *ainmanes*. We took photographs of each traditional *ainmane*, noted its location and collected information on the *ainmane* and on the *okka* to which it belonged.

While our attempt was to visit every standing traditional *ainmane* in Kodagu, we know of one or two that we have missed because they are difficult to access, for example, a Kudiya *ainmane*, way up the rugged hills in Cherangala.

Often, people whom we asked for directions came with us or sent guides to help us reach the *ainmanes*, especially those that were located far from the main road, with no motorable approach. They walked with us through paddy fields and coffee estates, along forest paths, across streams on narrow wooden foot-bridges, and up and down steep and sometimes slippery paths to the *ainmanes*.

Our visits were unannounced for several reasons. Prior communication was not easy since we had very few telephone numbers to contact at the start of the project. Given the terrain and difficulty of access, it would in any case have been hard to keep to pre-arranged appointments. Nearly all the *ainmanes* are located in villages and it would not have been fair to keep the people in the *ainmanes* waiting for us, interrupting their busy schedules, especially during the planting and harvesting seasons. Another concern was that if we had informed them ahead of time they would invariably have insisted on our having a meal with them. That would have involved spending a lot of time in each *ainmane.* They would also perhaps have prepared themselves with answers to our potential questions—answers that would therefore not have been spontaneous.

Without exception we were given a warm welcome in the *ainmanes* we visited, and the information we sought was readily given to us by the residents. They were impressed by the fact that we, a couple in our seventies, had taken the trouble to visit their *ainmane* and intrigued that we would voluntarily engage in a project of this kind. They were also keenly aware of the importance of preserving the information we sought. The fact that we were from Kodagu and were fluent in the Kodava language was a great advantage and helped us immensely. Many identified us as the translators of the *Pattole Palame*, and as the grandchildren of its author Nadikerianda Chinnappa. Some knew our parents and many had read or heard about us in the local media. That established our bona fides and we gained their confidence.

Since our visits were unannounced, the oral accounts given to us were spontaneous and unrehearsed. We realise that some of these narratives would not ordinarily have been told to strangers. That the informants were comfortable in sharing them with us is a reflection of their confidence in us, their support for the project, and their pride in their own history.

Many informants could not answer some of our questions such as the name of the *karanava/karanachi* (founder of the *okka* or the earliest remembered ancestor—male/female) and the history of the *okka*—where they came from, how they got their *okka* name, etc. There were instances where informants told us that they would seek the answers from their *karanava* the next time his spirit possessed their local medium. In many cases, we contacted the *pattedara* (headman of the *okka*), an elder of the *okka* or of its *aruva okka* (a friendly *okka* which performs the mutually agreed role of assisting this *okka* in rituals and ceremonies) to obtain the relevant information. Occasionally we were able to get the information from a knowledgeable elder in a neighbouring *okka*.

When we asked informants to tell us how old their *ainmane* was, they invariably estimated its age, since there were no records. Some traced their lineage to the ancestor who had built it and counted the number of generations that had lived in it. Assuming a generation to cover a time span of between twenty-five to thirty years[3] we arrived at an approximate estimate of the age of the *ainmane*. Occasionally informants told us that their *karanava* was '*el thale karanava*', meaning 'from seven generations ago', but this is only a figure of speech.

Many *ainmanes* did not have telephones to allow us to follow up and complete the information we sought. During our visits we therefore asked for the telephone numbers of contact persons belonging to the *okka* who could give us details that the informants could not provide, and could confirm or correct particulars that the informants were unsure about. This was most useful and often helped us in compiling all the information we needed about the *okka*, sometimes many months or even years after our visit. When the informants could not give us contact numbers, we tried to get the numbers by consulting neighbours whose telephone numbers we had, by checking the telephone directory for Kodagu and from the numbers we collected by scanning news items in the local newspapers. During the period of our project, as the years went by, cell (mobile) phones became popular in rural areas and contacting people became much easier.

There are no authentic written records of the histories of individual *okkas* or their *ainmanes*. It is only in the folk songs—the *mane pat* ('house song' that relates the history of the *okka*) and the *karana pat* (song about the *karanava*

3. Quite often we noticed informants taking sixty to 100 years (the expected lifespan of a person) as the duration of a generation, and using that number in this calculation—a common misconception.

and other famous ancestors of the *okka*)—that some of the history of the *okka* is preserved. In the tradition of oral folk songs, singers improvise as they sing and some of the details in these songs could be partly myth.[4] However these are 'living' songs that grow with time and include memorable events in the history of the *okka*. Unfortunately these folk songs[5] that are most common among Kodava *okkas* are gradually being forgotten. In Gouda *okkas* there is the tradition of *okkane*, a recital of the names of the ten *kutumbas* (founding families) and eighteen *gothras* (lineages) of the community, but not of the stories relating to the *okkas*.

Historical information narrated to us was vague on dates, and often there was confusion regarding which raja or war they were referring to. Where there was an item such as a sword gifted to an ancestor by a raja, the letter in Kannada inscribed on it in gold helped to narrow down the period of the ancestor—'Vi' referred to Veeraraja and 'Li' to Lingaraja. However, the confusion persisted because three of the Kodagu rajas were known by the name Veeraraja and two by the name Lingaraja.

Recently a few *okkas* have brought out books[6] (often as souvenirs during special occasions such as a hockey festival hosted by them) which include short accounts of their oral history. There have also been instances where the author of a book in the Kodava language has, in the introduction to the book, written about the donor who contributed to the cost of publishing the book, and about the *okka* to which the donor belongs. Information on *okkas* from such sources has been invaluable in helping us to correct, clarify and add to the oral histories that were narrated to us.

4. 'Myth is truth which is subjective, intuitive, cultural and grounded in faith.' [*A Handbook of Hindu Mythology* (2006), Devdutt Pattanaik (noted mythologist).]
5. See Appendix 12 for extracts from a *mane pat*.
6. We have copies of twenty-five such books from the *okkas* that we visited.

Oral narratives are not always reliable, but are useful as a starting point. Besides, folk tradition allows us to accept them as remembered history.[7] Often informants told us that the information they had was '*lo palame*' which translates roughly as 'so it is said'. We have tried to cross-check the information wherever possible. When we were given differing but plausible versions of the same story, we have accepted all the versions. These stories offer interesting insights into the history, the unique cultural practices and the way of life of the native communities of Kodagu. Other members of the *okka* may have their own versions of these stories. We welcome such versions and any other stories, additions or corrections to the information we have collected, which, if credible, will be incorporated in the website accompanying this book.

The fieldwork for this project has taken us to villages in Kodagu that we had not even heard of and to remote corners where the scenery literally takes one's breath away. While we were aware of the beauty of this land of hills and valleys, rivers and streams, viewing it through the seasons of the year was a fascinating experience. Our treasured memories are of vast stretches of bright green paddy (rice in the husk) fields, turning golden as the crop ripened; paddy seedlings being transplanted in flooded fields; harvested sheaves being threshed in yards; lorries overloaded with rice straw negotiating narrow roads; the fragrance of acres of white coffee blooms, brilliant against the rich dark green of the leaves; bright red coffee berries on the plants, turning brown as they were laid out to dry in yards; paths lined with ferns and wild flowers, swarming with butterflies; rough roads hugging the hillsides that we drove or walked on; blue and green hills everywhere

7. 'No one in oral societies doubts that memories can be faithful depositories which contain the sum total of past human experiences. Whether memory changes or not, culture is reproduced by remembrance put into words and deeds. The mind through memory carries culture from generation to generation.'—Jan Vansina, noted historian-anthropologist-folklorist, in his classic book *Oral Tradition as History* (1985). Peter Claus and Frank Korom in their book *Folkloristics and Indian Folklore* (1991) speak of 'the value of the study of oral tradition for the study of cultural history' and of 'legitimate uses of folklore for historical reconstruction of a culture's past.'

one looked; waterfalls and gurgling streams; and ancient dark forests dense with a variety of towering trees.

No less memorable was our experience with the people of Kodagu of all communities. The hospitality for which they are famed is best experienced in the villages. Even though we were strangers and went without prior intimation, the residents in every house we visited would stop whatever they were doing at the time to welcome us, often with the traditional pot of water and towel offered to guests. We were given refreshments and flowers and fruits from their gardens, and were warmly invited to the next festival to be held in the *ainmane* or the local temple. We have come across men dressed in their traditional costumes, dancing in the village green to the beat of drums during *Puthari.* Late in the evening we have seen men singing around a bonfire, practising for the local temple festival. And we have observed people busy at their daily chores, fetching water, clearing paths, trimming trees and plants, collecting firewood to be stocked ahead of the rainy season, tending to their fields and cattle, collecting mushrooms and wild ferns; women washing clothes by streams; children walking long distances to schools, playing hockey, cricket and football in open meadows or in harvested paddy fields, with crude hockey sticks and cricket bats fashioned from branches of trees, and fruits of various sizes for balls.

Appendix 2

KODAGU—THE LAND

Kodagu (Coorg), a district in Karnataka state, South India, lies on the summits and eastern slopes of the Western Ghats. The total geographical area of Kodagu is 4,109 sq. km. The district may be contained within a rectangle measuring approximately 100 km by 60 km.

The section of the Western Ghats mountain range that lies in Kodagu skirts the western and southern boundaries of Kodagu and is covered by dense forests. The summit of the Brahmagiri range in the west—the Brahmagiri peak (1,355 m) at Thalakaveri—is the source of the river Kaveri. Well south of here, in the same range, is the Thadiyandamol peak (1,717 m), the highest in Kodagu and the second highest in Karnataka. Other important peaks in Kodagu are the Pushpagiri peak (1,665 m) in the Subrahmanya range in the north-west and the other Brahmagiri peak (1,372 m) in the Marenad range in the south.

The terrain in Kodagu is hilly, undulating and forested, with meadows in the highlands, coffee plantations on the hill slopes, and rice fields along the valleys. Towards the east and north-east the land is barren and flat.

Currently, about a third of the district is covered by forests which support a variety of tropical birds, snakes and wildlife including elephants and tigers.

Reserve forests[1] cover over 1,000 sq. km of Kodagu. The most famous of these is the Nagarahole game sanctuary (about 640 sq. km) located in the south and south-east of Kodagu. It extends over the forest ranges of Nagarahole, Kalhalla and Thithimathi that adjoin the forests of Karnataka state in the east and the Wynad forests of Kerala state in the south.

Adjacent to almost every village are one or more *deva kads*[2] (sacred groves/ forests) that have existed from ancient times. Each of these is dedicated to a particular deity such as Ayyappa, Choundi, Bhagavathi, Bhadrakali or Madeva, and a small shrine to the deity or a simple platform in a clearing that marks the abode of the deity is located in the *deva kad*. Stones representing minor deities such as Guliga and Natha are also located in some *deva kads*. The sanctity attached to these forests has to a large extent helped in protecting the trees from being plundered and forest land from being acquired for private use. These sacred groves have also helped conserve the rich bio-diversity of the area (including rare medicinal plants) and provide an excellent habitat for small animals, birds and reptiles. However, in recent years, coffee plantations have encroached on parts of some of these sacred groves.

Since ancient times certain *okkas* living near the *deva kads* were appointed as *thakkas* with responsibility for maintaining these sacred forests. All the native communities of Kodagu are part of this unique tradition.

The south-west monsoon, which extends from early June until late September, brings heavy and continuous rainfall to most areas of Kodagu, decreasing as it passes from the hilly regions in the Western Ghats to the plains in the north-east. Deforestation and global climatic changes have caused a substantial decrease in the rainfall. The north-east monsoon

1. Forests under the management of the Forest Department, set apart for the protection of wildlife and trees in order to preserve the ecology of the area. Encroachment and hunting are prohibited in these forests.
2. Kodagu has 1,214 *deva kads*, varying from less than half an acre (0.2 hectare) to 350 acres (142 hectares) each, and together they cover 2,500 hectares or 25 sq. km (1991 survey).

from November to January is much less intense in Kodagu than the south-west monsoon.

Many rivers have their sources in the mountains of Kodagu and most of them flow eastwards. The river Kaveri, whose source is at Thalakaveri (a place sacred to all Hindus) in the Brahmagiri range of the Western Ghats in Kodagu, is revered as the mother goddess of the people of Kodagu. The Kaveri flows eastwards across the states of Karnataka and Tamil Nadu, before reaching the Bay of Bengal (Indian Ocean) at Poompuhar on the Tamil Nadu coast. Five kilometres to the east of Thalakaveri lies Bhagamandla, where the rivers Kanake and the mythical Sujyothi (believed to flow underground) join the Kaveri. Lakshmanatheertha, an important tributary of the Kaveri, rises from the Marenad range in the south, near Irpu.

The important rivers in Kodagu that flow westwards are the Barapole in the south, a small section of which forms the border with Kerala, and the Kumaradhara in the north, which similarly forms the boundary with Hassan district (Karnataka). These rivers flow down the Western Ghats and across the narrow coastal strips of Kerala and Karnataka respectively before reaching the Arabian Sea.

Many farmers in Kodagu are gradually moving away from cultivating rice, a staple but labour-intensive crop for which the district is famed, to cash crops such as coffee, cardamom, pepper and ginger which are relatively less labour-intensive and are commercially more profitable.

Coffee, a plantation crop, is now a major commercial crop, and Kodagu produces nearly forty per cent of India's coffee output. Coffee was introduced to Kodagu over 200 years ago, probably by the Moplahs of Malabar who traded with Arabia and Africa.[3]

3. It is believed that some time in the seventeenth century, Baba Budan who went on a pilgrimage to Mecca, brought some coffee seeds and planted them in his garden adjoining his home near Chikmagalur (Karnataka) on the Chandragiri hills in the Baba Budan range (named after him). The coffee that he planted was believed to have its origins in Koffa, Abyssinia. From the Baba Budan hills, coffee seems to have spread over parts of South India, although at the close of the eighteenth century it was considered a jungle produce. (*UPASI, 1893–1953*, edited by S.G. Spear, privately published, Coonoor, 1953. *UPASI* stands for *United Planters' Association of South India.)*

Pepper too is a plantation crop in Kodagu, grown by itself or as a mixed crop with coffee. Orange, another crop grown in Kodagu, has declined for the past many years, primarily because of pests. Cardamom is generally grown in shady areas at elevations of 900 m to 1500 m. Beekeeping is a thriving industry in Kodagu and 'Coorg[4] Honey' is famous.

With higher standards of living and the resulting interest in tourism, Kodagu, a land of spectacular scenery, has become a popular tourist destination. In recent years Kodagu has seen a surge in the number of tourists who come to enjoy the beauty of its hills, forests and the large variety of wildlife. In addition, there are many interesting sites of historical and religious significance, and treks for tourists to explore. Upscale resorts as well as homestays set up by the hospitable people of Kodagu now cater to the means and tastes of a wide range of tourists.

4. The name by which the British called Kodagu.

Appendix 3

A HISTORICAL ACCOUNT OF THE PEOPLE OF KODAGU

THE EARLY PEOPLE

The *mula nivasis* (earliest inhabitants) of Kodagu are commonly believed to be the nomadic Kuruba hill tribes, the forest-dwelling Kudiyas, Kembattis who tilled the land, Kodavas who were hunters and warriors, and Ammas, a priestly class. (See Appendix 5 for brief notes on the Communities of Kodagu). Of these, the Kembattis, Kodavas and Ammas are found only in Kodagu, whereas Kurubas and Kudiyas are found in the neigbouring areas of Karnataka and Kerala as well.

Very little is known about the early history of this region since there are no written records of this area or of its people till about the sixteenth century. There can only be conjectures about the earliest inhabitants of Kodagu and of their origins, based on information gathered from available archaeological data and anthropological sources, as well as myths and legends linked to known historical events. In particular, there have been many speculations on the origin of the Kodavas, the culturally dominant community in Kodagu since ages, because their customs and traditions are strikingly different from those of their neighbours. None of these speculations have been substantiated. The following hypothesis, where the early history of the world, myths and legends remembered in neighbouring areas and in the folk songs of Kodagu have been woven together, seems to be a plausible one.

It is a well-documented fact that 'Anatomically Modern Humans' originated some 2,00,000 years ago in the Rift Valley in Africa and that all of us on earth are descendants of these early people. From prehistoric times there have been movements of people from region to region for a variety of reasons—to escape severe weather conditions and in search of a secure habitat with adequate sources of water and food. These migrations occurred at different periods of time, sometimes separated by thousands of years.

According to archaeological research, the first migrations of Modern Humans from Africa are believed to have occurred some 1,25,000 years ago at a time of severe drought and falling sea levels, during a global ice age when water was locked up in vast sheets of ice. It has been established that at that time small bands of people from Africa travelled by foot over land routes along the coastal areas of Arabia (where fresh water springs supported them) to the Middle East and settled on the fertile banks of the Euphrates and Tigris rivers.

Groups from among these people moved on and formed new settlements in distant lands where they chose to put down their roots. Over a period of centuries, these people spread over all the continents of the world, and societies grew wherever people settled. Each group evolved biologically with unique features, as its members adapted to changes in weather, landscape, diet and culture, to form their own identity while retaining some of the cultural aspects of their ancestors.

Historians have inferred that over 3,000 years ago a few tribes from among these people who had lived for ages in the Middle East and in the region of the Caucasus travelled long distances, to escape droughts, famines and tribal rivalry, settling for generations at each new location before moving on to settle down where they felt safe. Some of these migrants came to India via land routes, crossing the Hindu Kush mountains in the north-west of the Indian subcontinent through mountain passes, and settled in the fertile Indus valley fed by rivers and rain. Over centuries they branched out and moved to different parts of India. Some of them moved south to areas in Rajasthan and Gujarat, and some went further south along the west coast as far as Malabar in the north of Kerala.

Seafaring developed during the first millenium BC, and trading began between coastal areas even as early as the sixth century BC. Trading contacts led to social interactions and migrations followed. Small groups of people from around Greece and the area around the Middle East came by sea, probably to escape persecution because of their beliefs, and landed all along the west coast of India including the Malabar coast. They could have intermingled with the other immigrants who had migrated along land routes, probably from the same stock of people from the Middle East, and settled here.

It is likely that from among these groups who came by sea and land and settled in the area now known as North Malabar, a small, closely knit band of hardy hunters and warriors with distinct physical features and similar cultural values migrated inland looking for a safe and secure area where they could put down their roots and practise their beliefs in peace. They went up the Western Ghats and having reached the region now called Kodagu, which was uninhabited then (except perhaps for some nomadic forest tribes along the fringes) and was sheltered by the hills around it, decided to settle there. These people probably formed the core of the Kodava community, and there is some evidence to indicate that they may be traced to the people of the Middle East and of the Caucasian region. This hypothesis also appears to find support in the oral traditions of Malabar and in the folk songs of Kodagu.

In the oral tradition of Malabar, among the elders in the area of Parassinikadavu, home of the original shrine and *samadhi* (tomb) of the rebel deity Muthappa (revered by Kodavas), it is said that a band of people who came by boats from across the seas sailed up the estuary of the Valapattanam river and landed in

Parassinikadavu, not far from Kannur. They spread to the nearby areas around Baithur, Payyavur and Wynad, where they lived for a period of time before moving further inland up the hills to Kodagu which did not then have defined borders. These early settlers could have been the forefathers of the Kodavas.

Parassinikadavu is a place of pilgrimage to this day, and many Kodavas go on annual pilgrimages to the shrines of their adopted patron deities—Muthappa in Parassinikadavu, Baithurappa in Baithur, Payyavurappa in Payyavur, and Thirunelli Pemmayya in Thirunelli, all located just south of the present-day borders of Kodagu. Besides, Kodavas also have rights and responsibilities during the festivals in these shrines and are treated with great respect by the local temple priests and officials. These pilgrimages and rights too give credence to the oral tradition of Malabar and the hypothesis noted above, since they indicate the enduring ties of the Kodavas with the places in Malabar where their forefathers might have lived before coming to Kodagu.

Some of the earliest folk songs in the Kodava language refer to the nameless 'gods' who came from across the seven seas, landed on the Malabar coast, and looking for a suitable place to settle, climbed up the hills and established themselves in Kodagu. These gods predate the arrival of the spirit-deities and village gods from Malabar and Tulunad,[1] as well as the pan-Indian Sanskritised gods to Kodagu. Is it possible that these early folk songs refer to the ancestors of the Kodavas who came from across the seas—ancestors, whom they by tradition deified as gods? This link between gods and ancestors might well have been long forgotten, and got confused with deities from Malabar who were 'brought' to Kodagu. It is our surmise that ancient, now-forgotten versions of these folk songs[2] could have referred to the deified ancestors of the Kodavas who came from

1. Such as Bhagavathi/Povvediamme and Pudiyodi.
2. Folk songs in the oral tradition, where history and legends are woven together, have always been adapted to new circumstances which change over time.

across the seas, and were identified only by the names of the places where they settled in Kodagu.[3]

Further, it is interesting to note that the folk songs of Kodagu also state that these gods did not find the place where they first landed in Malabar suitable to settle down, that they did not like the smell of fish or toddy (these are *prasadas* offered at the Muthappa temple in Parassinikadavu even today). So they moved further inland, and crossed the hills in their search for a suitable place to settle. This is very similar to what the oral traditions of Malabar claim, as noted earlier.

In the Kodava 'Wedding Song' that is sung even today, a verse refers to the early ancestors as '*mammarinja karana*' (literally, 'the ancestor who climbed up or crossed over to this land') which Nadikerianda Chinnappa, the author of the *Pattole Palame*, translated as 'ancestors who settled on this land'.

Warfare, hunting and living off the land were perhaps the only skills that these early settlers retained, purely for survival. They also appear to have held on to some of their ancient beliefs and traditional practices which included ancestor and nature worship.

They adapted to living in the dense forests of Kodagu and used bows and arrows to hunt wild animals such as boar and deer for meat. They also lived on what was available on the land—forest products such as yam, fruits, *ragi* and red rice that grew wild.[4]

These early settlers—the hardy hunters and warriors—having established themselves in their new environment, are believed to have made periodic raids into the neighbouring areas in North Malabar and South Canara[5] to plunder

3. They include the gods noted in the Songs of Seven Gods, of Five Gods, of Three Gods and of Two Gods. (See *Pattole Palame* by Nadikerianda Chinnappa, 1924.) See Appendix 7, Religious Practices.

4. Rice cultivation was believed to have been established well before the tenth century and rice became their staple food.

5. Dakshina Kannada district was known as South Canara during British times.

the goods they needed. The young men among them brought home wives for themselves and started their families.[6]

Other groups that came to Kodagu later might have migrated from neighbouring areas, and yet others were probably remnants of military settlements of the reigning dynasties in South India that exercised control over the region during various periods of history. They perhaps chose to settle here, attracted by the seclusion provided by the hills and forests, and the fertile soil.

EARLY SETTLEMENTS

Over time, more people migrated in small numbers from the neighbouring areas for various reasons and settled in Kodagu. Some perhaps came to escape tyranny and prejudices, and some in search of fertile land or new areas to practise their trades. These early immigrants included a few Jains and Tulu Goudas from neighbouring South Canara. All the *mula nivasis* and early immigrants lived in settlements called *ur guppes* (village settlements) within each *ur* (village). Many such *urs* dotted the region. Within an *ur guppe*, members of each community that followed its own trade lived in a *gudde mane*, a cluster of thatched mud huts close to each other, and the *gudde manes* belonging to the different communities together formed an *ur guppe.*

The villagers lived close to each other mainly to ensure mutual security against attacks from wild animals that were abundant in the thickly forested land and to jointly fight enemies or outsiders who came to loot and plunder. They shared the natural resources of the area and helped each other in times of need. Among these early inhabitants, tribes such as the Kudiyas lived deep inside the forests and the nomadic Kurubas lived outside the *ur guppes.*

6. One of the threats used to frighten small children in South Canara was to say, '*Kodagar bather, Kodagar bather*!' in Tulu, which means, 'The Kodavas are coming, the Kodavas are coming!'

HISTORY

That prehistoric people lived in this area, is evident from the dolmens (tombs of the Megalithic era) located at several places in Kodagu.[7] (These are locally referred to as *Pandava pares*). The early history of Kodagu till about the sixteenth century is unclear because there are no written records. The only stray references are in the stone inscriptions which refer to wars, heroes and grants of lands. It may be surmised that some of the powerful dynasties that ruled over large parts of South India at various periods of time, had control over all or parts of Kodagu (which then did not have defined borders).

The earliest recorded reference to Kodagu is in the Tamil literature of the Sangam period (second century AD) where it is stated that the Pandyan kingdom extended up to Kudakam in the west. Historians believe that Kudakam,[8] also called Kudumalenad,[9] is Kodagu. Other references are stone inscriptions dating from about ninth century AD. The earliest reference to the Kodavas—'Kodagaru'—is in the stone inscription dated AD 1174 found in Hunsur Taluk. The 'Kodagu District Gazetteer' (1993) says: 'Therefore one can conclude that these people had occupied the Kodagu region a few centuries earlier.' The Kannada dictionary written in verse form by Mangaraja in AD 1398 describes 'Kodavas' as *mlechas* (foreigners) given to hunting.

The *ur* or village was the basic unit of administration since the early days of recorded history. Kodagu and the areas surrounding it were under the control of local chieftains called *paleyagaras*, each of whom exercised authority over a section of the land. Over time, these chieftains became vassals of powerful dynasties and

7. See *Archaeology of Coorg* (1978) by K.K. Subbayya.

8. In Tamil, *kuda(m)* means 'west' and *akam* means 'inside'. It may be noted that Kodagu is referred to as 'Kodavu' in folk songs in the Kodava language. When the Kannada-speaking Haleri rajas started ruling the land in the early 1600s, Kannada became the official language and the rajas appear to have referred to 'Kodavu' as 'Kodagu'. The British, when they took over Kodagu in 1834, called it 'Coorg', and that name continued until Kodagu became part of Karnataka state in 1952, when it reverted to 'Kodagu'.

9. *Kudumalenad* means 'land of steep hills'—the Western Ghats.

laid the framework for the administration of the land that they ruled under their authority. Among these dynasties were the Kadambas and Chalukyas of Karnataka up to the seventh century. From about the eighth to the sixteenth century the *paleyagaras* became subordinate to the Chengalvas and Kongalvas who were vassals of successive dynasties that exerted control over parts of Kodagu. These dynasties were the Gangas of Karnataka in the eighth, ninth and tenth centuries, the Cholas of Tamil Nadu in the eleventh century, the Hoysalas of Karnataka in the twelfth to mid fourteenth centuries and the renowned Vijayanagara dynasty from the mid fourteenth to mid sixteenth centuries.

The Vijayanagara kings appointed *nayakas* (chiefs) to administer their vast territories that covered substantial parts of the present Karnataka and Andhra Pradesh states. The local *paleyagaras* of Kodagu were subordinate to these *nayakas*. It was only after the fall of the Vijayanagara kingdom in the battle of Talikota in 1565 (when it was defeated by the Bahmani Confederation of the Deccan kings) that the *nayakas* who were vassals of the Vijayanagara kings assumed independence, came into prominence and gave up some of the outlying areas to the local *paleyagaras* who then assumed the title of *nayakas*. Thereafter, Kodagu, which was one such area (larger than the present Kodagu), came to have defined borders, and for the first time the whole of Kodagu was ruled by the *nayakas* of Kodagu. At that time it was divided into twelve *kombus* (area defined by the limit up to which the sound of a *kombu*—a long curved horn—was heard)[10] and thirty-five *nads* (administrative divisions, each made up of a few *urs* or villages). Each *kombu* (a group of a few adjoining *nads*) was controlled by an independent *nayaka*.

Some of the famous *nayakas* in Kodagu are believed to be Ajjikuttira Achu Nayaka in Anjigerinad, Karnembavu in Thavunad, Nayakanda Utha Nayaka in

10. As attested to by Ferishta, the sixteenth-century historian in the service of the sultan of Bijapur, who wrote the history of India from the eleventh century to the seventeenth century.

Beppunad, Nayakanda Kollakongi Nayaka in Kadiathnad, Kaibilira Nayaka in Thavalagerinad, Machangada Nayaka in Pathukettunad and Mukkatira Nayaka in Mathur. Minor *paleyagaras* exercised authority over smaller areas.

It is believed that since about the fifteenth century the *paleyagaras* of Kodagu broke up the *ur guppes* and organised the landownership, in order to increase their revenue and facilitate collection of produce as tax. They allocated the land that was under their control to each of the *okkas* in their domain, for them to live on and cultivate. After the break up of the *ur guppes*, the *okkas* acquired substantial tracts of land and, independently, over a period of time, built their houses on the land allotted to them. These houses evolved to become the *ainmanes* of today.

There was constant fighting between the *paleyagaras,* who had their own private armies, both for enlarging their territory and for power. They got *kadangas*[11] (defensive trenches) dug along the boundaries of their territories to prevent armies of neighbouring areas from attacking them and to protect the land and the people from wild animals. There were other *kadangas* of varying sizes that had been dug even earlier. (Dodda Veerappa Raja who ruled Kodagu during 1687–1736 extended these ancient *kadangas.*) Smaller *kadangas* (*nishani kadangas*) demarcated villages, and *okkas* too built small *kadangas* (*pott kadangas*) around their land.[12] Some *okkas* fortified their houses and built *bakka pores* (guard's huts) in front, with guards keeping constant vigil, especially at nights and during the harvest season.

11. These *kadangas* are referred to in the Ganga inscriptions of ninth century AD. The largest of these, called *aramane kadangas* (palace trenches), are defensive earthworks about six m deep, three m wide and over 800 km long (*Encyclopaedia Britannica,* 1911), running up and down the hills and valleys of Kodagu, with *bakkas* (guarded passages) to cross over them. *Kadangas* are said to be unique to Kodagu and are not found anywhere else in India.

12. Many of these *kadangas* are not easily visible any more. They, especially the bigger ones, have become roads/ pathways or have been levelled. Some have been encroached upon for cultivation, and some are hidden under cover of thick vegetation.

Kadanga (ancient defensive trench) near the Allaranda *kaimada*

Around the start of the seventeenth century, a *nayaka* of the Keladi dynasty belonging to the Lingayath faith from Ikkeri in Shivamogga district of Karnataka, established himself in Paleri (Haleri) near Madikeri. Over a period of time he exploited the disunity among the *nayakas* of Kodagu and gradually subdued them. He appeased them with power, giving them the right to collect land revenue, and took control of the whole of Kodagu.

He was called Veeraraja, the first of the kings of the dynasty that ruled Kodagu, c. 1600 to 1834. This dynasty was known as the Paleri, Haleri or Ikkeri dynasty, and its kings were referred to as the Kodagu rajas, the Lingayath rajas or the Wodeyas of Kodagu.

Before the time of the Kodagu rajas, the land was sparsely populated. It consisted of the *mula nivasis* of Kodagu—the Kurubas, Kudiyas, Kembattis, Kodavas and Ammas, and a small number of early immigrants from the neighbouring areas—Jains and Tulu Goudas and a few others. Even during the time of the Kodagu rajas, the population of Kodagu 'did not exceed one lakh'.[13] Kodavas were the largest in number and the culturally dominant community in Kodagu since the early days.[14]

The Kodagu rajas confirmed the tenure over the lands that were already in the possession of the *okkas*—rights that had been given to the *okkas* by the *paleyagaras.* In addition, they gave the more prominent among the *okkas*—mainly Kodavas, Ammas, some Goudas and a few others—rights over even larger tracts of land and established *jamma*[15] land tenure for tax collection.

During their rule (1600–1834), the Kodagu rajas invited a large number of agriculturists from the neighbouring areas, mainly Okkaligas, Lingayaths, Tulu

13. 'Gazetteer of India', Kodagu District, 1993, p. 66. The current population of Kodagu is about 5.5 lakhs.

14. Kodavas formed the largest single group among the communities in Kodagu according to the 1931 Census. There have been no Census population counts by caste or community since the 1931 Census of India.

15. Permanent, hereditary rights of an *okka* over land that was lightly taxed (see Appendix 4 on Land Tenure).

Goudas and Heggades from the Kannada, Tulu and Malabar areas to populate Kodagu and bring more land under cultivation. They also invited much-needed artisans and skilled workers such as Airis (carpenters and smiths), Medas (drummers and basket-weavers), Hajamas (barbers), Madivalas (washermen), Koleyas (masons), Koyavas (agriculturists), Maleyas (practitioners of native medicine and *thanthras*), Kumbaras (potters) and Gollas (cowherds and cattle breeders) from the neighbouring areas. As an incentive to stay, all of them were offered *jamma* rights over portions of forest lands which they had to clear and make fit for cultivation. Yeravas (agricultural labourers) and other manual labourers were brought to service the needs of the agriculturists. A few of these people might have migrated into Kodagu even earlier in search of work. (See Appendix 5 for brief descriptions of the Communities of Kodagu.)

Most of these immigrants who came during the time of the Kodagu rajas (except for Kumbaras, Yeravas and other labourers) adopted customs and traditions that were similar to or close to those of the Kodavas and built their own *ainmanes*.

During the eighteenth century, Hyder Ali, an officer in the army of the Wodeyar of Mysore, usurped the Mysore kingdom and rose to power. He tried to subdue the people of Kodagu, but was repulsed. When Lingaraja I of the Haleri dynasty died in 1780, Hyder Ali assumed authority over Kodagu under the pretext of being a guardian to his sons and forcibly detained the princes (one of whom, Dodda Veerarajendra, also known as Dodda Veeraraja, was to become the next king of Kodagu) in Gorur. After Hyder Ali's death in 1782, his son Tippu Sultan shifted the captive princes to Periyapatna fort.

Tippu Sultan also made many attempts to exert control over all of Kodagu and enlarge his empire, but was unsuccessful. He was furious with the people of Kodagu who rose in rebellion from time to time and thwarted his attempts to enlarge his empire. In 1785 he invited them to a clearing near Bhagamandla for peace talks. When an estimated 70,000[16] of them (men, women and children, mainly Kodavas and Ammas) came there unarmed, Tippu Sultan's soldiers took them by surprise and forced them to march over rough terrain, through the jungles, to Seringapatam[17] and got them converted to Islam.[18] Many died on the way. The population of Kodagu was drastically reduced and several Kodava and Amma *okkas* became extinct. Tippu Sultan took control of Kodagu, and brought Muslims from the Mysore area and gave them the land of the deported *okkas*. However, unable to bear the severe weather and difficult living conditions in the wild, forested tracts of Kodagu, most of these Muslims returned to Mysore.

In 1788 Dodda Veerarajendra (1788–1809) along with his wife and brothers escaped from Tippu Sultan's prison in Periyapatna with the help of some brave and loyal Kodavas assisted by Hombale Nayaka[19] and Ismail Khan,[20] and returned to Kodagu. He defeated Tippu Sultan's battalion that was stationed there, took control of Kodagu and drove out the Muslim landlords installed by Tippu Sultan.

During the Third Anglo-Mysore War that started in 1791 (according to the 'Kodagu District Gazetteer', 1993), the British attacked Seringapatam and subdued Tippu Sultan. In the resulting chaos, an estimated 7,000 of the Kodavas and Ammas who were converted to Islam escaped and returned to Kodagu in 1791/1792. The converted Kodavas and Ammas were not taken back into their original communities (except for a few who returned unobtrusively and

16. Different accounts of this event have varying estimates of these numbers.

17. The name by which the British called Srirangapattana.

18. The able-bodied among these prisoners were trained to be soldiers in Tippu Sultan's army and they were called 'Ahamadis'. Dodda Veerarajendra requested the British to ensure safe passage back to Kodagu to those among the Ahamadis who were taken prisoners by the British during wars with Tippu Sultan or who sought refuge with the British.

19. Okkaliga army officer in charge of supervising the royal prisoners. He befriended and sympathised with Dodda Veerarajendra. When Dodda Veerarajendra regained control of Kodagu, Hombale Nayaka was rewarded with a *jagir* in Murnad, Kodagu, and was made a diwan in the king's court. He is the ancestor of the Keremane Okkaliga *okka* in Kodagu.

20. Officer in charge of the guards at Periyapatna fort and a good friend of Hombale Nayaka. He was rewarded with a *jagir* in Kodagu. His descendants, called Jagir Thurkas, are the Uddichanda *okka* in Bilugunda.

settled in their depleted *okkas*[21]) and they came to be known as Jamma Mapilles. Dodda Veerarajendra rehabilitated them—some in their own vacant *ainmanes* and others on newly allotted *jamma* land. He also offered refuge to the sizeable number of Roman Catholics from the coastal areas of South Canara, who too were forcibly taken to Seringapatam and converted to Islam by Tippu Sultan.[22] They too escaped from Seringapatam in 1791/1792 along with the others and because of the continuing battles in South Canara decided to accept the raja's offer to settle in Kodagu. Dodda Veerarajendra granted them land and assisted them in building St Anne's church in Virajpet. He also provided a stipend for its maintenance and procured a Catholic priest for them from Goa. This stipend was continued by his successors and later by the British. In 1799 the British defeated Tippu Sultan's army in the Fourth Anglo-Mysore War and Tippu Sultan was killed in Seringapatam.

The recurring wars with Tippu Sultan's armies in the late 1700s took a heavy toll on the population of Kodagu. Many of the raja's subjects, especially young men, died on the battlefield and the large number of people forcibly taken away by Tippu Sultan to Seringapatam resulted in the land being drastically depopulated. The raja then enticed more immigrants to the land and created border posts at the many mountain passes all along the borders of Kodagu to prevent the new immigrants from leaving Kodagu. Some of the later Tulu Gouda immigrants were given the land and *ainmanes* left vacant in the Bhagamandla and Napoklu areas by the many Kodava and Amma *okkas* made extinct by Tippu Sultan.

Later immigrants to Kodagu included a few Bunts from South Canara, Mahrattas and Moplahs. The Bunts and Mahrattas built traditional *ainmanes*.

---

21. We were told by eleven Kodava *okkas* that their elders who were converted by Tippu Sultan, returned to Kodagu, revived their *okkas* that were facing extinction with no males left, and reverted to their original status as Kodavas.

22. On 24 February 1784, on orders given by Tippu Sultan, 60,000 Roman Catholics, men, women and children were captured in Canara and marched to Srirangapattana. [*History of Bunts* (2008), by Krishnananada Hegde, p. 67; *Kodagina Ithihasa* (1974), by D.N. Krishnaiah, p. 247.]

Others who migrated in small numbers from the neighbouring areas were traders, manual labourers, skilled workers (who came initially for seasonal work), and Brahmins (brought to serve as priests in temples and to work in offices and courts). They tended to follow the customs and traditions of their native areas and did not build *ainmanes*.

Until British rule, Kodagu had no proper roads and only limited means of communication with the outside world. With the advent of the British in the 1800s, roads were built and commerce with the neighbouring areas increased. This resulted in a new set of migrants to Kodagu. Some were traders from Malabar and others were labourers who came to work in the paddy fields during sowing and transplantation seasons and in the coffee estates that were being opened up. During the paddy-growing season Billavas and Bunts from South Canara came to cultivate wetlands belonging to the bigger landlords on *vara* (lease—where the owners of the land were given about twenty-five to thirty per cent of the yield). A large part of this migration was seasonal.

Over the years, the changing demography of this region has resulted in a profusion of religious groups living in Kodagu, tolerant of each other's faith. The vast majority of them, including Goudas, Lingayaths and Kodavas, are Hindus. Next in numbers are Muslims, Christians and Jains. There are also small numbers belonging to other minor religious groups including Buddhists and Sikhs.

In 1807 Dodda Veerarajendra commissioned the *Rajendraname*—a record of the history of the Paleri kings of Kodagu. Because the letters and documents in the palace in Madikeri fort were destroyed during Hyder Ali's invasion, this history was reconstructed from whatever information was available and from memory. The *Rajendraname* was translated into English from the original Kannada in 1808 by Sir Robert Abercombie. Dodda Veerarajendra died in 1809. The other well-known Kodagu raja was his brother, Lingaraja II (1811–1820), who commissioned the *Hukum Nama* in 1811. It is a fascinating record with details on the prevalent justice system, administration, conduct of the raja's administrators, land tenure system, guidelines for land revenue collection and the responsibilities of farmers. This was translated into English by A.J. Curgenven. Robert Cole's *Manual of Coorg Civil Law*, 1871, was based on this translation.

The Kodagu rajas built four forts. Of these, only the one built by Mudduraja in 1681 in Madikeri (the capital of Kodagu) is well preserved. Originally a mud fort, it was renovated and the walls were strengthened with stones and mortar by Tippu Sultan. The buildings within it have been used as government offices since the time of British rule. The other three forts in Kushalnagar, Beppunad and Bhagamandla were wooden forts with mud walls. These were destroyed during the wars between the rajas and Tippu Sultan.

The rajas also built two palaces, a large one inside the Madikeri fort and a smaller one, the Nalnad (Nalknad) palace, in Kakkabe, both built with mud. The Madikeri palace was rebuilt in brick and mortar by Lingaraja II in 1814–1818. It was thatched until 1865 when it was tiled by the British. The Nalnad palace was built by Dodda Veerarajendra in 1792. It has a small, beautiful *mantapa* (ornamental pavilion) in front, built in 1796 to celebrate his marriage to Mahadevamma. There are some colourful murals on the walls of the palace which is now a popular tourist site.

There are two *gaddiges* (monumental tombs of the Lingayath rajas) in Madikeri, with striking architecture in the Mughal style. They were built in 1809 and 1821 in memory of Dodda Veerarajendra and Lingaraja II who were buried there. Their wives were buried next to them. Beside these is a third, similar *gaddige* built in 1834 for Rudrappa, a respected guru, the royal priest of the rajas. Also nearby are tombs of two Kodava diwans (high officials) of the Kodagu rajas—Biddanda Bopu (who served under Dodda Veerarajendra), and his son, Somaiah (who served under Chikka Veerarajendra). The tomb of

Lingaraja I (1775–1780), father of Dodda Veerarajendra, is in Madapur (north of Madikeri).

The last Kodagu raja, Chikka Veerarajendra (1820–1834) was deposed in 1834 by the British who took control of the territory. They called it Coorg and made it part of the East India Company's holding. Chikka Veerarajendra and his family were deported to Benares where he lived for fourteen years. He went to England in 1852 with his favourite daughter, Gowramma, whom Queen Victoria accepted as her god-daughter. Princess Gowramma was baptised and given the name 'Victoria'. Chikka Veerarajendra died in England in 1859.[23]

In 1837, there was a revolt against the British, mainly by the Goudas of Sulya and Puthur (which were formerly part of Kodagu and were transferred to South Canara by the British). The primary reason for the revolt was that they were required to pay tax on the produce of their land in cash, unlike the earlier practice of payment in kind or cash to the Kodagu rajas. The British put down the rebellion at Amara Sulya. This battle is referred to as the Amara Sulya *katakayi* (rebellion) of 1837.[24]

Kodagu was made a Chief Commissioner's Province of British India after Queen Victoria's proclamation of 1858.[25] In 1861, in recognition of their help in averting the 1857–1858 uprising in and around Seringapatam, the British proclaimed that 'the gallant people of Coorg' would be exempt from the Indian Arms Act, which was then called the 'Disarming Act'. This exemption to 'Kodavas by race' and to 'holders of *jamma* land in Kodagu' continues to apply to this day.

23. Gowramma married Col. John Campbell in 1860. She died in England in 1864, just short of twenty-three years of age. Her daughter Edith married Capt. Henry Yardley and they had a son, Victor Yardley. Edith died in 1934 at the age of seventy-three. Her son is believed to have died in a road accident in Australia in 1936.

24. When the soldiers from Kodagu who helped the British were offered a share of the Rs 20,000 that was looted from the Mangalore Treasury by the rebellers, they refused the offer and were rewarded instead with *jagir* lands and pensions for three generations, with horses, gold and silver medals, and broad cloth.

25. Queen Victoria's Proclamation of the 1 November 1858 to the Princes, Chiefs and People of India officially announced that the political authority of the East India Company had ceased to exist and that the Government of India had been transferred to the management of the Crown.

Although they do not need licences to possess guns, they now have to register their guns with the police.

The rule of the British ended in 1947 with India gaining independence. In 1952 Kodagu was made a part 'C' state with its own government, directly responsible to the central government. This continued until 1 November 1956 when the states were reorganised on a linguistic basis, and Kodagu was made a district of Mysore state which was renamed as Karnataka state on 1 November 1973.

Appendix 4

LAND TENURE

Jamma land tenure, a system that is unique to Kodagu, was established by the Kodagu rajas. It formalised the rights of the people over the land that they already possessed. *Jamma* land included stretches of *bhumi* (wetland) for cultivation of rice, *barike* (low-lying pasture land) for grazing cattle and *bane* (forest highland) for forest produce such as timber and firewood, and for grazing cattle. *Jamma* land was neither divisible nor transferable[1] and this helped in keeping the members of the *okka* united. *Jamma* land was enjoyed as a permanent, hereditary right of the *okka* and was recorded under the name of the *pattedara*, the current head of the *okka*. It was lightly taxed and was jointly owned, occupied and cultivated by all the members of the *okka*. Private ownership of land by individuals or nuclear families was practically non-existent in the past. The system of *jamma* land tenure continues to this day.

When the rajas granted *jamma* land, along with the land they gave the *jamma* landholders, families of labourers (Kembattis and Yeravas) to work on the land. These labourers were attached to the *okka*, and in a few cases to the land.

1. We have come across a few cases where, in the past, part or all of the *jamma* land of an *okka* was sold or given to another *okka*, when the *okka* which owned it could not cultivate or maintain it.

A distinctive feature of this tenure was that the revenue collected by the Kodagu rajas for *jamma* wetland was based not on acreage but on the quality of the land and the expected yield.[2] Wetland was measured in terms of the expected yield of paddy in *bhattis*[3] (baskets)—a practice that continues to this day. It was assessed nominally at Rs 5 for 100 *bhattis* of wetland (which amounted to about 1/20th of the value of the expected yield at that time) and could be paid in cash or in kind (as paddy). In return, *jamma* landholders were required to serve the rajas in various capacities[4]—as soldiers during times of war, as huntsmen and as guards. They were also obliged to supply the palace with produce from their land during festivals and wars.

The British too granted *jamma* land to some *okkas*. They framed laws that allowed partition of the *jamma* property of the *okka*. The revenue regulation of 1874 allowed for 'Maintenance division'. This did not break up the property of the *okka* but 'merely gave enjoyment rights to particular branches of the family'.[5] The British stopped granting *jamma* land in 1895.

Both *barike* and *bane* land were not taxed unless they were brought under cultivation.

Okkas that had no land at all were given '*sagu*' land (land for cultivation) that was assessed at the normal rate, which was twice that for *jamma* land. *Sagu* landholders were liable to render every type of service to the state, except military service. This ensured that cultivation did not suffer during times of war.

The rajas, and later the British, granted *umbali* land (wetland that was lightly assessed, at a fraction—about a quarter—of the rate for *sagu* land and, like *jamma*

2. This took into account factors such as availability of water, quality of the soil, weather in the area, location, etc.
3. Each *bhatti* holds eighty *seers* (a measure of volume) of harvested paddy. One hundred *bhattis* was the expected yield in those times from about three acres of paddy fields.
4. The *Hukum Nama* of Lingaraja II, 1811, defined the rights and duties of *jamma* landholders.
5. Lt Col. K.C. Ponnappa, *A Study of The Origin of Coorgs* (Bangalore: self-published, 1997), p. 9.

land, was not transferable) for valuable services rendered, and *jagir* or *jahagir* land (wetland that was free of assessment) for exceptional services rendered by individuals. The right to these lands was formalised by way of *sanads* (title deeds) and remained hereditary with the *okkas*.

Paisari land (wasteland) and forest land were the property of the rulers. Mountain slopes (parts of reserved forests) were leased to *okkas* residing in areas neighbouring the slopes, with the hereditary right to grow cardamom on the land. These leaseholds were free of assessment and were known as *jamma male* (*jamma* right to hills). Cutting trees and hunting were forbidden in these forest lands.

Lingaraja II had the cultivated land in Kodagu surveyed in 1815–1817 by Lt Connor to facilitate assessment of the tax to be paid.[6] Later, in 1906–1912, the British had an accurate survey of the land in Kodagu done by Gustav Haller.

6. This was a topographical survey. G. Richter, in his *Gazetteer of Coorg*, 1870, p. 422, writes '... his beautifully executed map on a scale of one mile to an inch ... he made no less than 118 triangulations .... and on his map every plot of cultivated land was carefully laid down.'

Appendix 5

COMMUNITIES

Some of the better-known communities in Kodagu, starting with the earliest inhabitants, are given below. Communities who do not have *ainmanes* are marked with an asterisk (*).

Kuruba* - Very early inhabitants of Kodagu who were nomadic hill tribes living on the fringes of Kodagu, also found in the neigbouring areas of Karnataka and Malabar.

Jenu Kuruba - A hill tribe found in the hills and forests of Kodagu and other parts of Karnataka, who traditionally collected wild honey from the forests and bartered it for a living. They are good hunters. They tamed wild elephants and were in charge of the royal elephants during the time of the Kodagu rajas. Their women wear their saris in the Kodava style but with the pleats in front. They speak a dialect of Kannada.

Betta Kuruba - They live deep in the forests and make baskets and mats for a living. They also work as agricultural labourers these days.

Halu Kuruba - Sheep breeders and blanket weavers.

Kudiya - Nomadic hill tribes living in the forests of the Western Ghats and found in the Karnataka and Malabar areas. They were among the very early inhabitants of Kodagu.

Poomale Kudiya - Branch of Kudiyas living in Kodagu. In the past their men and women earned their living by tapping toddy. They also wove mats and baskets and were good hunters. These days, Poomale Kudiyas work as agricultural labourers. They follow Kodava customs and dress, and speak the Kodava language.

Themale Kudiya* - Immigrants from Kerala who are not related to the Poomale Kudiyas. They collected honey in the past. They follow the dress, food habits and customs of Kerala and speak Malayalam.

Kembatti - Considered among the earliest inhabitants of Kodagu. Kembattis were bonded to *okkas* of the landed class (mainly Kodavas) in the past and worked as agricultural labourers in their fields. They belong to the scheduled castes, similar to those found in Kerala, Karnataka and Tamil Nadu. In the olden days, the relationship between Kembattis and the Kodavas was one of trust and friendship. When a Kodava died, some of the Kembattis attached to the *okka* followed the mourning rituals practised by close relatives of the deceased. Friendship between Kodavas and Kembattis is also evident in Kodava folk songs. In one song, Karikotta, believed to be a Kembatti, is given god-like status. Pannangalathamme, the deity of the Kembattis, is worshipped by Kodavas also and Kodavas along with Kembattis are often *thakkas* of Kembatti shrines. They follow the customs and dress of the Kodavas and speak the Kodava language. They play the pipes and horns during festive occasions and for the folk dances in Kodagu.

Kodava - Among the earliest inhabitants of Kodagu, Kodavas have been the largest and the dominant community since the early history of Kodagu. They were dominant probably because they were the landed class and were valuable to their rulers as warriors. Also, they have been the culturally dominant community in Kodagu.[1] There are many speculations regarding their origins since their customs

1. 'The Kodava, or Coorgs … are culturally dominant, giving the district its name, its image, and a substantial part of its political and economic leadership …' ['Kodava Song and the Public Non-Assertion of Difference', *Global Media Journal*, Australian Edition, Vol 4:2 (2010), by Dr John Napier, University of New South Wales, Sydney, Australia.]

are very different from those of the neighbouring areas. They were undoubtedly a community of warriors and hunters with martial traditions who, over time, took to agriculture, coffee growing and a variety of professions, especially in the armed forces. They have maintained their unique customs and cultural identity despite the influences of their Tulu, Malayalam and Kannada speaking neighbours. They are primarily ancestor worshippers and periodically propitiate their ancestors in the *Karanang Kodpa* ceremony. Their most important festivals are *Kail Polud, Kaveri Sankramana* and *Puthari.* They adopted elements of the Hindu religion from immigrants and priests who came to Kodagu. However, Brahmins have no role in any of their customs or rituals—unlike the practice among most Hindus. The Kodavas continue to wear their distinct traditional dress,[2] especially during festive occasions. They speak the Kodava language.

Amma - A community similar to Kodavas in all respects, except that they are vegetarians who follow some Brahminical practices. They are also referred to as Amma Kodavas. They are said to have been the indigenous priests of Kodagu but their origins are not known. Before the advent of Brahmins, they were the priests in many of the temples in Kodagu including the main ones in Thalakaveri, Bhagamandla and Igguthappa, and were known as Kaveri Brahmins. Now most of them follow other professions, primarily cultivation of paddy and coffee, although some continue to serve as priests in a few shrines. In 1834, the Ammas of Padinalknad were invited to Balamuri on the banks of the river Kaveri by Thimmappayya, a Brahmin in the court of the raja, and were given the sacred thread worn by Brahmins in a traditional investiture ceremony. They became disciples of the Sri Ramachandra Matha in Shimogga. Later, Ammas of Kiggattnad

2. The Kodava man's attire is a long *kupya* (coat/tunic, usually black; white for special occasions) and *chele* (red and gold sash) with a *peeche kathi* (dagger) tucked in the sash, and a red-and-white checked scarf or a white turban tied around his head. The Kodava woman wears her sari with the pleats tucked in at the back of the waist and the loose end secured over her right shoulder. She covers her head with a *vasthra* (long veil) tied back at the nape of her neck.

also adopted the sacred thread when they became disciples of the Udupi Ashta Matha. The remaining Ammas became followers of the Subrahmanya Matha in Dakshina Kannada.

Jaina - Early settlers who were probably here as early as eighth century AD, during the rule of the Chengalvas and Kongalvas who were Jains. After the fall of the Kongalvas, Jainism gradually disappeared in Kodagu. The small number of Jains now in Kodagu belong to the Digambara sect and the Kashyapa *gothra* (lineage traced back to ancient sages). Since marriage within a *gothra* is forbidden, they marry Jains from outside Kodagu. Although they are strict vegetarians and their religion requires them to be non-violent, they offer chicken to the spirit-deities Pashana-murthi and Kuliya outside the house during their *theres/kolas* (performance rituals in honour of deities). They celebrate *Kail Polud* and *Puthari*, besides Jain and Hindu festivals. They speak Kannada (mainly) and the Kodava language.

Heggade - Early settlers about whose origin there are many theories. It is likely that they came in groups from neighbouring Malabar, Tulu and Kannada areas at different points in time. Some were possibly a very early offshoot of the Kodavas. Yet others are believed to have been soldiers of the Hoysala kings, who stayed back in Kodagu. The more recent Heggade immigrants were invited by the Kodagu rajas from South Canara and were given *jamma*, *umbali* and *jagir* land. They are cultivators and warriors who conform to Kodava customs and language. '*Thodangl kathi ullannake nanga Kodavada kuda*' is a saying among them, implying that they are as close to Kodavas as a sword to its clasp.

Gouda - Cultivators from the Puthur and Sulya areas of South Canara that were part of Kodagu until 1834, they are a large community of Vaishnavites (worshippers of God Vishnu or Venkataramana). A few are very early immigrants and the rest came in waves, mainly during Dodda Veerarajendra's time towards the end of the eighteenth and beginning of the nineteenth century. They were invited by the raja to populate areas that were depleted when large numbers of Kodavas and Ammas were captured and taken away by Tippu Sultan. The Goudas settled mainly in the Bhagamandla, Napoklu and Madikeri areas and gradually became close to the Kodavas in their cultural traditions. They follow most of the Kodava customs and festivals although they have retained some of their native customs (such as the *dhare* ceremony at weddings and the *thali* worn by married women). Besides Kodava festivals they celebrate *Yugadi, Bishu* and *Kidasa* (worship of paddy after planting is completed). Their most important ceremony is *Hari Seve* to God Venkataramana. In the past, they dressed like Kodavas during their wedding ceremonies and when dancing in the *ur mand* and *nad mand* during *Puthari*. These days they rarely participate in the *Puthari* dances and only dance the *Bolakat, Peeliyat,* etc., in temple yards during temple festivals, wearing the *kupya* and *chele*. In some *okkas* even that has stopped.[3] The women, especially older women in villages, continue to wear their saris in the Kodava style, but with the pleats in front. They speak Are-bhashe (literally 'half language'), a mix of Halegannada (old form of Kannada), Tulu and Kodava *thakk* and are therefore called Are-bhashe Goudas. They are also called Tulu Goudas.

Okkaliga Gouda - Kannada-speaking Okkaligas (agriculturists) from the Mysore, Hassan and Chikmagalur areas. Invited by the rajas, they came in large numbers and initially settled in the north of Kodagu. They adopted Kodava customs and observe both Kodava and Hindu festivals. Many of them who married Kodavas came to be known as Jamma Kodavas or Ede Kodavas, and cannot be distinguished from the Kodavas. Some intermarried with Goudas and can hardly be distinguished from them. Those who remained as Okkaliga Goudas are few in number. They speak both Kannada and Kodava languages.

3. When they decided to stop dancing, the *okkas* offered a silver staff to God Igguthappa asking to be excused from dancing during *Puthari*. The same procedure was followed by some Golla *okkas* also when they stopped dancing.

Lingayath (Veerashaiva)* - The Lingayath sect has followers from many communities. Those who came to Kodagu were Kannada-speaking agriculturists and traders of the Veerashaiva faith. A few of them came to Kodagu during the time of the later Chengalva rule; more came during the time of the Lingayath rajas. They have some *mathas* (monasteries) in the Somwarpet area in the north of Kodagu where the rajas gave them land. They are vegetarians, Shaivites (worshippers of Shiva) and observe Hindu festivals.

Airi - Early immigrants from Malabar who were carpenters (*mara-airi* or *achari)*, goldsmiths (*ponn-airi* or *thatta*) and blacksmiths (*irumb-airi* or *kolla*). They were called Thachayiri and helped in building the *ainmanes*, temples and palaces of Kodagu. They follow Kodava customs and speak the Kodava language.

Meda* - Early settlers in Kodagu who were drummers, basket-weavers and agricultural labourers. They beat the *pare* drum for festivals and dances, and during hunts. They also weave baskets and fish traps from cane, reed and bamboo. They worship Kali and spirit-dieties. Their customs are similar to those of the Kodavas and they speak the Kodava language. Their women wear their saris in the Kodava style.

Hajama/Nayinda - Barbers, who are also drummers and pipers. They are believed to have come from the *moodu seeme* area (eastern parts) of Karnataka. They follow many Kodava customs, speak the Kodava language and have a role in Kodava marriage and death ceremonies. It is said that there are only five *jamma* Hajama *okkas* in Kodagu. They intermarry with other Hajamas who came to Kodagu later.

Madivala - Washermen who came from the Kannada areas. They have a role in Kodava ceremonies (such as weddings and funerals) and in temple ceremonies. They speak the Kodava language. Their womenfolk wear their saris in the Kodava style.

Koleya - Workers who work with mud, building walls, etc. They belong to the Koleyan (also called Maniyani) community in Kerala and are believed to have 'come' to Kodagu with Goddess Adi Pudiyodi. They follow Kodava customs and speak the Kodava language.

Koyava - Early immigrants from Kerala who are agriculturists. They follow Kodava customs and speak the Kodava language.

Yerava* - A nomadic tribe who are believed to have been brought as slaves or to have migrated to Kodagu in the seventeenth century from Wynad in Kerala and from the Mysore region. In the past they were agricultural labourers bonded to *okkas* of the landed class. Nowadays they work on their own paddy fields and as paid agricultural labourers. During the time of the Kodagu rajas, they were recruited as soldiers in the army and were hired as trusted servants to royalty. Their beliefs and practices are similar to those of other Hindus. Their language has many words from Malayalam and old Kannada. Their women wear saris in the Kodava style but with the pleats in front.

Marangi* - Similar to Kembattis, but a separate community, Marangis are much smaller in number than Kembattis and are believed to have been bonded to Ammas in the past. They work as agricultural labourers. These days, some of them have intermarried with Kembattis.

Brahmin* - Namboodris from Malabar and Brahmins from the Kannada areas. While a few of them came to Kodagu even before the time of the rajas, the majority of them came during the time of the rajas to officiate as priests in temples and to work in offices and courts.

Bunt - Tulu-speaking agriculturists and traders who came from South Canara during the rule of the Kodagu rajas. They celebrate Kodava festivals as well as *Hari Seve* and follow most of the Kodava customs. They gave up their native '*aliya kattu*' (matrilineal) customs and adopted the patrilineal system common in Kodagu. They speak Tulu and Kodava languages. Only five Bunt *okkas* in Kodagu had traditional *ainmanes*—called *malla illu* in Tulu—of which only two are still standing.

Golla/Aimbokka - Cattle-breeders belonging to the Yadava *kula* (race) who originally came as palanquin-bearers from Vijayanagara. They were given land to cultivate and *jamma male* land by the Kodagu rajas, and took to agriculture. They speak the Kodava language and worship Krishna and Venkataramana. They were also called '*aimbokkas*' because '*aimbad* (which means fifty) *okkas*' of their community came to Kodagu. They follow many of the Kodava customs and speak the Kodava language. Brahmins officiate at their marriages. They used to dance the Puthari *kol* dance in the village *mand* but that stopped some years ago.[4]

Christian* - Mainly Roman Catholics from South Canara who had been persecuted and captured by Tippu Sultan and who later escaped from the prison in Seringapatam. Dodda Veerarajendra gave them refuge in Kodagu. He granted them land, assisted them in building a church in Virajpet, and procured a Catholic priest for them from Goa.

Kumbara* - Potters from South Canara, Mysore and Malabar who came to Kodagu during Dodda Veerarajendra's time. They are worshippers of Venkataramana and speak Tulu, Kannada, Malayalam and a dialect of their own.

Kapala* - Believed to be descendants of Abyssinian Siddhis who came to Kodagu from Malabar in the seventeenth century to work as the rajas' guards and executioners. They are now very small in number and live mainly in the Yavakapadi area. Their customs are similar to those of the Kodavas and they speak the Kodava language with a mix of Tamil and Malayalam words. They have no *ainmanes*, but have a *kaimada* to their *karanava*—Bolthajjappa (probably Katala Bolthu, referred to in the ballad of Kaliyatanda Ponnappa).[5]

Kaniya - Astrologers and spiritual guides from Malabar who later took to agriculture. They have adopted many Kodava customs and speak Malayalam and Kodava languages.

---

4. See footnote 3 on page 153.
5. See *Pattole Palame*.

Jamma Mapille - Descendants of the Kodavas and Ammas who were captured by Tippu Sultan in 1785, taken to Seringapatam and converted to Islam. When they escaped from Seringapatam and returned to Kodagu in 1791/1792, the majority of them were not taken back into their original communities. Dodda Veerarajendra rehabilitated them in Kodagu, some on land previously owned by them and the rest on land that was given to them with *jamma* rights. Since they depended on the Moplahs/Mapilles[6] of neighbouring Malabar to guide them in the religious practices of Islam, they were called Jamma Mapilles. Up to the end of the nineteenth century they followed many of the social customs of the Kodavas and joined them in the group dances held during *Puthari*. Some of them continue to do so and a few make offerings to village deities to this day. In one Jamma Mapille *okka* we were told that they worshipped Ayyappa until recently. Some of them were the *thakkas* of their *ur*, and some continue in that role. In the past, some had *thakkames* in village shrines. Jamma Mapilles and Kodavas treat each other with mutual respect and friendship. In some villages, Jamma Mapilles and Kodavas have roles in each others' festivals and shrines/mosques.

Jagir Thurka - Descendants of some of the Muslims who were brought by Tippu Sultan from the Mysore area and were given land of the deported Kodava and Amma *okkas* as *jagirs*. Most of them left, unable to bear the living conditions in Kodagu. Other Jagir Thurkas are descendants of the family of Ismail Khan who helped Dodda Veerarajendra escape from the prison in Periyapatna. They were given *jagirs* by the raja in the Kunda and Bilugunda areas.

Banna - Washermen from Malabar, who are also drum-beaters. They perform *theres/kolas* in honour of deities and ancestors, at which time they also act as oracles. Their customs and language are similar to those of the Kodavas.

6. Muslim traders from Malabar.

Panika - They came from Madayi in Malabar, where they served in shrines. They take part in *theres* of ancestors and in other *theres/kolas* of deities such as Ayyappa, Bhagavathi, Sarthavu and Povvadi, as well as of spirit-deities Nari Bhutha, Pade Beera, etc. They follow Kodava customs and language.

Paleya* - Tulu-speaking Ajala Paleyas (from South Canara) and Malayalam-speaking Aramane Paleyas (from Malabar). They are spirit dancers who do *kola* of spirit-deities such as Vishnu-murthi, Pashana-murthi, Panjurli, Angara, etc. Some of them also perform *theres* of ancestors. Some of their customs are similar to those of Kodavas.

Maleya - They came from Malabar and are proficient in *nat vaidya* (native medicines) and *thanthras* (mystic rites in the worship of Shiva). They generally perform *theres* of ancestors and *kolas* of Vishnu-murthi, Ajjappa, Kuttichatha and other spirit-deities. Their customs are similar to those of Kodavas.

Komati* (Shetti/Vaishyas) - Telugu-speaking trading caste.

Bune Patta/Beene Patta/Cheeni Patta - Originally singing mendicants from Malabar, they follow all Kodava customs and speak the Kodava language. Since they are very small in number they have intermarried with Kodava Nairs and Kodavas.

Moplah/Mapille* - Traders from Malabar who follow Islam.

Banya/Ganiga - Traditional oil extractors from Malabar and South Canara areas. They speak the Kodava language. Being a small community, they found it difficult to find brides/grooms and joined the Are-bhashe Gouda community in 1962. But they continue to be identified as Banyas.

Balegara/Telugu Banajiga - Originally bangle sellers, who came from the Mysore, South Canara and Telugu regions. They speak a mixture of Tamil and Telugu.

Kodava Nair - Originally from Kodathur near Neeleshwar in Kasargod district of Kerala. They are similar to Kodavas in most respects and follow all Kodava customs and speak the Kodava language. They claim to have 'come' to Kodagu with God Sarthavu.

Shivachaliya* - Farmers and traders from the Mysore areas.

Devanga* - Weavers and farmers who came during the time of the rajas. They speak Kannada and Telugu.

Jamma Marathi - Mainly business folk, who migrated from South Canara. They are small in number and speak a mix of Marathi and Kannada languages. (They had one *ainmane* with beautiful carvings which is no longer there.)

Most of the early immigrant communities spoke the Kodava language and followed Kodava dress, customs and manners. Some of the immigrants who came during the latter part of the rule of the Kodagu rajas kept their separate identity, although they followed the customs, dress and language of the Kodavas.

The *ainmanes* and the rituals conducted in some of the non-Kodava *ainmanes* are so similar to those in Kodava *ainmanes* and the residents are so fluent in the Kodava language, that, on a casual visit, one hardly notices any difference between them and the Kodavas. There are many villages where even today members of all the different communities join together to celebrate the harvest festival or a temple festival with song and dance. Some communities also have a role to play in each others' festivals.

In the past, Jamma Mapille *okkas*, like many of the other communities in Kodagu, celebrated *Puthari*, the harvest festival. Even today, they ritually cut *kad* (new ears of paddy) from their paddy fields during *Puthari*. They have a role in some Kodava festivals and village shrines, and some Kodava *okkas* have roles in Muslim festivals and mosques. In fact, unity between the different communities in the villages appears to have been the norm in Kodagu.

Appendix 6

LANGUAGES

Kodagu is now inhabited by a mosaic of people of different faiths and cultures, resulting in a number of languages being spoken in the district. Most of the early inhabitants and settlers in Kodagu speak Kodava *thakk*, the mother tongue of the Kodavas. Eminent linguists such as Prof. M.B. Emeneau (Professor Emeritus, University of California, at Berkeley) and Dr R. Balakrishna (Department of Linguistics, Annamalai University) consider Kodava *thakk* to be an independent, early Dravidian language, which incorporated words from languages spoken in the neighbouring regions. It is an oral language that does not have a script of its own, and is written in the Kannada script, since Kannada was the court language of the Kodagu rajas.

The massacre and forcible deportation of a large number of Kodavas by Tippu Sultan, and the immigration of a large number of outsiders invited into Kodagu by the Lingayath rajas during their reign (1600–1834), changed the demographics and the language pattern of the region. The people brought in by the rajas included farmers, labourers and skilled artisans, mainly from the neighbouring Kannada and Tulu areas in Karnataka, and traders and artisans from the North Malabar areas. As a result Kannada is now spoken by about a third of the population of Kodagu. (The total population of Kodagu according to the 2011 census is 5,54,519.) Next in number are those who speak Malayalam and those who speak the Kodava language. Tulu, Tamil, Urdu, Konkani and Telugu are the other major languages spoken in the district.[1] There are a number of dialects spoken in Kodagu, including Are-bhashe that is spoken by a large number of Tulu Goudas.

1. According to the Census of India, 2001, Kannada is spoken by 35% of the population of Kodagu, Malayalam by 23%, Kodava *thakk* by 17%, Tulu by 9%,Tamil by 6% and Urdu by 3%.

Appendix 7

RELIGIOUS PRACTICES

Primarily ancestor worshippers, the early inhabitants of Kodagu also pay homage to nature, worshipping the earth, the sun, water and fire—practices that predate religion. Ayyappa, god of the hunt, and river goddess, Kaveri, are among the earliest of their local deities.

They pray to their ancestors and seek their blessings every day. On special occasions, each *okka* ritually worships its ancestors at the *karana thare,* the sacred ancestor platform, or the *kaimada*, the sacred shrine to ancestors, both of which are located near the *ainmane*. These rituals and the unique ceremonies related to ancestor worship—*Karanang Kodpa* and *Karana There*—define the identity of the early inhabitants of Kodagu. (See brief descriptions of these ceremonies on pages 90–93.)

Elements of nature worship continue to this day among the early inhabitants of Kodagu. The earth is worshipped before ploughing paddy fields. The sun is prayed to every morning when the front door (that almost invariably faces east) is opened to let in the rays of the rising sun. Water from the well is worshipped during the Ganga *puje* ceremony by a bride or by the mother of a newborn child. Kaveri (Kaveriamme, the mother goddess) is worshipped only as water, both in the sacred Kundike pond at Thalakaveri and in every house during the *Kaveri*

Sankramana festival (see pages 101–102). The sacred lamp in the *ainmane* which is lit and prayed to daily is also witness to all important ceremonies such as weddings and funerals. None of these ceremonies have priests presiding over the rituals.

For the very early inhabitants, living in the dense jungles of Kodagu, the primary source of food was meat obtained by hunting. They worshipped Ayyappa, god of the hunt, in primitive forest shrines that consisted of simple earthen platforms erected in clearings in the forests, and made votive offerings of small bows and arrows, and terracotta dogs to him. Ayyappa is worshipped in this manner to this day. However, over time, the identities of some of the early deities have become confused and their names are occasionally intermixed. For example, the ancient deity Ayyappa is confused with the Sanskritic god Sarthavu.

Besides these, the early inhabitants worship their ancient gods who came to Malabar from across the seven seas and 'migrated' to Kodagu. Their coming to and settling in Kodagu is narrated vividly in their folk songs. These gods are perhaps the earliest to 'come' to Kodagu. They are called by the names of the places where they settled (for example, Igguthappa settled on the Iggutha hill, Palurappa in Palur, Pannangalathamme in Pannangala, Rudraguppelamme in Rudraguppe, etc.).[1] The most revered of them is Igguthappa, the god of rain and foodcrops.

These gods were later inducted into the Hindu pantheon of gods and given Sanskritic names by the Brahmin priests who were employed by the Lingayath rajas. For example, Igguthappa is now identified with Ishwara or his son Subrahmanya, and Palurappa with Ishwara. There are a few exceptions such as Pannangalathamme[2] who has no Sanskritic identity. There are temples in Kodagu to these gods. Among them, the temples to God Igguthappa in Padi, Ammangeri, Nelji and Perur are very popular.

1. See 'Songs of Gods and Goddesses', *Pattole Palame*.

2. Pannangalathamme came to Kodagu from Malabar with her brothers, and became the deity of Kembattis. The priests in her shrines are Kembattis. She is popular with all the native communities of Kodagu who worship her as the goddess who blesses childless couples with children.

The religious practices of the early inhabitants of Kodagu have been significantly influenced over time by those in the neighbouring areas of Malabar in Kerala and the Kannada and Tulu-speaking areas in Karnataka. The various spirit-deities to whom they pay obeisance, and whose presence is marked by stones planted near the *ainmanes*, as well as the village gods to whom they built shrines within the confines of the *ur*, appear to have been 'brought' from the neighbouring areas. These spirit-deities and village gods predate the pan-Indian Sanskritic gods (Ishwara, Vishnu and Krishna, etc.) who were introduced to Kodagu by immigrants and by Brahmin priests. The process of Sanskritisation of religious practices among the early inhabitants of Kodagu is ongoing.

Spirit-deities are semi divine folk-deities worshipped as tutelary spirits, each with a limited sphere of influence. Many of these deities were adopted from the cultural practices in Tulunad and Malabar, and some of them have now become identified with Sanskritic gods.

Most of the spirit-deities are represented by simple unhewn stones embedded in mud or stone platforms built around the base of sap-exuding trees, some near the *ainmane* and some in a clearing in the jungle, not far from the *ainmane*. The belief is that these deities need to be appeased periodically to ward off evil and in fulfilment of vows made to them. Ritual offerings to them include chicken, cooked or puffed rice and arrack or liquor, except to Natha (the snake god), who is offered milk and flowers. During the annual festivals of each of these deities, and on ritual occasions, people go from their *ainmanes* in traditional attire to propitiate the deities.

People have a close relationship with these spirit-deities with whom they talk in a very intimate manner, telling them their problems and asking for guidance and favours. This is unlike their relationship with the classical Sanskritic gods who are regarded with awe and are more distant.

Some of the commonly worshipped spirit-deities are:

Ammanuru - God Venkataramana's younger sister (from Kannambadi)
Angara/Potta - Guardian spirit of oxen
Anji kut murthi - Group of five deities: Eth Kuliya, Rahu Kuliya, Panjurli, Pashana-murthi and Potta
Path kut murthi - Group of ten deities. The five deities in Anji kut murthi and five more: Thotha, Kuttichatha, Bhairava, Karuvala and Nuchuta
Bhumi Kuliya/Guliga - Spirit guarding the land and cattle
Kallurti - Helpful but mischievous female spirit
Kavala - Guardian spirit who protects villages
Kole/Beera - Spirit of a hero who died a violent death, such as Kaliyatanda Ajjappa and Kannanda Doddayya
Kuttichatha - Mischievous spirit-deity of *thanthras* or mystic rites
Male deva - Spirit of the hill
Mandana-murthi - The deity at the Kakotparamb shrine, also known as Kariappa[3]
Mariamma - Associated with epidemics, believed to cause famine if not appeased
Mrithyu Kuliya/Guliga - A minor deity associated with death
Nari puda - Spirit of a tiger killed in a hunt
Natha (snake god) - Dravidian deity of fertility, later identified with Subrahmanya, a Sanskritic deity
Nuchuta - Attendant to Goddess Parvathi
Panjurli - Spirit of the boar,[4] guardian of agricultural classes
Pashana-murthi - Foremost among the spirit-deities, the deity who presides

3. Another name of Karikotta chandala who was transformed into a god. ('Song of Two Gods', *Pattole Palame*).
4. In Tulunad, Panjurli is a male deity who stands for Varaha, Vishnu's incarnation as the boar who lifted and saved the earth when it was submerged in water. *Panji* means pig or boar in Tulu. In Kerala, Panjurli is a female deity, Varahi, one of the *saptha mathrikas*, the seven mother-goddesses.

over death and suffering, is responsible for the well-being of children, and is the guardian deity of the house and its precincts

Puda/Bhutha[5] - Spirit of a dead ancestor

Thammacha - Guardian spirit of the *yala male* (cardamom hills), patron god of Poomale Kudiyas

Nearly every village in Kodagu has shrines to one or more *ur devas* (village gods, such as Bhagavathi/Povvedi, Bhadrakali, Kethrappa and Sarthavu), and the communities in the village join together to celebrate the festivals held in these village shrines. These village gods migrated to Kodagu from the neighbouring areas of Malabar and Tulunad, and there are local folk songs that narrate the stories of their 'coming' to Kodagu. Most of these village gods were originally outside the fold of Brahminical Hinduism. They were inducted into the Hindu fold later, some as forms of Shiva and of Parvathi, wife of Shiva.

The most common of these shrines are to Bhagavathi/Povvedi (a form of Parvathi, Shiva's wife, a Sanskritic deity), to Bhadrakali (a fierce form of Parvathi), and to Sarthavu[6]/Shasthavu, the Sanskritic name for Ayyappa, the ancient god of the hunt. Other village gods include Choundi, Kali (both fierce forms of Parvathi), and Kethrappa (Kshethra Pala, a Vedic deity, guardian of the lands/fields).

Many of the shrines to these village gods have non-Brahmin priests from one or more of the following communities: Okkaligas, Kodavas, Airis and Panikas. *There/kola* performances to propitiate some of these deities are held in some *ainmanes* and in their shrines during their annual festivals. Ritual offerings to the deities include chicken, goats and pigs, as well as arrack or liquor.

5. *Bhutha* literally means 'of the past'.

6. See 'Song of Sarthavu', in the *Pattole Palame*. Sarthavu is the son of Shiva and Vishnu (in female form), and is therefore also called Hari-Hara *puthra*.

There are also temples in Kodagu to Sanskritic gods. The majority of them are dedicated to Ishwara/Shiva, probably the influence of the Shaivite (worshippers of Shiva) Lingayath rajas, who ruled Kodagu for more than two centuries.

In these temples, daily worship is offered by Brahmin priests from South Canara (Tulu-speaking) or Malabar (Malayalam-speaking) and only vegetarian offerings are made. But on certain occasions, such as temple festivals, animals are sacrificed by non-Brahmin priests to the deity or to the spirit-deities established in the temple premises. The Brahmin priest leaves the temple at that time and returns to resume his duties only after the temple premises are thoroughly cleaned and ritually purified.[7]

Traditionally, the affairs of each of these shrines and temples are overseen by one or more prominent *okkas* in the village who are referred to as *deva thakkas* and *bhandara thakkas*. These *thakkas* could be from any community. (See Appendix 10 on *Thakkame*.)

DEITIES OUTSIDE KODAGU

Some of the *okkas* in Kodagu have patron deities whose temples are located just beyond the present-day borders of Kodagu. This tradition was probably prevalent since ancient times. Muthappa, the rebel god and hunter, is an ancient deity whose main temple is in Parassinikadavu in North Malabar, on the banks of the Valapattanam river. Also referred to as Ponn Muthappa, he is revered by the native communities of Kodagu. There are a few shrines to him in Kodagu also.

Not far from Parassinikadavu are temples to Baithurappa (a form of Shiva), in Baithur and in Payyavur in North Malabar, just south of Kodagu. Baithurappa, the patron deity of many *okkas* in south Kodagu, is closely associated with the people

7. For example, in the Bhadrakali temple in Kuklur, the Brahmin temple priest leaves the temple during the annual temple festival when large numbers of animals are sacrificed.

of Kodagu and offerings of rice are taken to these temples by *eth por* (loaded on the backs of pack-oxen) during annual pilgrimages even today.[8] Traditionally the people of Beppunad and Yedenalknad go to Baithur and the people of Padinalknad and Kadiathnad go to Payyavur. Another place of pilgrimage in North Malabar, just south of Kutta in Kodagu, is the temple in Thirunelli to Pemmayya, the patron deity of *okkas* in the south-east of Kodagu.[9] God Venkataramana, whose temple is in Thirupathi in Andhra Pradesh, is the patron deity of Goudas. They go to Thirupathi on pilgrimage and worship God Venkataramana in their *ainmanes* in a ceremony called *Hari Seve*.

SOME UNIQUE RELIGIOUS PRACTICES

During our fieldwork we heard of three unique religious practices prevalent in certain pockets of Kodagu. These practices were very likely adopted from areas neighbouring Kodagu.

Nara bali (Human sacrifice)

There are stray references to the practice of *nara bali* (human sacrifice) in the distant past, to deities such as Bhadrakali, in shrines located deep in the forests of Kodagu. These sacrifices were offered at times of deep distress, to appease a deity whose anger was believed to have caused terrible calamities such as an epidemic for which the people knew no remedy. It is believed that until about 200 years ago, humans were sacrificed as offerings to Kattemad Amme (Goddess Bhadrakali) at her annual festival in a forest shrine in Kattemad, and to Bhadrakali at her shrine in Bellur.

There is a popular legend, that every year, the *okkas* in the village of Kattemad took turns to offer an unmarried man from the *okka* as *nara bali* to the fierce

8. The Puggera *okka* is the *thakka* for the temple in Baithur; the Boverianda and Mundyolanda *okkas* are *thakkas* for the temple in Payyavur.

9. The Ajjamada *okka* is the *thakka* for this temple.

Goddess Kattemad Amme to appease her. The man who was to be sacrificed would remain 'ritually pure' and go to the shrine in a trance and lay his head on the sacrificial stone. The *there* (priest possessed by the spirit of Bhadrakali) would then decapitate the man's head. According to the legend, the *nara bali* ritual was not held one year because the *okka* whose turn it was, had no one to offer. The *okka* was cursed by the goddess and soon became extinct. The following year, the *okka* that had to offer *nara bali* told the *there* '*bappa kalakad*' which has a dual meaning—'next year, we will offer' as well as 'next year, a goat'. Since then only goats are offered at this shrine.

In the Bhadrakali shrine in Bellur, it is said that when they could not find a man (*al*) to offer to Goddess Bhadrakali, the Panika priest at the shrine told the goddess '*bappa kalakad*', again with the same dual meaning. The following year, the Panika offered a goat (*ad*) at the festival, declaring to the goddess, '*alallamma, ad*!' (It is not a man, but a goat!) Since then, only goats are offered at this shrine too. When the priest makes the offering, he repeats the same words, and makes a cut on his own finger to allow human blood (as a token) to drop on the sacrificial goat.

Bethale seve (Worship in the nude)

There is another unusual custom practised during the annual festival in the forest shrines to Korchandale Ayyappa in Ballamavati and to Vana Bhadrakali in Hathur, where only women are allowed. In the past, women devotees worshipped the deity in the nude and wore white saris on their way back from the shrine. Men and boys would not look at them for fear of the god's curse. These are similar to the practices in some remote villages in the areas neighbouring Kodagu.[10]

Nowadays in Ballamavati, women devotees from the surrounding villages remain 'ritually pure' on the day preceding the festival day. Before daybreak on

10. Worship of the female deity, Yellamma, by women in the nude (signifying without ego) was apparently common in certain parts of Kerala, Karnataka, Andhra Pradesh and Maharashtra.

the day of the festival they walk to the Ayyappa shrine draped in white cotton saris with no underclothes, carrying on their heads new earthen pots filled with rice, ground rice and jaggery given to them by Madivala, Airi and Maleya women. They also take with them ghee and wicks given by Gouda women to light lamps in the shrine. On reaching the shrine, the women cook the rice and jaggery in freshly drawn water to make *payasa* on improvised hearths made of rough stones, using freshly broken twigs as firewood. They also knead the rice powder, jaggery and turmeric into dough and prepare *ottis* (flat rice bread). If a vow was made, a *thrishula* (trident) is offered to the deity. There are many such *thrishulas* in this forest shrine.

Pommangala (Mangala ceremony for cross-dressed children)

Yet another ritual that appears to have become common practice since about fifty years is *pommangala*, celebrated in the Puth Bhagavathi temple in Birnani. If a child has health problems during birth, a vow is made to Goddess Puth Bhagavathi to grant good health to the child. In fulfilment of the vow, two or three days prior to the temple festival (which is held on *Yugadi* or new year's day in April), parents dress the child as a bride in the case of a son, or as a bridegroom in the case of a daughter, and perform all the ceremonies for the child, as in a traditional *mangala* (wedding) in their individual houses. Friends and relatives are invited for the occasion and a grand feast follows. That evening all the boys and girls dressed as brides and bridegrooms along with their *mava* (mother's brother) and family members assemble in the *mand*. Those dressed as brides carry *kalashas* (pots with water for rituals) on their heads; those dressed as bridegrooms carry a cane and a bamboo shield each. They then proceed to the temple for a community *puje*, accompanied by a wedding band playing *volaga* music with horns, pipes and drums.

Appendix 8

NARI MANGALA

One of the unique ceremonies among the early inhabitants of Kodagu was *nari mangala* (literally, tiger wedding)—a ceremony to honour a person who had killed a tiger. According to folk songs both men and women were so honoured.

In the olden days, when Kodagu had dense jungles teeming with wild animals, killing a tiger, the most ferocious of the animals, was an act of great bravery that was cause for celebration. The weapons used to hunt wild animals those days were bows and arrows and the broad-bladed Kodava war-knife—the *odi kathi*. Later, primitive blunderbusses and flintlock guns stuffed with gun powder and lit with wicks (*thiri thok*) were used. These weapons were no match for the fast-moving wild animals, and the hunt often ended in a mortal combat—a physical struggle between man and beast. Many a hunter died fighting the ferocious animals.

The *nari mangala* ceremony has not been heard of in recent decades. Hunting was forbidden by the Wildlife Protection Act of India of 1972, and has in fact been on the decline in Kodagu since the early 1960s.[1]

1. Examples of a few who were honoured with *nari mangalas* within living memory are: Kodimaniyanda Chami Madayya in Naladi, 1958; Morkanda Devayya in Shirangalli, 1966; Kalmadanda Madayya in Madikeri, 1971; and Muddanda Thimmiah (who shot a tiger in self defence) in Surlabhi, 1982.

On the day the tiger was killed or on the following day, a grand celebration was held to honour the tiger killer. If the tiger was killed by a man, he was dressed like a bridegroom in a white *kupya,* red *chele* and white turban. If it was a woman, she was dressed in a grand red silk sari, like a bride, and adorned with bridal jewellery.

The tiger killer was taken in a procession from the *ainmane* to the *nad mand* accompanied by the people of the *nad* and a band with pipes, horns and drums. The carcass of the slain tiger (or at least its skin or tail) was suspended from bamboo scaffolding in the *mand*. If the hunter was a man and a gun was used to kill the tiger, its barrel was decorated with a red silk scarf called an *oja*, and the hunter walked holding the gun with its muzzle pointing forward. If a gun was not used, the *oja* was used as a veil on his head. If the hunter was a woman, the coils of her hair were decorated with the *oja*.

A *murtha*, similar to that in a wedding ceremony, was performed in the *nad mand* for the tiger killer, and he/she was blessed by all the assembled people. During the *murtha*, the *nari mangala* song praising the tiger killer and describing the valorous fight was sung by a group of four men beating *dudis*. This was followed by a grand feast in the *mand* for all the assembled people. From that day onwards the tiger killer enjoyed a higher social status in the community and, if it was a man, he was entitled to sport a *komba meese* (mutton-chop moustache).

If it was a panther or a leopard that was killed, the ceremony was held in the *ur mand*, and not on such a grand scale.

Appendix 9

MANE PEDAS

All the members of an *okka* have a common *mane peda* or *okka* name (literally 'house name') which is distinctive. It essentially denotes the lineage of the *okka* and serves as its surname. It is believed that *mane pedas* existed from ancient times and were given by the *paleyagaras*. It was the Kodagu rajas who formalised them in official land records and *sanads* (title deeds). The rajas gave new *mane pedas* to those who did not have them and to the new immigrant clans, so that every *okka* had its own individual name. This was done in order to identify each *okka* in land records and to facilitate systematic tax collection.

Initially the *okka* names were simple and short, and often denoted a trait relating to the *okka*, the location of its *ainmane* or the name of its *karanava*.[1] Over time, the suffix '*da*', '*anda*' or '*ra*' (meaning 'belonging to') was added to the *okka* name.[2]

1. There are many stories, a few quite amusing, on how *okkas* got their names. These stories are based on tales that were handed down in the *okka*, on *lo palame* (hearsay), or on guesses. It is said that when the king's representatives went around the land giving names to *okkas* who did not have them, some were named after trees, fruits, animals or parts of the body, etc., and others on what they happened to be doing when they were given the names. Some names were derived from the location of the *ainmane* or the name of the *karanava* of the *okka*.

2. Different families of an *okka* may spell their *mane peda* differently, even in the Kannada script which is phonetic, but especially in English. For example, a vowel in the name is sometimes elongated even if it is not so pronounced, because that was once the fashion.

In the past, some of the smaller communities (for example, Airi, Madivala) who did not have *mane pedas* were identified only by their community names. Many of their *okkas* have now adopted and registered[3] new, distinctive, *okka* names for themselves, since this gives them an identity and a sense of dignity. Kembatti *okkas*, who were earlier identified by the names of the *okkas* to which they were bonded, now have their own unique *mane pedas* with the suffix '*kuttada*',[4] for example, Badakuttada.

It was not uncommon in the past for an *okka* that had very few members and therefore could not cultivate its land, to invite a family or a branch of another *okka* (from the same or another community) to settle on part of its land and cultivate it. This land was either given on lease or as a gift. In a few cases, the invited group gradually assumed the *mane peda* of the original *okka* and, over time, claimed to be a *bhaga* (branch) of that *okka* and attempted to assume rights in its *ainmane*. In some of these cases, the group was accepted as a branch by the members of the original *okka*. In other cases, the original *okka* rejected any relationship with the invited group even though the 'new' group became known by the same *mane peda*. Some of these groups who were not accepted built their own *ainmanes*.

In a variation of the above situation, there are cases where two totally separate *okkas* having the same *mane peda* live close to each other, but have very little in common. The *okka* which came later claims to be a *bhaga* of the older original *okka* but has no rights in its *ainmane*. It is said that in some cases the newer *okka* consisted of immigrants who acquired land adjacent to that of the first *okka*, lived on friendly terms with it and, over a period of generations, having gradually established relationships with it, started addressing its members as relatives and assumed its *okka* name.

---

3. The declaration of change of name is attested to by a notary and published in the local newspapers to inform the public. Some also get it registered in the *taluk* office.

4. The suffix '*kuttada*' identifies the *kudi* (family) to which the *okka* belongs. In some cases it identifies the *okka* to which it was bonded in the past.

In yet another case we were told that an unrelated family that was asked to look after the land of an *okka*, most of whose adult male members had been taken away by force by Tippu Sultan, occupied the land and took on the *mane peda* of the original *okka*. In this case the new family that assumed the *mane peda* was not accepted as a branch of the original *okka*.

There are instances where the same *mane peda* (for example, Mukkatira, Kotera) is held by many separate *okkas* that belong to the same community but are not related to each other and live in different villages. The unique identity of the *okka* in that case is indicated by the village name attached to the *mane peda*. For example, there are Mukkatira *okkas* that are called Devanageri Mukkatira, Arapatt Mukkatira, Kunjalageri Mukkatira, etc. Intermarriage between these unrelated *okkas* with the same *mane peda* is not uncommon. There are a few cases where *okkas* belonging to different communities have the same *mane peda* (for example, Mukkatira,[5] Charimanda). Each *okka* is unique and we have treated it as such.

When there were no male members left in an *okka* and it faced extinction, a common tradition in the Kodava community and in other communities of early inhabitants was for that *okka* to invite a man from another *okka* to marry an unmarried girl or a widow from its *okka* to help continue the *okka* and preserve its name. If the man agreed to change his *mane peda* and carry the *okka's mane peda* himself, the marriage was called *okka paraje*. If he allowed only his children from this marriage to carry the *okka's mane peda*, it was called *makka paraje*. There are also cases where a boy was adopted from another *okka* and made a member of the *okka* facing extinction in order to carry forward its lineage and *mane peda*.

5. Our list has twenty-seven Kodava *okkas*, thirteen Gouda *okkas*, one Amma *okka* and one Golla *okka*, all with the *mane peda* Mukkatira. In the past, the title 'Mukkati' ('*munn*' means 'ahead' and '*kati*' means 'show') was given to the man who held the torch in a temple 'showing the way ahead'. Over time his *okka* was called by the *mane peda* 'Mukkatira'. There were many Mukkatis in different temples and that lead to many Mukkatira *okkas*. The saying goes '*urkor Mukkati*' which means 'for every village a Mukkati'. Similarly 'Kotera' means 'of the *kote* or fort'. Hence many *okkas* who had roles in the raja's fort acquired the *mane peda* 'Kotera'.

Occasionally the rajas gave an immigrant *okka* the *jamma* land and *ainmane* of an *okka* that had become extinct. The new *okka* often assumed the name of the extinct *okka*, even if it belonged to a different community, especially if the extinct *okka* was a well-known one. It also assumed the *thakkame* responsibilities—the traditional rights and duties relating to the area or the local shrine—if any, of the extinct *okka*.

There are cases where an *okka* or a *bhaga* of an *okka* changed its *mane peda* for a variety of reasons. The *bhaga* then became a separate *okka*, sometimes with its own *ainmane*. Occasionally the changed *mane peda* was the same as that of another existing *okka*.

In days long past, some *mula nivasis* who were already following Kodava customs were accepted as Kodavas. Being a patrilineal society, if a Kodava man married a girl from another community, she was accepted as a member of his *okka*. This practice is also observed in most of the native communities in Kodagu. In the past fifty years or so there have been a few rare cases where a non-Kodava, a long-time resident of Kodagu, having married a Kodava girl, sought acceptance into the Kodava fold and was admitted as a Kodava with a new *mane peda*.

The information we were given during the fieldwork shows that in the past there have been a few *okkas* who moved from one community to another, often to the socially dominant Kodava community. They were accepted and quickly adapted to the community to which they moved. Rev. Richter writing about this in 1870 says, 'Even within the memory of the present generation strangers were received by and incorporated with the Coorgs.'[6]

Many of the early Tulu Gouda immigrants kept their old family name or the name of the village they came from as their *mane peda*, sometimes adapting to

6. *Gazetteer of Coorg*, G. Richter, 1870, p. 231.

the custom in Kodagu by attaching the suffix '*da*', '*anda*' or '*ra*' to the *mane peda.* Often they got themselves new *mane pedas.* Some who came later assumed the *mane pedas* of the extinct Kodava and Amma *okkas* whose lands and *ainmanes* were given to them by the Kodagu rajas. Many a time, brothers—sons of a common Gouda ancestor—gave themselves distinct *mane pedas* although they belonged to the same clan. Some of these brothers built their own *ainmanes* and now celebrate their traditional ceremonies separately.[7] In such cases all these *ainmanes* have been included in this project.

7. While these *okkas* are now aware of their common ancestry, that might well be forgotten in time.

Appendix 10

THAKKAME

Thakkame (literally 'the right to speak for') stands for the institution of headmanship or leadership with respect to a geographical region or a shrine, and was likely introduced even as early as the rule of the *paleyagaras*. It is a traditional, hereditary role that was assigned to prominent *okkas* in the area. The duties and responsibilities attached to that role follow age-old unwritten rules. Although *thakkames* could be assigned to *okkas* of any community, the majority of them are held by Kodava *okkas*. Whereas a *thakkame* is assigned to an *okka*, the current *pattedara* of that *okka* is the *thakka* (headman) who officiates, and he (or his representative from the *okka*) has to carry out the prescribed duties and responsibilities of a *thakka*. Some villages, *nads* and shrines have *thakkas* from more than one *okka* and community.[1] These days, since the local administration and courts provide many of the services that were the *thakka's* responsibility in the past, the role of a *thakka* is largely ceremonial.

There are many kinds of *thakkames*, each with a different responsibility and ceremonial role. One group of *thakkames* has responsibility over matters relating

1. For example, Kadiyathur has six *ur thakkas* from different communities, including Kodavas, Goudas and Heggades.

to the welfare of the inhabitants in various geographical jurisdictions. Thus, the *ur thakka* is the headman of an *ur* (village). He presides over the council of elders that resolves disputes within the village, and has the lead role during community dances, sports and other events. In the past he was also responsible for the welfare of pilgrims who passed that way. The *nad thakka* is the headman of a *nad* (a group of villages) with similar responsibilities. In the past he was also responsible for collecting taxes. The *desha thakka* or *seeme thakka* is the headman of a *desha/seeme* which is a group of *nads*. In the past, he was the representative of the ruler in that *desha/seeme* and was responsible for carrying out the ruler's dictum in that region. The *mand thakka* is responsible for the maintenance of the *ur* or *nad mand* (village green).

The other group of *thakkames* has responsibilities relating to the village shrines. All the communities in the village join to celebrate the festivals at these places of worship. Traditionally each shrine is under the care of one or more of the prominent *okkas* in the village, called *deva thakkas* and *bhandara thakkas*. These *thakkas* are also responsible for the shrine in the *deva kad* (sacred grove) which is attached to the village shrine. The *deva thakka* is responsible for the administration of the shrine, for the maintenance of its property and for organising festivals. The *bhandara thakka* is responsible for safe-keeping of the *bhandara potti* in which the money offerings made to the deity by devotees, jewellery of the deity, processional images and other paraphernalia related to the festivals are kept. The *bhandara potti* is normally kept in the *ainmane* of the *bhandara thakka*. The *kavukara thakka* officiates as a 'festival priest' only during the temple festival and maintains the temple accounts for the festival.

There are many instances of shrines belonging to one community having *deva thakkas* from other communities besides their own. Most shrines that belong to non-Kodava communities have at least one local Kodava *okka* as a *thakka*. This also applies to the *thakkame* of some mosques. On the other hand, there are instances where a Jamma Mapille *okka* offers a *therige* (tribute) of rice and oil at a Bhagavathi temple or is responsible for the upkeep of a temple *ambala* (roofed structure on a raised platform where villagers and elders meet to settle disputes).

Some *okkas* have *koyime* (customary rights) during festivals in temples to Ishwara, Bhagavathi, Bhadrakali, etc. These rights entitle them to perform the *kudre* (horse) or *ane* (elephant) dance during a local temple festival, with horse and elephant-shaped cane frames fixed around the bodies of the dancers; or the right to dance with *chouri* (yak-tail whisks), *peeli* (peacock feathers), *komb* (stag horns) or *bill* (bows). There is also the *koyime* which gives the *okka* the honour of cooking special dishes (such as *kuyya* rice) or of taking *eth por* (pack-oxen laden with rice as votive offering), oil, lamps, etc., for the temple festival.

There have been cases where, because of quarrels with villagers, an *okka* has given up its *thakkame* or, having lost the trust of the people, has been relieved of it. The *thakkame* has then been passed on to another *okka* of that area that was deemed to be suited for the role. When an *okka* acquired *jamma* land of an extinct *okka* or when it exchanged its *jamma* land with that of another *okka*, it also assumed the *thakkame* rights, if any, of the extinct/other *okka*.[2]

2. The Gouda *okkas* Surthale and Kudupajje got the land and the *thakkame* of the Amma *okkas* Paruvanda and Porera, who were the *seeme thakkas* in the Bhagamandla area, after the latter were annihilated by Tippu Sultan's soldiers and became extinct. Cheerammanda (Amma *okka*, now known as Kodiyammana) exchanged their *jamma* land with Baimana (Gouda) and in the process they gave them their *thakkame* related to the Payyavur temple in Kerala.

Appendix 11

FOLK SONGS AND FOLK DANCES

FOLK SONGS

The *mula nivasis* of Kodagu have a large repertoire of traditional folk songs in the Kodava language that are colloquially called *balo pat* because they start with the words '*Balo, balo*'. *Bal* or *balo* is a common blessing meaning 'live long' and *pat* means 'song'. A *balo pat* traditionally starts with a prayer to the almighty, the earth, the sun and the moon. This chant is believed to be similar to the invocation at the beginning of the songs in the *Sama Veda*,[1] which is regarded as the primordial source of all Indian music.

Balo pat songs are sung to the beat of *dudis* played by the singers. They are also called *dudi kott pat*, which means 'song sung to the beat of the *dudi*' played by the singers. The *dudi* is a small two-sided bronze, copper or wooden drum whose flat ends are covered with tightly stretched hide.[2] It is held in the left hand and is beaten with a thin, curved cane stick held in the right hand.

1. One of the four Vedas, the sacred Sanskrit scriptures of Hinduism.
2. The hide used for the *dudi* in the past was that of wild animals—the skin of the *mucha* (a species of monkey) for the right side that is beaten with the stick and the skin of the *udumb* (iguana, large lizard found in the wild) for the left side. These days, since there are hardly any monkeys or iguanas left in Kodagu, goat skin is used—the skin of a male goat for the right side, since it is thicker and produces a deeper sound, and that of a female goat for the left side.

While their origins are unknown, these folk songs have been handed down the generations and are believed to be ancient.[3] In the tradition of oral literature, any singer could improvise on them, and the songs owe their vibrancy to the many anonymous authors who have crafted them. Occasional improvisations continue to be made, but today most singers stick to the memorised versions, some of which have been printed in compendiums such as the *Pattole Palame*.

The songs coming under the category of *balo pat* include the *desha kett pat* (song of the land), *mangala pat* (wedding song), *batte pat*[4] (song for the way that describes the *ainmane*), *polichi pat* (song sung in praise of the dead), *mane pat*[5] (song of the *okka*) which often includes the *karana pat* (song of ancestors), and *Puthari pat* (*Puthari* song). Besides these, there are the *chavu pat* (sung during death ceremonies), songs of gods and goddesses (describing each deity and the history of his/her 'coming' to Kodagu, sung at village temple festivals), and ballads of legendary heroes (describing their valour and adventures).

Other songs include the *kodichi pat* (a collection of humorous songs of *kodichi*, the dancing girl) and the *joyi/thali pat* (songs of *joyi*, the mendicant, with the refrain '*thali lellela*') sung during *Puthari*.[6] Versions of the *joyi pat* sung during the *Bod Namme* festival[7] are peppered with bawdy comments.

There are also songs that were commonly sung in the past during agricultural operations. These include the *uyya pat* and *nati pat* (that are sung when

3. ' … a core musical repertoire of the Kodava, the *dudi kot pat* … conveying texts grounded in ancestor worship, accounts of localised deities and heroes, the relationship of the Kodava to adjacent regions, and the minutiae of life-cycle rituals, these songs are presented in a melodic style …. austere and limited' …
' …. the *dudi kot pat* form a crucial means of self-identification, and of resistance to both Sanskritization … and the exoticizing gaze of the broader community.' [John Napier, *Global Media Journal*, Australian Edition, vol. 4:2 (2010).]

4. See pages 21–24 for an extract from the English translation of the *batte pat*.

5. See Appendix 12 for a section of a *mane pat* translated into English.

6. The *Pattole Palame* has a collection of many of these folk songs.

7. *Bod* means to beg and *namme* means festival. *Bod Namme* is an unusual temple festival observed in some parts of Kodagu, where male dancers in different guises sing *bod* songs that poke fun at and abuse their gods, masters and onlookers, as they dance the *bodat*, begging and teasing those around for money.

transplanting paddy seedlings). The *eth pat* (sung when driving pack-oxen) is rarely heard these days.

Women of the Gouda community sing a variety of folk songs in the Kannada language. They include *sobane* songs, which are sung during different wedding rituals. Other folk songs are sung during *Hari Seve* celebrations, during naming ceremonies and when women work at their chores. They also sing folk songs during transplanting and other agricultural operations, and during *Puthari*. These latter songs are similar to the songs sung by the *mula nivasis* on those occasions.

Other communities too sing many of the folk songs sung by the *mula nivasis* besides their own folk songs. Some of these songs are sung for their folk dances.

In addition, women sing lullabies and songs for children, and songs for the graceful *ummathat*—the folk dance performed by women.

FOLK DANCES

The native communities of Kodagu perform a variety of folk dances during festive occasions. These dances are unique to the region and are common to most of the communities, except for some that are specific to some communities.

Since time immemorial every village has land set apart for an *ur mand* (village green), and every *nad* (group of villages) for a *nad mand*, an open space for community activities such as folk dances and sports at the *ur* and *nad* levels, respectively.

There are a variety of folk dances that are performed by men in their traditional attire in the *mand* during the *Puthari* festival and in yards in front of shrines during temple festivals. The *Puthari* dancers dance in a large circle going round in a counter-clockwise direction to the beat of songs sung by four men who stand in the centre of the circle around a lit pedestal lamp, beating *dudis* as they sing. Many communities take part in these dances. During community dances in temple yards, besides singers with *dudis,* there could be musicians who beat the *pare* (a large drum made of wood and stretched hide, beaten with heavy sticks), and others who play the drone-pipe, cymbals and horns.

The *Puthari* dances include *kol* dances (also known as *Puthari kol*) danced in the *mand* by men holding canes which they strike together as they dance, and *pariya kali,* a stylised mock fight between a pair of men who dance holding shields and canes. Also during *Puthari,* young boys dressed as *kodichi* (dancing girl) and *kunda* (dancing boy) dance to the *kodichi* songs, striking cymbals as they dance.

Dances by men during festivals in shrines to village gods such as Bhagavathi and Sarthavu include *bolakat* during the *Bolak Namme* (festival of lights), *kathiyat* where the dancers hold *odi kathis* (war-knives) as they dance, *chouriyat* where they hold yak-tail whisks, *kombat* where they hold stag horns, *peeliyat* where they hold peacock feathers and *billat* where they hold bows and arrows.

During certain temple festivals individual men dance the *kudreyat*—horse dance, where the dancer positions himself inside a hollow cane frame that resembles a horse and prances like a horse, and the *aneyat*—elephant dance, where the dancer similarly uses a hollow cane frame that resembles an elephant.

Other dances by men are *kappeyat* where the dancers hop like frogs and *pambat* where they sway like snakes. *Volagathat* is a freestyle dance that men, women and children dance at weddings and other social gatherings to the traditional *volaga* music played with horns, pipes and drums.

During the *Bod Namme,* generally held during the festivals at the Bhadrakali temple, *bodat* is performed by youngsters to the beat of *dhols* (large drums). In some villages these dancers—traditionally, one from each *okka*—dance in various guises imitating different communities. They go from house to house, often all through the night, dancing the *bodat* and singing humorous and sometimes bawdy *bod* songs. They also loudly abuse those around them, especially their masters and the gods, all in fun, and collect gifts of paddy, rice or money from their masters and onlookers. The *chooleyat* (part of *Bod Namme*) is performed by one or two men dressed as dancing girls, holding mirrors or cymbals as they dance to the beat of *dudis*.

Women perform the graceful *ummathat*. The dancers hold brass cymbals and strike them as they dance around a lamp in a large circle to the beat of a variety of songs sung by four women. In the past it was danced only in *ainmanes* during the *Puthari* festival, and in temple yards during festivals dedicated to Goddesses Bhadrakali and Bhagavathi. *Thaliyathat* is danced by women of the Kodava and Kudiya communities during temple festivals. The dancers hold *thaliyas* (plates) on which lit lamps are placed.

Jamma Mapilles dance *dappu at* near their mosques, mainly in Emmemadu and in Kondangeri, while singing songs in Arabic and beating a percussion instrument called *dappu*. *Yeravat*, a dance with swaying movements to the beat of *dudis*, is unique to the Yeravas and is danced by both men and women. They also dance *suggi kunitha*, a variety of harvest dance to the beat of *dudis* and *cheeni*, a wind instrument, and *pandalat* during death ceremonies. *Mandiyat* is danced by Yerava women. Kurubas dance *kolat* with sticks in their hands—a dance of speed and beauty; *suggi kunitha*, a harvest dance; and *dollu kunitha*, where they beat *dollus* (large drums) as they dance. Other tribal communities who are small in number have their own folk dances.

In the past, it was a matter of pride for every member of the various native communities in Kodagu to know how to sing folk songs and perform folk dances. Singing and dancing at festivals was mandatory. While it is no longer so, there is currently a revival of interest in these folk arts and experienced elders teach and encourage youngsters to learn them.

Appendix 12

AN EXTRACT FROM A *MANE PAT*

PARADANDA *MANE PAT*

The Paradanda *okka* claims descent from a Namboodri Brahmin, who they believe was the eldest member in the house when God Igguthappa came to Kodagu. They were made the *deva thakka* of the temple to God Igguthappa. The following is a translation of a condensed extract from their *mane pat* which is sung in the *balo pat* style. It describes the life of their famous ancestor, Diwan Ponnappa, who is referred to as a *karana* of the *okka*.

Live long and be blessed my friend,
Listen to the words of this song,
The song that we four youths
Sitting on the *aimara*
Of this *nal kett mane*, sing
With copper *dudis* in our hands.

Listen, listen, O people,
In the golden land of Kodagu
In days long ago

When kings ruled this land
In the village of Naladi
In the Paradanda *okka*
Was born a baby boy,
A boy named Ponnappa
Destined to be a hero.

When hero Ponnappa
Grew to be a man
He wished to make his name
In the teachings of those days,
Learning *thanthras* and *manthras*
From the *thanthri* at Kaleghat
In neighbouring Malabar.

To the *thanthri's* abode he went,
And greeting him with respect
Told him the reason for his coming
'Serving at the feet of the five *murthis*
And the ten gods of the netherworld,
Thanthras and *manthras*
I wish to be taught
In forty-eight days,' he said.

The Kaleghat *thanthri*
Agreeing to this,
In forty-eight days
Not missing a single day

Taught him the occult arts
Of *thanthras* and *manthras*,
To change the human form
And to make things disappear.

Ponnappa took leave of his teacher
Having proved his skill
By turning two *palachi* leaves
That his teacher had given him
Into snorting bulls.
The *thanthri* instructed him
Not to forget Igguthappa.
And to establish *sthanas*
For the five *murthis*
And the ten gods of the netherworld.

Ponnappa the hero
Was made the *karyakara*
Of the great king Dodda Veerappa.
In his court one day
The king said these words:
'Listen, listen, O people,
Ajjikutti Achu Nayaka of Kiggatnad,
Kollekongi Nayaka of Kadiathnad, and
Utha Nayaka of Beppunad
These three *nayakas*
Do not pay me taxes.
How shall we subdue them?'

All who heard him
Were silent and said no word,
Except Ponnappa the brave, who said:
'Listen, listen, O Lord,
If you give me a hundred men
In six months time
I will curb their arrogance
And bring them to you.'
The great Dodda Veerappa
Agreed to this
And gave him a hundred men.

In twelve days time,
Ponnappa's team of hundred
As *sanyasis* by day
And as hunters by night
Tracked the errant *nayakas.*
Kollekongi was captured.
The one called Utha Nayaka
Went into hiding.
Achu Nayaka of Kiggatnad
When he returned from a hunt
In the darkest hour of the night
Ponnappa attacked and captured him.

King Dodda Veerappa, greatly pleased
Asked Ponnappa
What he wished as a reward.

Ponnappa asked for the land
That belonged to Utha Nayaka.

The Lingayath king granted him
All that he wished for
And naming him his diwan
Asked that he collect taxes
From Nalayiranad
For the royal treasury.

Ponnappa the famous
Went about the land
As one of the *desha thakkas*
And as the *deva thakka*
Of God Igguthappa.

As time passed
Ponnappa stopped paying homage
To God Igguthappa
And to the gods of his house.
He stopped giving the taxes
Due to the king
And raised his own army
Of more than two hundred
Paleyas and Kapalas.

Angered by this
The king asked his men

To bring Ponnappa to him.
But Ponnappa with his army
Went to Nalnad palace
And routed the king's men.

When all was peaceful,
The king thought of a plan
To capture Ponnappa.
He told him he had found
A bride suitable for him
From the Bonda Mukkatira *okka*.

Unaware of the trap
When Ponnappa went to Nalnad palace,
The king's men captured him.
Ponnappa then
With *thanthras* and *manthras*
Transformed himself
Into a fly and flew away.

Back in human form
As he drank water from a stream
The king's men who followed him
Attacked and killed him.
Ponnappa became known as
The *kudi beera* of his *okka*.

The king's men then

Burnt down the mud house
Of the Paradanda *okka*
And killed every one of them
Man, woman and child.

At that time, O friend,
A girl from the Thennira *okka*
Given in marriage
To the Paradanda *okka*
Was in her parent's house
With her two little sons.
Fearing for their lives
They fled from there
And hid in the house
Of a Gouda *okka*—
The Kadlera in Kuyyangerinad.

Meanwhile, O friends,
God Igguthappa
Was angry that there was none
From the Paradanda *okka*
To bring oxen laden with rice
For his temple festival.
Not only that,
The spirit of *kudi beera* Ponnappa
And the ten gods of the netherworld
Began troubling the people of Naladi.

The king who consulted
The *kaniya* from Ammangeri
Was told the cause
And was asked to find
If any man or woman
From the Paradanda *okka*
Had survived the massacre.

When the king sent his drummers
Proclaiming this message,
The two Paradanda boys
In the Kadlera house
Disclosed their identity
And were given the land
That was theirs by right.

So now there were people
Of the *deva thakka okka*
To take oxen laden with rice
For the Igguthappa festival.
God Igguthappa blessed them
And the people of the *nad* were happy.

This song that we have sung,
Let us now lay aside
And pray to the *Adi Mula*.
Adi Mula Le Lle Lo!

(Translation of an extract of the Paradanda *mane pat* from the book *Paradanda Manethana mathu Kunjilageri Mukkatira Manethana*, 1990, by Paradanda G. Chengappa)

Appendix 13

SUMMARY TABLES OF *AINMANES*

The two tables in this appendix give counts of *ainmanes* by communities.

Table 1 classifies all the traditional *ainmanes* that were functional when we visited them during the fieldwork for this project (24 April 2003 to 15 May 2008), by the community to which they belong and the kind of *ainmane*:

a) *mund mane* (square structure built around a sunken inner courtyard open to the sky);
b) *othe pore* (rectangular, one-winged structure—the most common kind);
c) *madak mane* (rare, L-shaped structure).

Table 2 classifies the information that we collected on all the *ainmanes* in Kodagu, by community and by whether the *ainmane*:

a) is traditional and functional (hence visited for this project);
b) is non-traditional, having been rebuilt in a non-traditional way, but is functional and serves as an *ainmane*;

c) belongs to an *okka* that had an *ainmane* earlier, but has no *ainmane* now (the old one having fallen, been brought down, been in a dilapidated condition, abandoned or not rebuilt). Some of these are now private houses or are not considered as *ainmanes.*

The list of traditional *ainmanes* that we visited (Table 1, and column 1 of Table 2) has been verified and is complete. But the information in Table 2 on *ainmanes* that are not traditional or belong to *okkas* that have no *ainmanes* now is likely to be incomplete and subject to errors, because collecting that information was not part of this project. This is information that we heard of or read about in newspapers during the course of the fieldwork. Yet Table 2 gives a good indication of the large number of *ainmanes* that are no longer in the traditional style or are simply no longer there.

It should be noted that the number of *ainmanes* in these tables is slightly larger than the number of *okkas* or *mane pedas* that they belong to, because some *okkas* have more than one *bhaga*, each with its own *ainmane.*[1]

Besides these numbers we have compiled a list of about hundred *mane pedas* that have become extinct. This list is based on information that we happened to hear of or read about during our fieldwork, and is therefore incomplete.

1. Among the visited ones for which we have information that we have verified, the 683 *ainmanes* are associated with 582 *mane pedas*; i.e., the ratio of *mane pedas* to *ainmanes* is 85%.

TABLE 1: Number of Traditional *Ainmanes* in Kodagu

(visited between 24 April 2003 to 15 May 2008)

Community	*Mund mane*	*Othe pore*	L- Shaped	Total number of *Ainmanes* visited
Kodava	79	353	2	434
Gouda	4	128	-	132
Heggade	1	36	-	37
Amma	1	13	-	14
Airi	-	14	-	14
Jamma Mapille	-	12	1	13
Kembatti	-	10	-	10
Hajama	-	5	-	5
Golla	-	4	-	4
Madivala	-	4	-	4
Okkaliga Gouda	-	3	-	3
Bunt	-	2	-	2
Jagir thurka	-	2	-	2
Jaina	-	2	-	2
Koyava	-	2	-	2
Banya	-	1	-	1
Balegara	-	1	-	1
Banna	-	1	-	1
Kodava Nair	-	1	-	1
Koleya	-	1	-	1
TOTAL	85	595	3	683

TABLE 2: Summary of *Ainmanes*/*Okkas* in Kodagu

Community	Traditional *Ainmanes*[1]	Non-traditional (rebuilt) *Ainmanes*[2]	No *Ainmane* now[3]	Total number of *Okkas*[4]
Kodava	434	226	395	1055
Gouda	132	94	95	321
Heggade	37	7	16	60
Amma	14	7	13	34
Airi	14	9	28	51
Jamma Mapille	13	5	31	49
Kembatti	10	4	28	42
Hajama	5	1	10	16
Golla	4	13	14	31
Madivala	4	9	5	18
Okkaliga Gouda	3	1	3	7
Bunt	2	1	1	4
Jagir thurka	2	-	-	2
Jaina	2	-	-	2
Koyava	2	5	4	11
Banya	1	1	2	4
Balegara	1	-	-	1
Banna	1	1	4	6
Kodava Nair	1	1	6	8
Koleya	1	-	2	3
Kaniya	-	4	6	10
Panika	-	2	1	3
Bune Patta	-	-	5	5
Maleya	-	-	3	3
Jamma Marathi	-	-	1	1
Kudiya	-	-	1	1
Kumbara	-	-	1	1
TOTAL	683	391	675	1749

1. *Ainmanes* that were built in the traditional style and are functional—the focus of this book.
2. *Ainmanes* that were rebuilt, but not in the traditional style, and are functional—not covered in the book.
3. *Ainmanes* that are dilapidated/fallen/brought down but are not rebuilt; those that are abandoned; those now used as private houses, or those that are not now considered as *ainmanes*.
4. *Okkas* or *bhagas* of *okkas* for which we have information on whether they have *ainmanes* or not.

Appendix 14

TIME SEQUENCE OF SOME IMPORTANT EVENTS IN HISTORY

BC

Around 2,00,000	Anatomically modern humans emerge in the Rift Valley in Africa.
2,00,000 to 6,000	Stone Age. Age of the hunter-gatherers. Use of chipped stone instruments.
1,25,000 to 75,000	Periods of migration of anatomically modern humans out of Africa.
4,000 to 2,000	Early farmers in the Indus Valley. Use of polished stone instruments.
3,500 to 1,500	Indus Valley Civilisation.
Around 3,000	Early pyramids of Egypt.
Around 2,000 to 500	Bronze Age.
Around 2,000	Origins of Judaism.
1,500 to 600	The Vedas—oldest sacred literature of the Hindus.
1,500 onwards	Indo 'Aryan' overland migration into India from the north.
Around 1,000	Origins of trading by sea-going vessels.
900 to 500	*Mahabharatha* written by Vyasa pertains to this period.

800 to 30	Indo 'Aryan' migrants spread from the north to the south and east of India.
628	Birth of Zoroaster, founder of Zoroastrianism. (Parsees).
599 to 527	Mahavira, founder of Jainism.
563 to 483	Buddha, founder of Buddhism.
327/6	Alexander (of Macedonia) invades north India and conquers Punjab.
About 200 onwards	People who came by boats from the Middle East, Greece and the surrounding areas settle on the west coast of India, including Malabar, where some of the Indo 'Aryan' migrants had already settled. Around this time the core group of the Kodavas probably entered Kodagu from the North Malabar area.
50	Start of the Iron Age.
AD	**Beginning of the Christian Era**
About 4 BC to AD 30	Life of Christ.
570 to 632	Prophet Mohammed, founder of Islam.
600 to 750	Foundations of Islam.
Around 1192	Start of the conquest of north India by the Mongols.
1469 to 1538	Guru Nanak, founder of Sikhism.

Appendix 15

MAPS

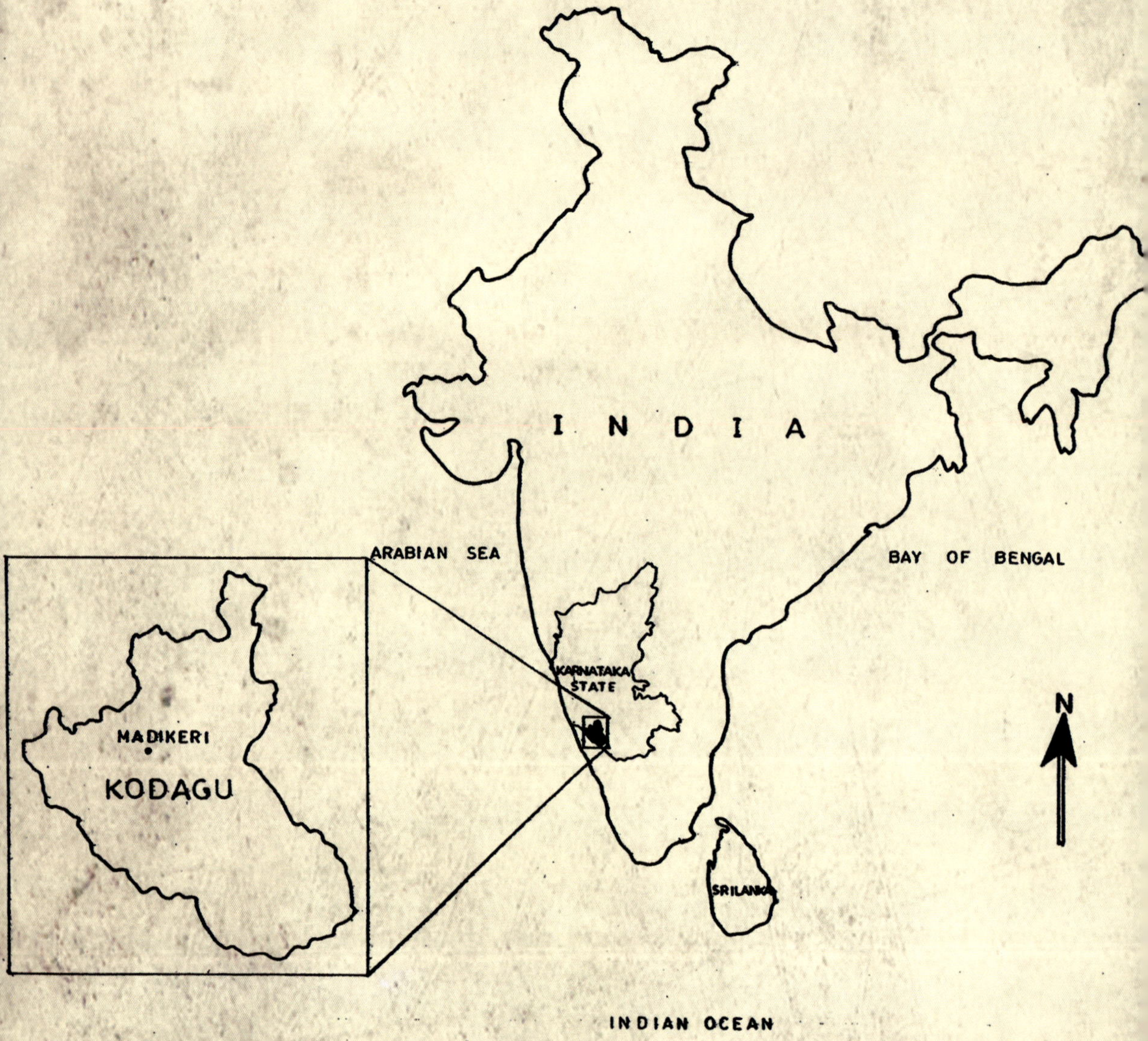

Map locating Kodagu in India.

Map of Kodagu divided into nine sections.

Nine section maps of Kodagu with numbers indicating the location of *ainmanes*

Index to the location numbers in the section maps—nine tables, one for each section map—with corresponding *okka* names of the *ainmanes*. The index also notes the village where the *ainmane* is located.

When an *okka* name is common to more than one community, the community to which the *okka* belongs is indicated with the following alphabets: (A) – Amma; (Gd) – Gouda; (Gl) – Golla; (Hg) – Heggade; (Hj) – Hajama; (Jm) – Jamma Mapille; (K) – Kodava.

INDEX FOR MAP A – BY LOCATION # ON MAP

***Okka* name**	**Village**	**Location #**
Soorthale/Surthale	Thannimani	1
Kaveri mane (Hj)	Thavur	2
Ermekalu	Thavur	3
Kudukuli	Thavur	4
Nidyamale	Bhagamandla	5
Koodakandi mane -1	Thavur	6
Kolibailu mane	Thavur	7
Chettijana/Shettejana -1	Chettimani (Padakal)	8
Allangada	Kundacheri	9
Mukkati - 4 (Gd)	Kundacheri	10
Anjanda	Kundacheri	11
Koorana -2	Kolagadala	12
Bellamane	Kolagadala	13
Mukkati -2 (*Balya*) (Gd)	Kolagadala	14
Koorana -1	Kolagadala	15
Mukkati -3 (*Sanna*) (Gd)	Kolagadala	16
Cheerammana	Kolagadala	17
Naliyammana/Naliyammanda	Kolagadala	18
Ajjinanda	Kolagadala	19
Baddira	Kolagadala	20
Kompulira -2	Bettathur	21
Apadanda	Bettathur	22

Chimmanda -2	Bettathur	23
Podanolana	Kopatti	24
Dayana	Kopatti	25
Chennapanda	Kopatti	26
Annachi mane -1 (Dodda Annachi)	Kolagadala	27
Nangaru mane	Korangala	28
Kuyyamudi	Sanna Pulicot	29
Kaveri mane (Gd)	Sanna Pulicot	30
Udiyana mane	Sanna Pulicot	31
Thothiyana	B.Badaga	32
Shettejana -2	B.Badaga	33
Panathale	Charandeti	34
Kekada	Kottur	35
Baimana/ Bymana	Kottur	36
Thelappanda	Aivathoklu (Bengur)	37
Pattamada	Bengur	38
Ponnachettira -2	Bengur	39
Kalmadanda	Bengur	40
Kunchettira	Bengur	41
Mandappanda/Mandapanda	Bengur	42
Chokira -3 (K)	Bengur	43
Koodakandi mane -2	Bengur	44
Paithadiyanda	Aivathoklu (Bengur)	45
Kotholira	Aivathoklu (Bengur)	46
Yadekeri -1	Ballamavati	47
Chokira -1(Gl)	Ballamavati	48
Neravanda -2	Ballamavati	49
Airira -2	Ballamavati	50

Madeyanda	Ballamavati	51
Appachettolanda	Ballamavati	52
Thapanda	Perur	53
Moovera/Muvera -1	Perur	54
Manavattira -1	Nelji	55
Thumbera	Nelji	56
Chettineravana	Nelji	57
Maleyanda	Nelji	58
Mandira -1	Nelji	59
Achandira -2	Nelji	60
Thotathanda	Kunjila	61
Nambudumanda	Kunjila	62
Kalyatanda	Kunjila	63
Kotera -2	Kunjila	64
Uthukuttada -3	Kunjila	65
Pongera	Kunjila (Ammangeri)	66
Koleyanda (Kopira)	Kunjila (Ammangeri)	67
Kambeyanda	Kunjila	68
Paradanda	Naladi	69
Allaranda -1	Naladi	70
Mechanda	Kakkabe (Pariyangeri)	71
Udiyanda -1	Kakkabe	72
Apparanda	Yavakapadi	73
Karthanda	Yavakapadi	74
Madanda -1	Yavakapadi (Karangeri)	75
Barike/Barikera -2	Marandoda	76
Perubayi	Cherangala	77
Parivarana	Cherangala	78

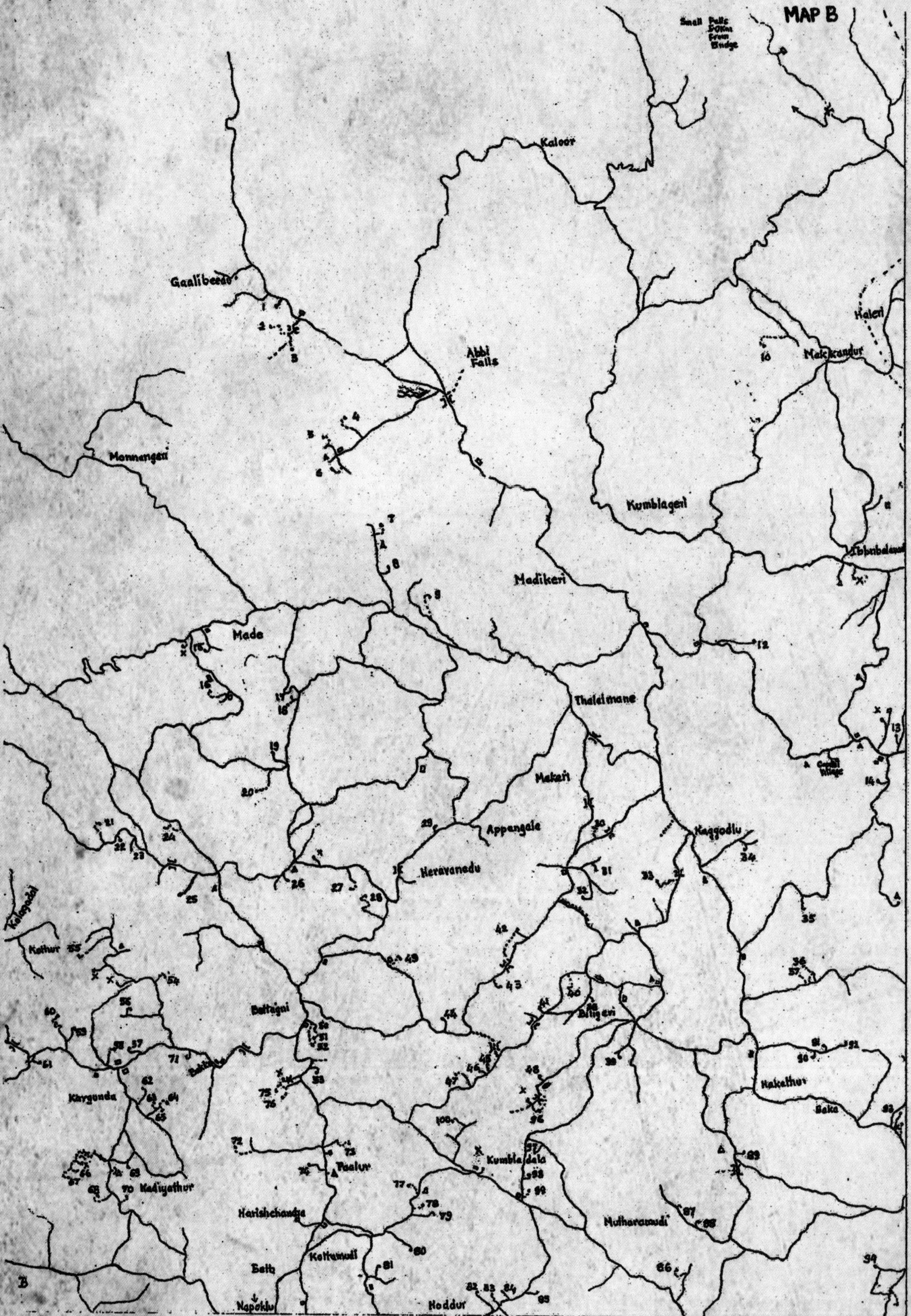
MAP B
Kaloor
Gaalibeedu
Abbi Falls
Monnangeri
Kumblageri
Madikeri
Made
Thalaimane
Makeri
Appangala
Heravanadu
Kaggodlu
Hakathur
Kumbaladala
Harishchandra
Kottumudi
Napoklu
Hoddur

INDEX FOR MAP B – BY LOCATION # ON MAP

Okka name	Village	Location #
Pandira	Galibeedu	1
Kochana	Galibeedu	2
Ayyapadakanda	Monnangeri – 1st	3
Achapattira	Monnangeri – 1st	4
Ammachimaniyanda	Monnangeri	5
Kuttamaniyana	Monnangeri -1st	6
Paikera -2	Katakeri	7
Achalapadi	Katakeri	8
Chimmanda -1	Katakeri	9
Kumbugoudana	Makkandur	10
Nandineravanda	Ibbnivalavadi	11
Ponnachettira -1	Ibbnivalavadi	12
Kottakuttada -1	Kadagadala	13
Koravanda -2 (*Keeda*)	Kadagadala	14
Muddiyana	Made	15
Huli mane -1	Made	16
Kolyada	Made	17
Huderira	Made	18
Deshakodi	Made	19
Huli mane -2	Made	20
Kadyada (Huliyana mane)	Avandur	21
Ponnachana -1	Avandur	22
Urolana	Avandur	23
Anche mane	Avandur	24
Mandodi -1	Kargunda	25
Mottera / Motra	Heravanadu	26
Kallambira	Heravanadu	27
Ningappana -1	Heravanadu	28
Mukkati -7 (Gd)	Appangala	29
Chondira (Thirodi)	Mekeri	30
Odiyana	Mekeri	31

Kangira (Kangeri)-1(Gd)	Mekeri	32
Chettolira-2	Kaggodlu	33
Mandrira /Mandri mane	Kaggodlu	34
Baddana mane -2	Kaggodlu	35
Kunjilana mane -4 (Thevooru mane)	Kaggodlu	36
Honnukoti mane	Kaggodlu	37
Kannachanda -2	Biligeri	38
Parlakoti -2	Biligeri	39
Paikera -1	Biligeri	40
Kaleyanda (Kalekoti)	Biligeri	41
Poojarira	Arvathoklu	42
Mootera/Mutera	Arvathoklu	43
Jabbanda	Arvathoklu	44
Thennira -2	Arvathoklu (Bettageri)	45
Govindammana	Arvathoklu	46
Kolumadanda	Arvathoklu	47
Baledi	Arvathoklu	48
Thalooru mane	Arvathoklu	49
Chaliyanda -1	Bettageri	50
Katrathanda	Bettageri	51
Chandandira	Bettageri	52
Poudanda -1	Bettageri	53
Kodapalu	Kargunda	54
Ajjetira (Hg)	Kargunda	55
Napanda -1	Kargunda	56
Motteyanda	Kargunda	57
Baichana/Bychana	Kargunda	58
Guddana	Kargunda	59
Pudiyathanda	Kargunda	60
Bodanda -2	Aivathoklu (Bengur)	61
Kuttetira	Kadiyathur	62
Neiyani mane	Kadiyathur	63
Kunjilana mane -1	Kadiyathur	64
Poreyana -1	Kadiyathur	65
Mukkati -6 (Gd)	Kadiyathur	66

Kenjana-1	Kadiyathur	67
Thorera -1	Kadiyathur	68
Koppada -1	Kadiyathur	69
Machanda (Hg)	Kadiyathur	70
Mandetira	Kadiyathur (Bakka)	71
Soodana mane/Sudana mane	Palur	72
Poduvada	Palur	73
Neravanda -3	Palur	74
Pudineravana -1	Palur	75
Pudineravana -2	Palur	76
Baddana mane -1	Kuyyangeri	77
Kadlera mane	Kuyyangeri	78
Thambanda	Kuyyangeri	79
Chourira/Chowrira -1	Podavada	80
Mandeda (Hg)	Podavada	81
Korana	Podd (Hoddur)	82
Mundotira	Podd (Hoddur)	83
Koodanda	Podd (Hoddur)	84
Chettimada (Gd)	Podd (Hoddur)	85
Bylemane/Bailemane	Mutharamudi	86
Paremajlu -2	Mutharamudi	87
Paremajlu -1	Mutharamudi	88
Deraje	Mutharamudi	89
Balyatana (Bettageri)	Hakathur (Paka)	90
Padyana (Mayeti)	Hakathur (Paka)	91
Ammatanda -3(*Keeda*)	Hakathur (Paka)	92
Pacharanda	Margod	93
Kompulira -1	Ikola	94
Poreyanda	Ikola	95
Kunjilana mane-2	Kumbaladala	96
Devajana -2 (Thammachana)	Kumbaladala	97
Neravanda -1	Kumbaladala	98
Thekkada	Kumbaladala	99
Kullachana	Kumbaladala	100

MAP C
Murnad
Napoklu
Padi
Balamuri
Kottandi
Kiggal
Keikad
Kirundad
Parane
Halgonda
Koken
Kolakeri
Bavali
Malambetti
Chamiyel
Marandoda
Chelavara
Karoda
Kadanga
Palangala
Male
Thirike
Kettoli
Kedamallur
Thomara
Edamakki
Peggala
Heggala

INDEX FOR MAP C – BY LOCATION # ON MAP

Okka name	Village	Location #
Baduvanda	Kodambur	1
Pandanda -2	Kodambur (Murnad)	2
Kunjilana mane -6	Kodambur	3
Almachanda	Murnad Badaga	4
Kotera -5	Murnad-Badaga	5
Madeyanda	Murnad-Badaga	6
Appachanda -2	Murnad-Badaga	7
Bariyanda	Murnad-Badaga	8
Mekanda	Podd (Hoddur)	9
Neravanda -4	Podd (Hoddur)	10
Chourira/Chowrira -2	Podd (Hoddur)	11
Vanchira	Podd (Hoddur)	12
Achappanda -2 (K)	Podd (Hoddur)	13
Kanganda -1	Napoklu	14
Areyada -2	Napoklu	15
Thirodira	Napoklu	16
Shivachaliyanda	Napoklu	17
Kundairira	Napoklu	18
Ajjettira (K)	Napoklu	19
Keletira	Napoklu	20
Kullattira/Kulletira	Napoklu	21
Boppanda -1	Napoklu	22
Kallengada -2	Napoklu	23
Kombanda	Napoklu	24
Ketolira -1	Kolakeri	25
Kannambira	Kolakeri	26
Kundyolanda	Kolakeri -W	27

Kandanda	Kolakeri -W	28
Kaliyanda - 2	Kolakeri -W	29
Kaliyanda -1	Kunjila	30
Padeyanda -2	Kaikad	31
Nayakanda - 2	Kaikad	32
Kaddaniyanda -1	Kaikad	33
Kaddaniyanda -2	Kaikad	34
Chotteyanda -2	Kaikad	35
Bollanda -1	Kaikad	36
Bittira	Kirndad	37
Mukkatira -1(Gd)	Kirndad	38
Padeyanda -1	Kirndad	39
Devajana -1(Hosa Olike)	Kirndad	40
Appaneravanda	Kirndad	41
Chermandanda -1	Kirndad	42
Chermandanda -2	Kirndad	43
Naleyanda -1	Kirndad	44
Naleyanda -2	Kirndad	45
Natolanda	Kirndad	46
Kannanda	Bavali	47
Devanira	Bavali	48
Biddanda -2	Bavali	49
Naliyanda	Bavali	50
Elthanda/Althanda	Bavali	51
Kochamanda	Bavali	52
Kuttanjettira	Beth	53
Bollepanda -1	Beth	54
Chokira -2 (K)	Beth	55
Bollepanda -2	Beth	56
Chokira -1 (K)	Beth	57
Cheeyanakuttada	Beth	58
Badakuttada	Beth	59

Doddakuttada	Beth	60
Bakeerana	Balamberi	61
Guddemane/Guddera -1 (*Balya*)	Balamberi	62
Ponnachana-2	Balamberi	63
Cheeyappana/Cheeyappanda	Balamberi	64
Palandira	Balamberi	65
Ichodiyanda	Balamberi	66
Guddemane/Guddera -2 (*Cheriya*)	Balamberi	67
Pebbatanda	Balamberi	68
Kotera - 1	Balamberi	69
Thothiyanda	Balamberi	70
Podeyanda	Balamberi	71
Angira (Airira)	Balamberi	72
Periyanda -1(K)	Balamberi	73
Kottakeriyana	Balamberi	74
Katrathana	Balamberi	75
Nadanda	Balamberi	76
Changanda -1	Balamberi	77
Biddanda -3	Balamberi	78
Cheriyatanda	Konanjangeri	79
Bolkaranda	Konanjangeri	80
Porkada	Konanjangeri	81
Kadira	Konanjangeri	82
Mandathanda	Konanjangeri	83
Bellathanda	Konanjangeri	84
Bairikundira	Konanjangeri	85
Mallada	Konanjangeri	86
Chottera -2	Kunjalageri	87
Kameyanda	Kunjalageri	88
Chottera -1	Kunjalageri	90
Charamanda/Charmanda	Kunjalageri	91
Vallanda	Kunjalageri	92

Cheeyandira -1	Kunjalageri	93
Kuliyakkanda	Kunjalageri	94
Allappira -1	Kunjalageri	95
Mukkatira -2 (K)	Kunjalageri	96
Battakalanda	Kunjalageri	97
Mundanda -2	Kunjalageri	98
Paleyanda	Nalkeri (Pemmad)	99
Kethira	Nalkeri (Pand-mad)	100
Kunhira/Kunjira -2	Nalkeri (Thonur)	101
Moolera/Mulera	Nalkeri	102
Mevada	Nalkeri	103
Mandetira	Nalkeri (Mugur)	104
Kotera -4	Nalkeri	105
Kambeeranda/Kambiranda -2 (*Cheriya*)	Murnad-Badaga	106
Mukkatira/Muckatira-4 (K)	Murnad-Badaga	107
Buttanda	Kiggal	108
Pudiyokkada	Kiggal	109
Ammanda -3	Kiggal	110
Palanganda -2	Ikola	110a
Padinjaranda	Kiggal	111
Ammatanda -1(*Keeda*)	Kiggal	112
Pemmanda (Hg)	Maithadi	113
Cheeruda	Maithadi	114
Iychettira	Maithadi	115
Balekuttira -1	Maithadi	116
Kunhira/Kunjira -1	Maithadi	117
Mundachadira -1(*Mek mane*)	Maithadi	118
Kundachira	Maithadi	119
Mundachadira -2 (*Keeda mane*)	Maithadi	120
Ammanda -2	Maithadi	121
Iyyamanda	Maithadi	122
Chappanda -1	Maithadi	123

Alathanda	Maithadi	124
Neelimadu mane	Bollumad	125
Changoolanda/Changulanda -1	Bollumad	126
Palachanda -1	Bollumad	127
Mathanda -1	Bollumad	128
Mathanda -2	Bollumad	129
Pandianda -1 (*Cheriya/keeda*)	Bollumad	130
Codanda	Kadanga-Murur	131
Baltikalanda	Kadanga-Murur	132
Ballachanda	Kadanga-Murur	133
Bachettira	Kadanga-Murur	134
Ammanda -1	Kadanga-Murur	135
Mandepanda -2	Kadanga-Murur	136
Balyanda (K)	Kadanga-Murur	137
Kangira -1(K)	Kadanga-Murur	138
Kangira -2(K)	Kadanga-Murur	139
Mookairira	Arameri	140
Bachira	Arameri	141
Kandrathanda	Arameri	142
Udiyanda -3	Arameri	143
Kotera -6a	Arameri	144
Kotera -6b	Arameri	145
Ittira -1	Chamiyal	146
Koovalera/Kuvalera	Chamiyal	147
Puttichanda	Bollarimad	148
Pemmanda -1(K)	Kadanur	149
Annarkanda	Kadanur	150
Kanathanda -1 (*Kodil*)	Kadanur	151
Palecanda	Kadanur	152
Poyyetira -1	Kadanur	153
Ammanichanda -1	Kadanur	154
Changachanda -2	Kottoli	155

Changachanda-3	Kottoli	156
Muttal mane	Kottoli	157
Pattada	Botoli	159
Nayakanda -3	Botoli	160
Ammanakuttanda	Botoli	161
Bollepanda/Bollyappanda - 3	Botoli	162
Kambanda	Botoli	163
Achappanda -1 (K)	Peggala	165
Allappanda -2	Kedamullur	166
Maletira -2	Kedamullur	167
Mullairira	Kedamullur	168
Kullachanda	Arapatt	169
Mukkatira -1 (K)	Arapatt	170
Kodira	Arapatt (Poddamani *keri*)	171
Pandanda -1	Arapatt	172
Nerpanda -2	Arapatt	173
Bidderianda	Arapatt (Podavada *keri*)	174
Nambiyappanda -2	Poddamani	175
Nambiyappanda -1	Poddamani	176
Chelmanda/Chelamanda	Poddamani	177
Ithichanda	Karada	178
Patrapanda -1	Karada	179
Nadikerianda -1	Karada	180
Palengada -1	Palangala	181
Palengada -2	Palangala	182
Paleyanda	Palangala	183
Karineravanda	Palangala	184
Mechura	Palangala	184a
Bachamanda -1(A)	Chelavara	185
Pattacheravanda	Chelavara	186
Kolimada	Chelavara	187
Mundyolanda	Chelavara	188

Boverianda/Bovverianda	Nariandada	189
Battiyanda	Nariandada	190
Kolira	Nariandada	191
Beliandra/Biliyana/Boliyanda	Nariandada	192
Pokkulanda	Nariandada	193
Thotambail	Nariandada	194
Manhapura/Manjapura	Nariandada	195
Kikkare	Kokeri	196
Biddanda -1	Kokeri	197
Moodera/Mudera	Kokeri	198
Machanda -2 (K)	Kokeri	199
Kummanda	Kokeri	200
Chenanda -1	Kokeri	201
Cheruvalanda -1	Kokeri	202
Aiyettira/Iyettira	Marandoda	203
Mottepanda	Marandoda	204
Meriyanda	Marandoda	205
Annadiyanda -1	Marandoda	206
Annadiyanda -2	Marandoda	207
Choyamadanda -1 (*meke mane*)	Marandoda	208
Choyamadanda -2(*keeda mane*)	Marandoda	209
Mukkatira -5 (Gd)	Marandoda	210
Achiyada/Acheyada	Podavada	211
Ballanda -1 (*Adil*)	Podavada	212
Ballanda -2 (*Kodil*)	Podavada	213
Chelyanda -2	Halgunda	214

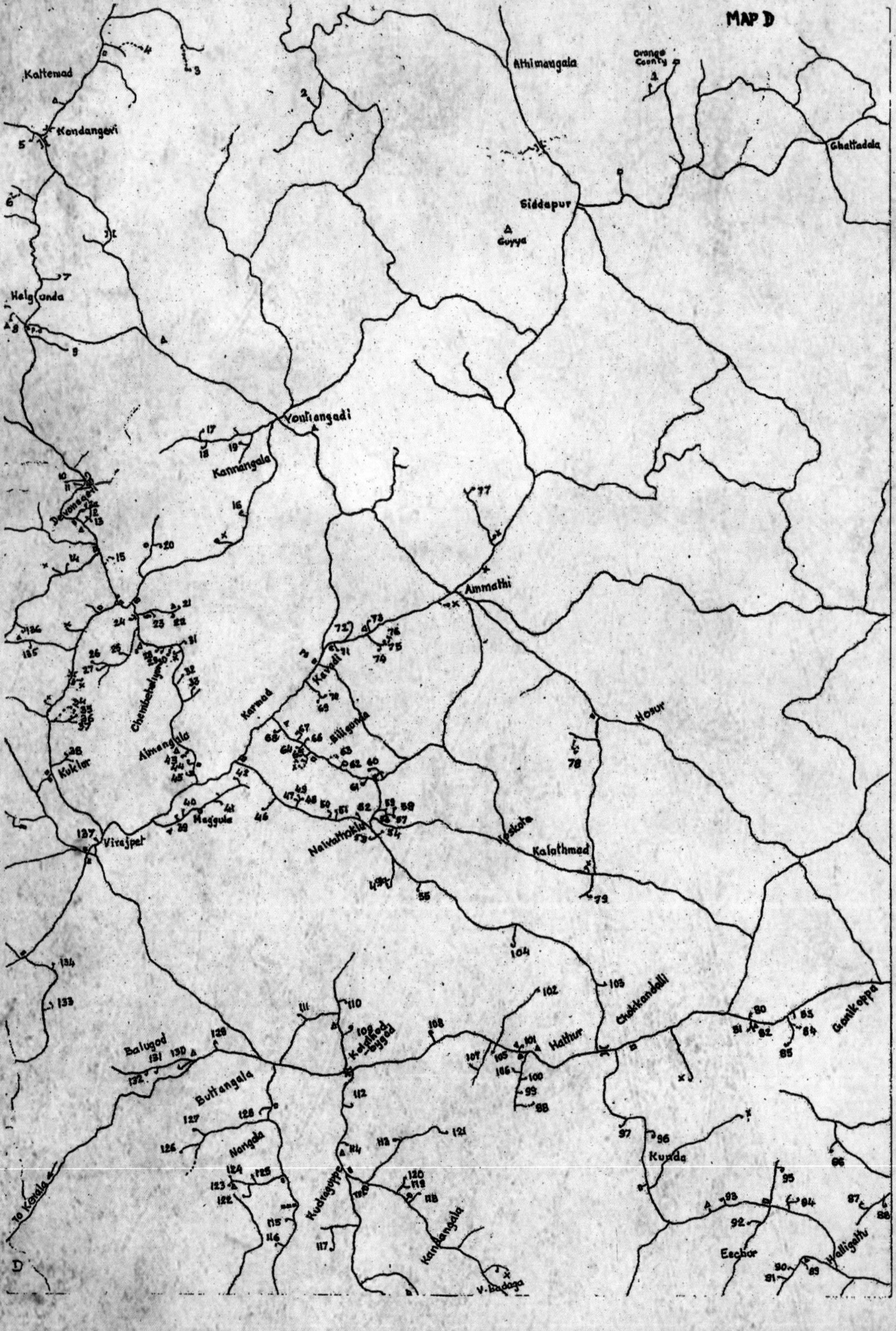
MAP D
Kattemad
Kondangeri
Athimangala
Orange County
Ghattadala
Siddapur
Guyya
Helgunda
Youtiangadi
Kannangala
Devanageri
Ammathi
Kavadi
Karmad
Biligunda
Kukler
Virajpet
Haggula
Nalvattokla
Hosur
Hoskote
Kalathmad
Chokkandalli
Hathur
Balugod
Buttangala
Nangala
Kudregundi
Kandangala
Kunda
Eschur
Walligathi
V. Badaga
To Kerala
D

INDEX FOR MAP D – BY LOCATION # ON MAP

Okka name	Village	Location #
Kukkanooru	Kardigod (Sidāpur)	1
Kukkera	Arekad	2
Bidrupane	Kattemadu	3
Sadera -1	Kattemadu	4
Kuppandare/Kuppandira	Kondangeri	5
Periyanda (Jm)	Kondangeri	6
Koppada -2	Halgunda	7
Pandikanda	Halgunda	8
Machetira	Halgunda	9
Ichanda -3	Devanageri (Thalakatkeri)	10
Puggera -1	Devanageri	11
Mukkatira/Muckatira -3(K)	Devanageri	12
Ichanda -1(*Paleya mane*)	Devanageri	13
Ichanda -2 (*Mek*)	Devanageri	13a
Allappanda -1	Devanageri	14
Jaina -2	Devanageri	15
Marga mane	Kannangala	16
Changachanda -1	Kannangala	17
Koranda	Kannangala	18
Macharanda	Kannangala	19
Porkonda -1	Chembebeliyur (Mudiyap)	20
Charimanda -2 (K)	Chembebeliyur	21
Somayanda/Someyanda -2	Chembebeliyur	22
Chembanda -1	Chembebeliyur	23

Mandepanda -1	Chembebeliyur	24
Chembanda -2	Chembebeliyur	25
Coluvanda -1(*Kodil mane*)	Chembebeliyur	26
Koluvanda -2 (*Adil mane*)	Chembebeliyur	27
Balyamanda	Chembebeliyūr	28
Chotteyanda -1	Chembebeliyur	29
Airira -1	Chembebeliyur	30
Kundira -1	Chembebeliyur	31
Ajjinikkanda -1	Chembebeliyur	32
Charimanda -1 (K)	Chembebeliyur	33
Kuttanda -1	Kuklur	34
Kuttanda -2	Kuklur	35
Monnanda -1	Kuklur	36
Thathanda	Kuklur	37
Maletira -1	Kuklur	38
Chovanda	Maggula	39
Kottiyanda -1	Maggula	40
Kuppachira -1	Maggula	41
Puliyanda -2	Maggula	42
Bollachanda	Aimangala	43
Kundranda -1	Aimangala	44
Mekathanda -1	Aimangala	45
Kolumanda	Nalvathoklu (Aimangala)	46
Mandeda (K)	Nalvathoklu	47
Kalyapanda (K)	Nalvathoklu	48
Mukkatira/Bonda Mukkatira -5a (K)	Nalvathoklu (Bonda)	49
Mukkatira/Bonda Mukkatira -5b (K)	Nalvathoklu (Najugod)	49a
Duddiyanda	Nalvathoklu	50
Chillavanda -1	Nalvathoklu	51

Kannadiyanda	Nalvathoklu	52
Patteyoda	Nalvathoklu	53
Jagalukuttada	Nalvathoklu	54
Puchanda	Nalvathoklu	55
Uthukuttada -1	Bilugunda	56
Billirakuttada	Bilugunda	57
Bannakuttada	Bilugunda	58
Thambakuttada	Bilugunda	59
Uddichanda -1	Bilugunda	60
Uddichanda -2 (*Keeda mane*)	Bilugunda	61
Inanda -1	Bilugunda	62
Uppangada -2	Bilugunda	63
Madappanda -1(*Mek mane*)	Bilugunda	64
Madappanda -2 (*Keeda mane*)	Bilugunda	65
Kopuda	Bilugunda	66
Inanda -2	Bilugunda	67
Allappira -2	Bilugunda	68
Kuttanda -3	Kavadi-Karmad	69
Baduvamanda	Kavadi-Karmad	70
Nellamakkada -2	Kavadi	71
Kavadichanda	Kavadi	72
Mukkatira -7 (K)	Kavadi	73
Nellamakkada -1	Kavadi	74
Uddappanda	Kavadi	75
Paleyathanda	Kavadi-Karmad	76
Bommanda	Ammathi	77
Pandianda -3	Hosur-Ammathi	78
Kollira	Kalathmad	79
Jammada -1	Kaikeri	80

Muduvanda	Kaikeri	81
Thapanera	Kaikeri	82
Vedappanda	Kaikeri	83
Achappanda (Hg)	Kaikeri	84
Kuppanda -2	Kaikeri	85
Kadyamada	Arvathoklu (Gonikoppa)	86
Machiyanda	Halligattu	87
Mookalera	Halligattu	88
Achiyanda	Halligattu	89
Boovadira/Buvadira	Eechur	90
Hajamara (Kelchira)	Eechur	91
Madrira	Eechur	92
Theethamada	Eechur	93
Sannuvanda -2	Mugutageri	94
Manepanda/Maneyapanda	Kunda	95
Kodandera	Kunda	96
Kademada -2	Kunda	97
Kongepanda	Hathur	98
Kalengada -2	Hathur	99
Chendanda -3	Hathur	100
Dodda mane	Hathur	101
Hanchina mane	Hathur	102
Bott mane	Hathur	103
Somayanda/Someyanda -1	Kolathod-Baigod	104
Puliyanda -3	Kolathod-Baigod	105
Chappanda -3	Kolathod-Baigod	106
Kelappanda	Kolathod	107
Muruvanda	Kolathod	108
Nayada	Buttangala	109

Mukkatira -6 (K)	Buttangala	110
Ponnakachira -1	Buttangala	111
Ponnira -1	Buttangala	112
Meniyanda	Rudraguppe	113
Konganda	Rudraguppe	114
Kokkera	Rudraguppe	115
Pollanda	Rudraguppe	116
Kalyappanda (Hg)	Rudraguppe	117
Mechiyanda	Kandangala	118
Mookachanda	Kandangala	119
Balladchanda	Kandangala	120
Mandamada	Kandangala	121
Kambeeranda/Kambiranda -1	Nangala	122
Chendrimada	Nangala	123
Kuppanda -1	Nangala	124
Chotranda	Nangala	125
Channira/Chennira	Nangala	126
Guddanda	Nangala	127
Buttianda/Bittianda -1	Nangala	128
Puchimanda	Balugod	129
Machettira	Balugod	130
Chendanda - 2	Balugod	131
Moorira -1	Balugod	132
Kabbachira	Arji	133
Karthachira	Arji	134
Ammeyanda	Bollarimad	135
Onerira (Bellarimadu mane)	Bollarimad	136
Jaina -1	Virajpet	137

MAPE

Kandangala
Tea Shop
Badaga
Kuttandi
B Shettigeri
Parekalageri
Theralu
Badagarekeri
Marenad

E

INDEX FOR MAP E – BY LOCATION # ON MAP

Okka name	Village	Location #
Chemira/Chemeera -1	V. Badaga	1
Malavanda/Malanda	V. Badaga	2
Ammanichanda -2	V. Badaga	3
Kolathanda	V. Badaga	4
Nambudumada -2	V. Badaga	5
Nadu mane	Rudraguppe -2nd	6
Mudagadde/Moodagadde	Rudraguppe -2nd	7
Chandura -1	Kandangala	8
Appanderanda	Kandangala	9
Mullengada	Kandangala	10
Annira/Anneera (A)	Kuttandi	11
Bananda -1	Kuttandi	12
Bananda -2	Kuttandi	13
Cheranda	Kuttandi	14
Karthamada -1	Kuttandi	15
Pandimada -1	B.Shettigeri	16
Chottemada	B.Shettigeri	17
Ajinira	B.Shettigeri	18
Namera -1	Kongana	19
Kalimada -2	Parakatageri – Pookola	20
Nellira	Birnani	21
Buttianda/Bittianda -2	Theral	22
Bollera -1	Theral	23
Kayapanda -1	Badagarakeri	24
Mallengada	Badagarakeri	25
Anneera -2 (K)	Badagarakeri	26
Meederira	Badagarakeri	27

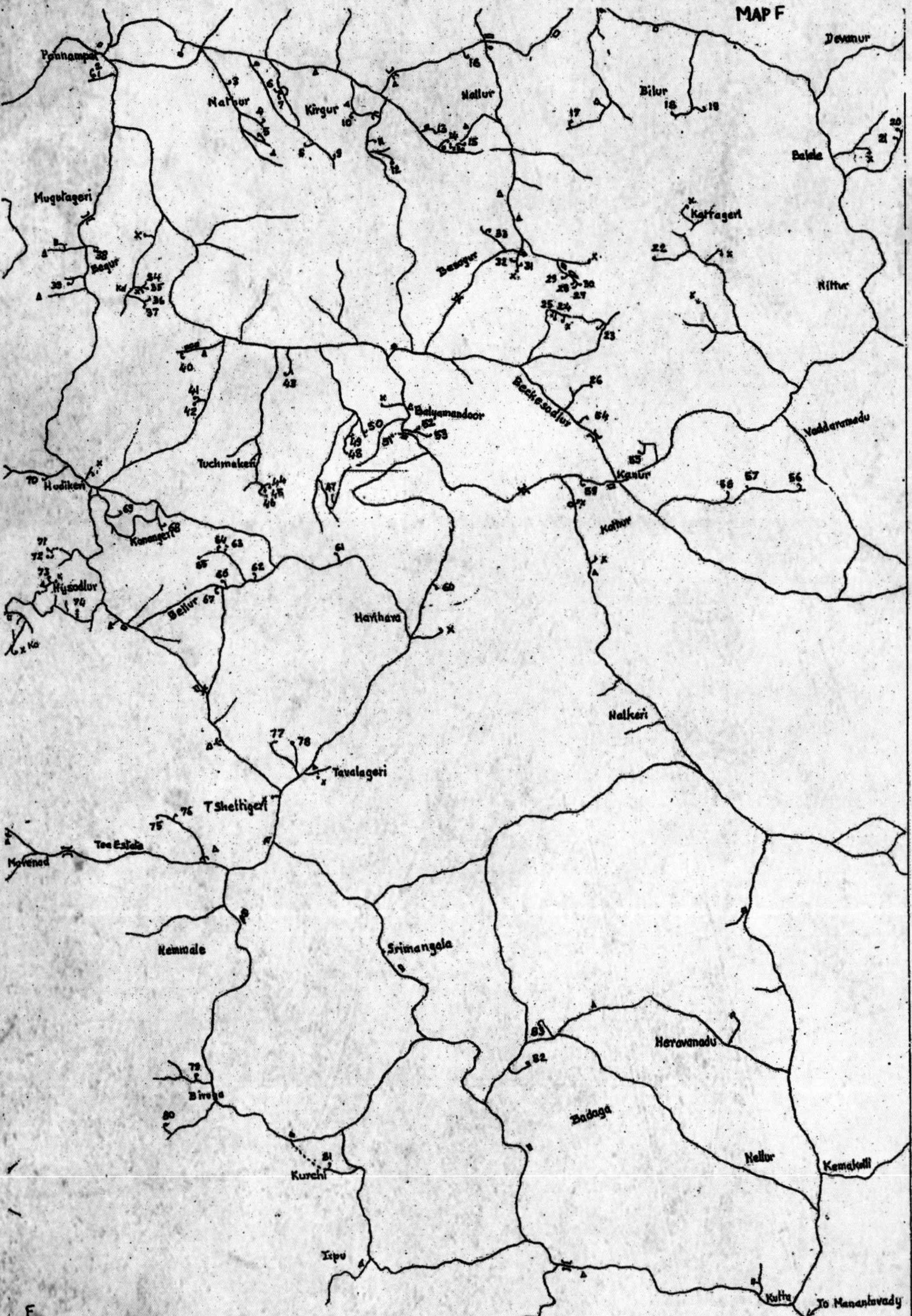
MAP F
Ponnampet
Devanur
Kirgur
Nallur
Bilur
Balele
Mugutageri
Begur
Kattageri
Besagur
Nittur
Beekesodlur
Balyamandoor
Tuchmakeri
Hudikeri
Kanur
Kaltur
Vaddaramadu
Konangeri
Hysodlur
Bellur
Harihara
Nalkeri
Tavalageri
T Shettigeri
Tea Estate
Mavenad
Kemmale
Srimangala
Heravanadu
Badaga
Nallur
Kurchi
Irpu
Kutta
To Manantavady

F

INDEX FOR MAP F – BY LOCATION # ON MAP

Okka name	Village	Location #
Alira -2	Katrakolli - Hudoor	1
Alira -3	Katrakolli - Hudoor	2
Korakuttira	Mathur	3
Panikuttira	Mathur	4
Puthamane	Mathur	5
Pokkalichanda -2	Kirgur	6
Kakera	Kirgur	7
Kodengada	Kirgur	8
Chiriyappanda -1	Kirgur	9
Cheppudira -2	Kirgur	10
Kokkengada	Kirgur	11
Cheppudira -1	Kirgur	12
Theetharamada	Nallur	13
Pullangada -1	Nallur	14
Puchimada	Nallur	15
Chetrumada	Nallur	16
Biddamada	Bilur	17
Adengada -2	Bilur	18
Kandera	Bilur	19
Adengada -1	Devanur (Balele)	20
Addengada	Devanur	21
Machangada -1	Kottageri	22
Machamada -1	Beckesodlur	23
Mallamada	Beckesodlur	24
Theethamada	Beckesodlur	25

Telugu Banajigara	Beckesodlur	26
Paruvangada -2	Besagur	27
Paruvangada -1	Besagur	28
Kokkalemada -1	Besagur	29
Aramanamada -1	Besagur	30
Chettimada (K)	Besagur	31
Bachamada/Bachammada	Besagur	32
Mechamada	Besagur	33
Kallichanda -1	Nadikeri	34
Mapanda	Nadikeri	35
Muddiyada -1	Nadikeri	36
Maniyapanda/Manipanda	Nadikeri	37
Alira -1	Begur	38
Kakamada -2	Begur	39
Ajjikuttira -1	Chikkamundur	40
Mundumada	Chikkamundur	41
Korkanda	Chikkamundur	42
Pemmanda -2 (K)	Tuchamakeri	43
Kottangada -1	Tuchamakeri	44
Karthamada -4	Tuchamakeri	45
Puttangada	Tuchamakeri	46
Kottangada -3	Balyamundur	47
Acharamada	Balyamundur	48
Chandangada	Balyamundur	49
Uppangada -1	Balyamundur	50
Kottangada -2	Balyamundur	51
Machimada -1	Balyamundur	52
Machimada -2	Balyamundur	53
Karthangada	Balyamundur	54
Kechamada -2	Kanur	55

Chiriyappanda -2	Kanur	56
Ottemada/Vottemada	Kanur	57
Chottekmada	Kanur	58
Hemmachi mane	Kothur	59
Theethira -2 (*keeda*)	Harihara	60
Kallengada -1	Bellur	61
Balera	Bellur	62
Mallangada	Bellur	63
Bollimada	Bellur	64
Pandimada -2	Bellur	65
Noorera/Nurera -1	Bellur	66
Ittira -2	Bellur	67
Katikuttira	Hudikeri-Konageri	68
Chekkera	Hudikeri-Konageri	69
Daddera	Hudikeri (Ponnampet)	70
Chonira	Hysodlur	71
Kodangada	Hysodlur	72
Kotramada -1	Hysodlur	73
Kechamada -1	Hysodlur	74
Kattera -1	T.Shettigeri-Vagare	75
Chotteyandamada -2	T.Shettigeri-Vagare	76
Thadiyangada	Thavalageri	77
Kaibilira -1	Thavalageri	78
Iyyamada -1	Beeruga	79
Upparara	Beeruga	80
Ajjamada	Kurchi	81
Kotrangada	Kumtoor	82
Kallangada	Kumtoor	83

MAP G

Muthuru
Maldare
To Polibetta
To Periyapatna
Tittimathi
Devarapura
Gonikoppa
Mayamudi
Balaji
Dhanugala
Konkanakatte
Suluged
G

INDEX FOR MAP G – BY LOCATION # ON MAP

Okka name	Village	Location #
Balyanda (A)	Mayamudi (Balaji)	1
Mallanda	Balaji	2
Andamada	Mayamudi (Rudrabeedu)	3
Bananda -3	Mayamudi (Dhanugala)	4

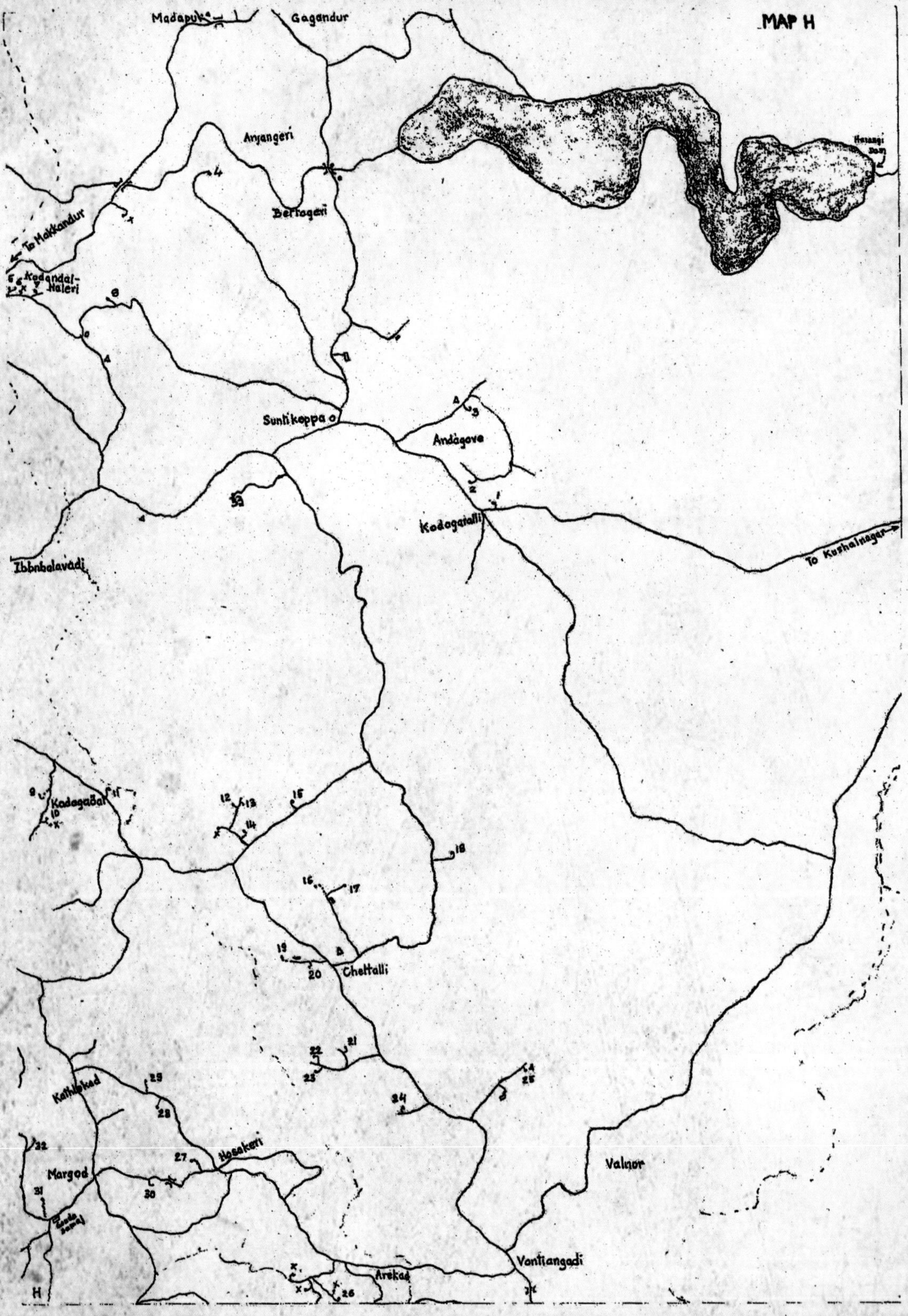
MAP H
Madapur
Gagandur
Anjangeri
Bettageri
Harangi Dam
To Makkandur
Kodandal-Haleri
Suntikoppa
Andagove
Kodagaralli
To Kushalnagar
Ibbnbalavadi
Kodagadal
Chettalli
Kathlekad
Margod
Hosakeri
Valnur
Vontiangadi
Arekad

INDEX FOR MAP H – BY LOCATION # ON MAP

Okka name	Village	Location #
Jaggaranda -1	Kodagaralli	1
Mollera -1	Andagove	2
Chikkanda	Andagove	3
Kalachettira	Anjanageri-Bettageri	4
Aimaniyanḍa	Kadandal - Haleri	5
Airira -3	Kadandal - Haleri	6
Muddura	Kadandal - Haleri	7
Maruvanda -1 (*Meke*)	Kandankolli - Haleri	8
Ajjeeranda	Kadagadala	9
Madetira	Kadagadala	10
Kechetira	Kadagadala	11
Ballaranda -1 (*Keeda*)	Chethalli (Eerale-Olamudi)	12
Ballaranda -2	Chethalli (Eerale-Olamudi)	13
Cholappanda -1	Chethalli (Eerale-Olamudi)	14
Adikera -1	Chethalli (Eerale Olamudi)	15
Kongetira	Chethalli (Cherala Srimangala)	16
Cheralathammanda	Chethalli (Cherala Srimangala)	17
Mechana	Chethalli (Cherala Srimangala)	18
Putherira/Putharira -1	Chethalli (Cherala Srimangala)	19
Mullanda	Chethalli (Cherala Srimangala)	20
Battira -1	Chethalli (Cherala Srimangala)	21
Periyana -1	Chethalli (Cherala Srimangala)	22
Lakkandra	Chethalli (Cherala Srimangala)	23
Ayyandra (Belliyana)	Chethalli (Cherala Srimangala)	24
Karnayana -1	Chethalli (Kudlur)	25
Thondiyanda	Arekad	26
Bolloorumane (Paleyana)	Hoskeri (Margod)	27
Boddanda	Hoskeri (Margod)	28
Kenjana -2	Hoskeri (Margod)	29
Mallandira	Hoskeri (Margod)	30
Baduvandra	Hoskeri (Margod)	31
Thondimane/Thondira	Bakka- Margod	32
Yenkana	Chethalli (Nargane)	33

MAP I

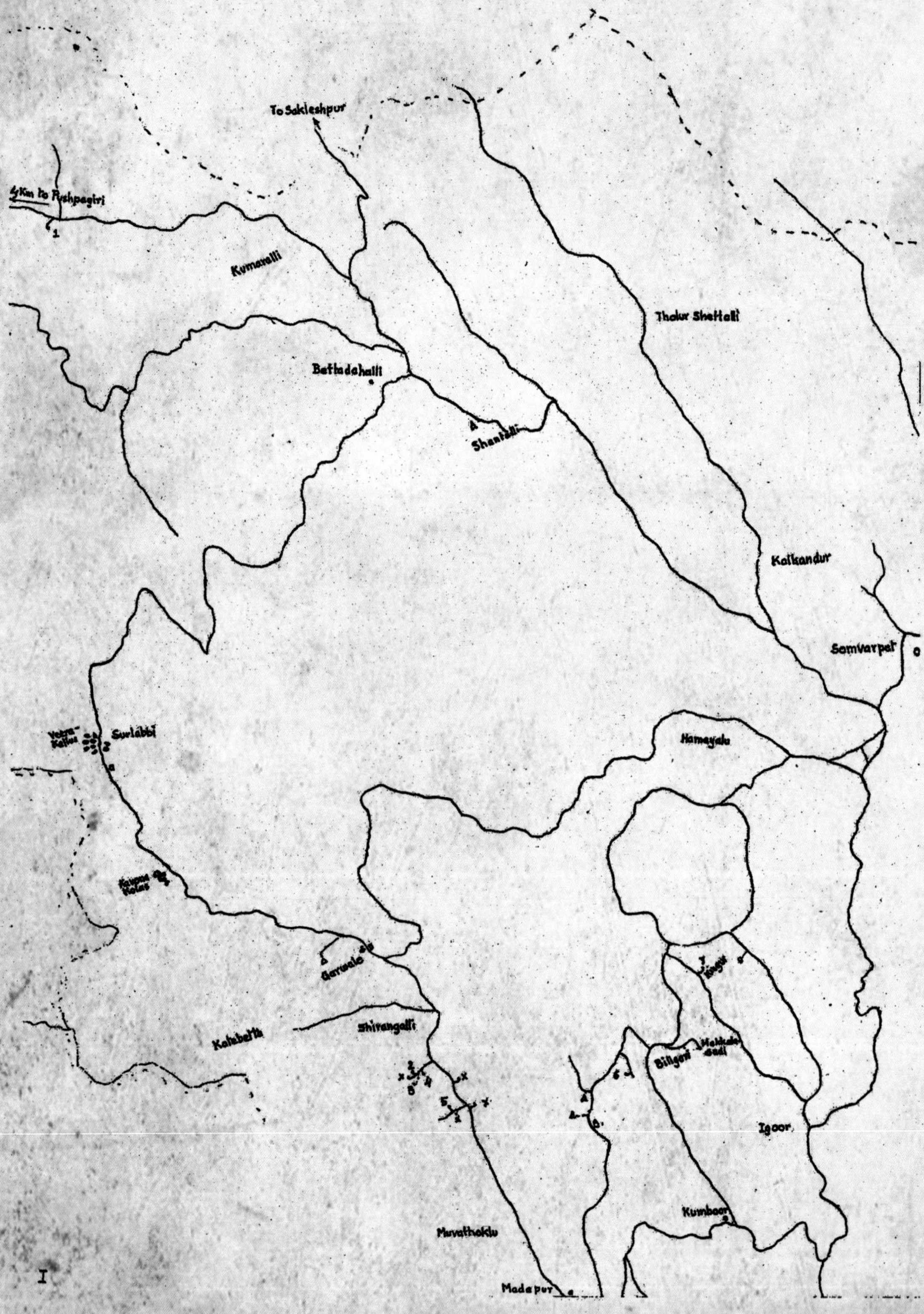

To Sakleshpur
4 Km to Pushpagiri
Kumaralli
Thakur Shettalli
Bettadahalli
Shantalli
Kalkandur
Somvarpet
Surlabbi
Hanayalu
Garwale
Shirangalli
Kalebetta
Bilgeri
Igoor
Kumbaor
Muvathoklu
Madapur

I

INDEX FOR MAP I – BY LOCATION # ON MAP

Okka name	Village	Location #
Hanchettira -1	Kumaralli	1
Morkanda -2 (*keeda*)	Shirangalli	2
Motanalira -2	Shirangalli	3
Uddinadanda	Shirangalli	4
Naganda	Muvathoklu	5
Allachanda (Alibilira)	Biligeri (Somwarpet taluk)	6
Senera	Kirgandur	7

Appendix 16

SKETCHES OF FLOOR PLANS OF TYPICAL *AINMANES*

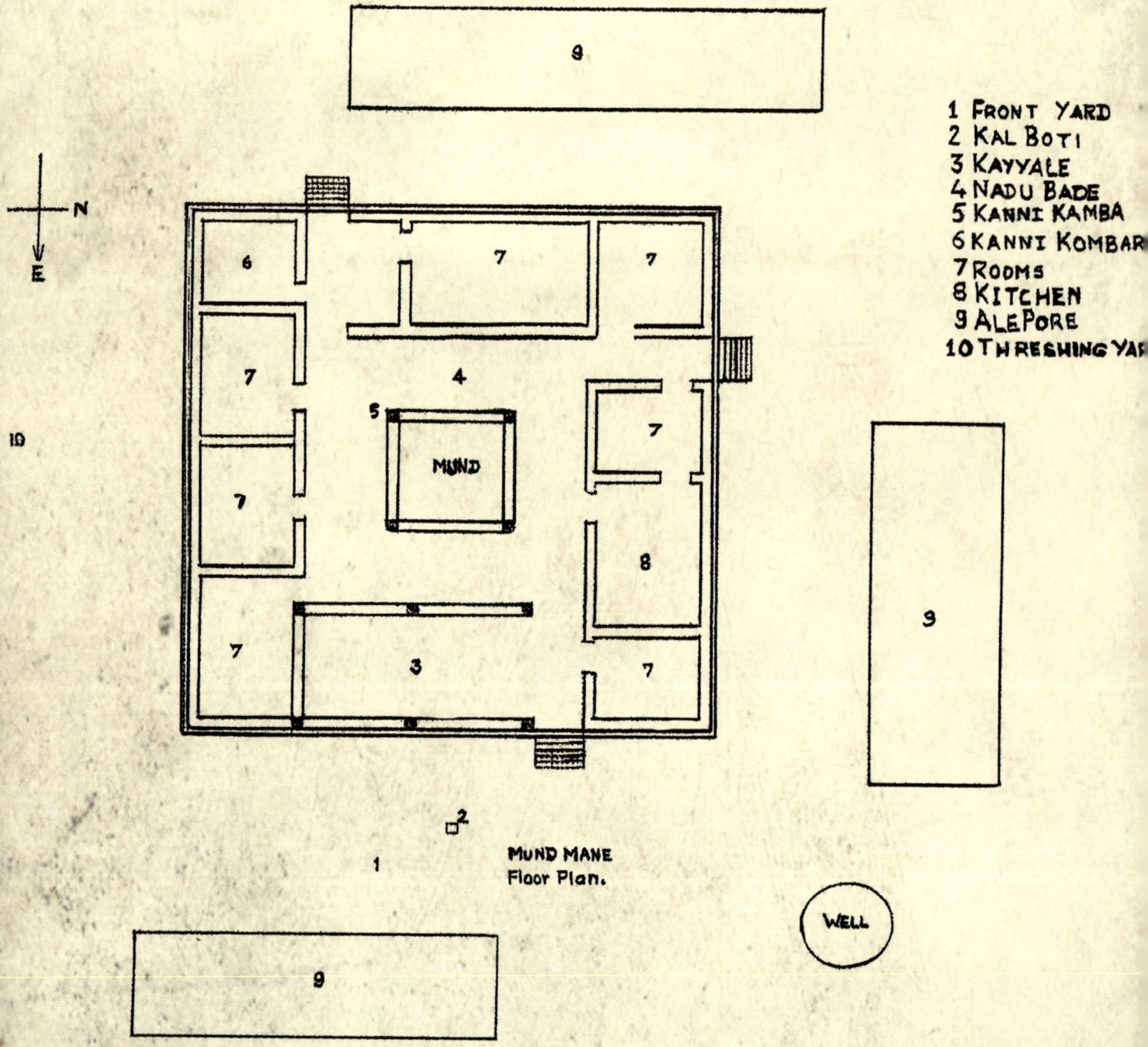

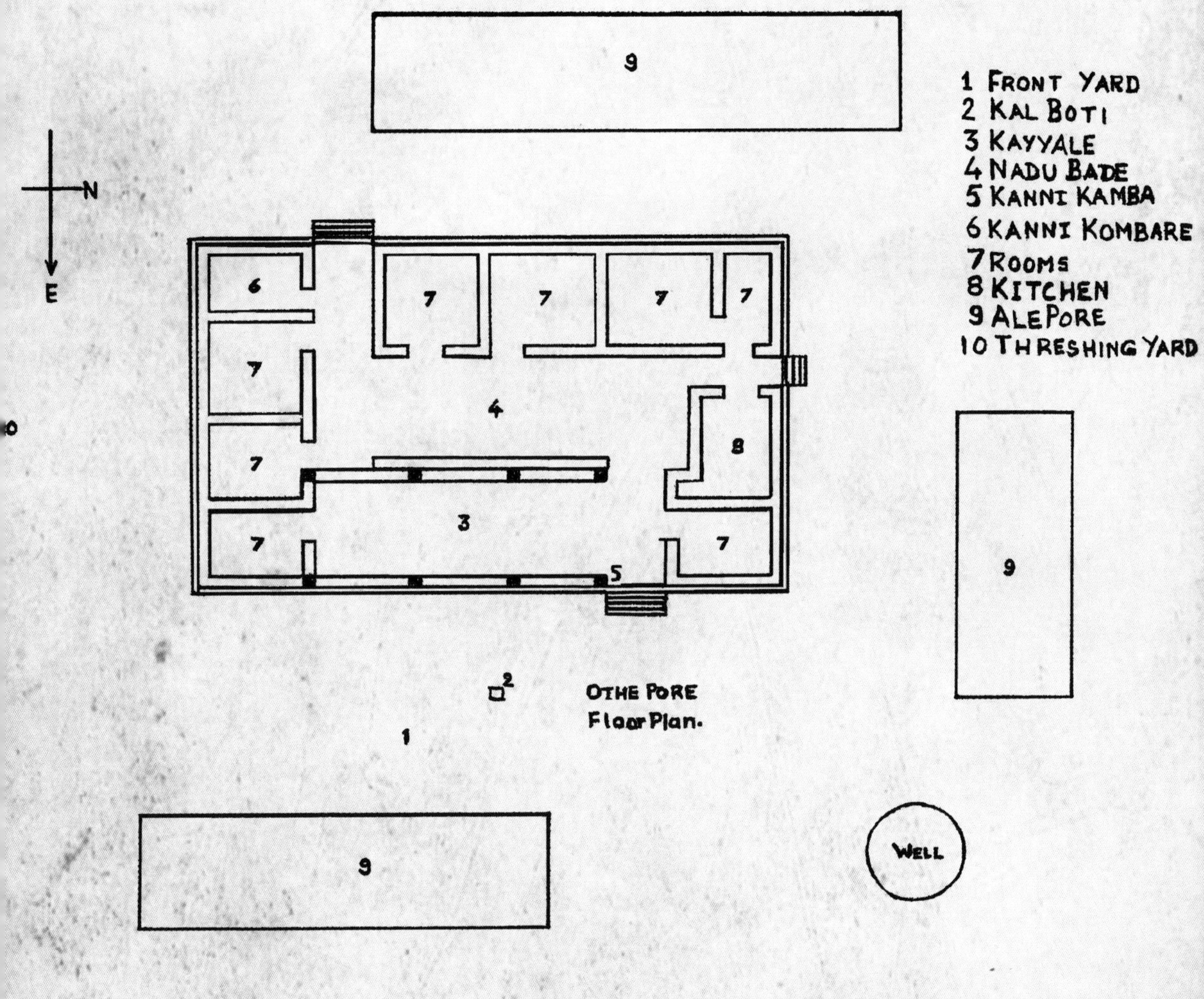

OTHE PORE
Floor Plan.

Appendix 17

INFORMATION IN THE WEBSITE ON TWO *AINMANES*

BOVERIANDA

Community: Kodava.

Date visited: 5th Nov 2003, 12th May 2005.

Location – Village: Nariandaḍa (Cheyyanḍāṇé Post)

Type of *ainmane:* 52 feet long and 51 feet wide *mund mane* with two roofs. It has a small yard in front with a well to the north-east of the house. A lane near the well leads up to the yard from the paddy fields below (that belong to the Battiyanda *okka*). The large verandah (about 30 feet long and 9 feet wide) is seven feet above ground level and has a 3-tiered *thethi* (with two narrow ledges between the tiers) all around the house. Cement steps lead up from the yard to the verandah which has many photos on its walls. Besides the traditional wooden *aimara* on the eastern and southern sides of the verandah (on which only elders may sit), there is a long cement *aimara* on the western side (built about 15 years ago, on which women married into the *okka* may sit). In the past, women married into the *okka* did not enter the house through the main entrance door in the verandah. They used either the door to the rear (west) or the one to the north of the house. (This custom is not strictly followed these days). The *nellakki* has a triangular niche (*gud*) in the western wall where the sacred lamp is kept, and a hanging lamp dedicated to Payyavurappa. Besides the traditional wooden *aimaras* around the *mund*, the *nellakki* too has cement *aimaras* all along its eastern, southern and northern walls, on which women married into the *okka* may sit.

Direction facing: East.

***Kall boti*:** Simple three feet high stone pillar in the threshing yard to the south of the house.

Age: About 250 years old.

Original *ainmane*? No. This is the third one, and was built by Poonacha *ajja*. The first one, built by *Karanava* Beeracha about 500 years ago, was in Naduvenkott, where the Choundi/Vishnu-murthi *kota* is – some distance away from the current house. When Vishnu-murthi established himself in the *kanni kombare* of that house (now a Vishnu-murthi shrine), they found it difficult to maintain it unpolluted, so they gave up that house and Beeracha's son Poonacha built another *ainmane* nearby at Thirike Kandi. That second *ainmane*, a *mund mane*, was burnt down by Tippu's soldiers.

Woodwork: The verandah has a beautiful carved door-frame with a Gajalakshmi panel on top and a simple window with some carving on its frame.

Electricity in the *ainmane*: Yes.

Telephone in the *ainmane*: No.

***Kanni kamba*:** Pillar in the north-west corner of the *mund*, near the sacred lamp.

***Kanni kombare*:** Room to the south-west corner of the house.

Floor: Only the verandah and *nellakki* were cemented, sometime after 1983. All the rooms have cowdung-washed mud floors.

Roof: Tiled in 1928.

Number of rooms: 12 (including the *kanni kombare* and kitchen). The kitchen to the right of the *mund* is now used only for rituals during festivals such as Puthari. There is a new large kitchen outside the house to its north.

Attic: Large airy hall, with only benches kept there. The staircase leading up to it is from the *nellakki*.

***Kaimada*:** A tiled building on a raised location to the right of a lane leading from the *ainmane* to the Bhagavathi temple. It was rebuilt in 1989 after it was damaged by rain. The *gudi* in the *kaimada* has two Deepa Lakshmis and eight bronze images of ancestors, each about six to eight inches high. The largest image has long ear-lobes and hands folded in prayer; one (its leg is broken) is wearing *kupya-chele* and *peeche kathi*, and holding a gun; two small ones with folded hands; one with a turban, *kupya-chele* and *peeche kathi* holding a spear/stick; one holding a spear; one holding an *odi-kathi*; and a small image of a lady holding cymbals.

***Al rupa*:** In the past they used to immerse a silver *al rupa* in the *kundike* at *Thalakaveri*. That is rarely done now.

Temples/shrines nearby: Nariandada Bhagavathi (built by the Boverianda *okka*) and Ayyappa temple, both on Boverianda land. There is a *sthana* of Bhumi Kuliya near the *ainmane* and two *sthanas* of Natha, one by the paddy fields and one near the *kaimada*.

Festivals celebrated in the *ainmane*: Puthari. Bhumi Kuliyang *kodpa* (in Adare, when they offer chicken). Ajjappa/*Karana there* is held occasionally if there is a vow or when the surviving spouse of an elderly couple dies (see *There/Kola* below).

Number of members in the *okka*: About 300, none of whom resides in the *ainmane*; three families live near it.

Book on the *okka* and Family tree: *'Boverianda okkada vamshavali'* written in Kannada by Dr.B.C.Uthaiah in 2001 has information on the *okka* and the Family Tree going back to the *Karanava* (around the year 1600), covering 12 generations. A framed copy of the Family Tree is kept in the verandah of the *ainmane.*

Name of *Karanava*: Beeracha, who built the first *ainmane.*

Name of *Aruva okka*: It used to be Cheyyanda. But some years ago, the Boveriandas decided not to have *aruvas.*

***Thakkame* rights of the *okka*:** *Ur thakka* for Nariandada village. *Thakka* of the Nariandada Bhagavathi temple and the Ayyappa temple nearby. Fore-most *thakka* of the Payyavur temple in Kerala. They take *akki eth por* to the Payyavur temple *namme.* They also have the *koyime* to take *akki eth por* to the Malethirike temple in Karada and to the Ponnola Ishwara temple in Chelavara, during the festivals at those temples.

***Pattedara*:** B.M.Cariappa (in Virajpet).

President of the *okka*: Shyam Thammiah (in Mysore).

***Mand* nearby:** The *ur mand* in Nariandada is not being used now and is overgrown with wild plants. (The path in front of the *ainmane*, past the Battiyanda fields, leads to the *ur mand*). Beliyane *mand* in Karada and Pebbattane *mand* in Chelavara are the two *nad mands.*

***Ambala* nearby:** There was one in the past, behind the Bhagavathi temple. Not any more.

***Deva kaad* nearby:** The sacred forest dedicated to goddess Bhagavathi (about six acres) was converted to Revenue land when the shrine fell into disuse many years ago. It is surrounded by land belonging to the Boveriandas, and has not been encroached upon.

***Thutengala* of the *okka*:** There are three. One for cremation of married adults (to the right of the road to Shyam Thammiah's house); another a little further down to the right to bury unmarried adults; and a third one near the Bhagavathi temple, to bury children.

Year when last wedding held in the *ainmane*: 15 years ago.

***There/Kola* in the *ainmane*:** Ajjappa/*Karana there* is held occasionally if there is a vow or when the surviving spouse of an elderly couple dies and they observe *manek kutuva* (ceremony to bring their spirits home). The songs of *Karanava* Beeracha and Poonacha *ajja* (*Karana paat*) are sung in the *mund* to the beat of *dudis* and many *theres* (including those of Poonacha and Appayya *ajjas* – see story) are held through the night, ending with the *Karana there* in the morning when the one possessed by *Kadi Karana* Beeracha answers questions put to him. The *there* ends at the *kaimada* where pigs and chicken are offered to the *Karanava*.

Folksongs sung in the *ainmane*: The *Karana paat* of ancestors Beeracha and Poonacha is sung during Puthari and during *Karana there*.

Singers of folk songs in the *okka*: Yes, a few.

Paintings/drawings on walls: Have not heard of it.

***Kadanga* nearby:** Yes, around the *ainmane*.

Stories related to *okka* name:

- Elders used to say that the ancestors of this *okka* lived on Kabbe hill over 500 years ago and used to go to the Bori *paramb* (meadow) at the foot of the hill to get salt from Malabar. Hence they were called Borianda, which became Boverianda. In Payyavur, the priest and Korathacha said that the name comes from "Bahu veeran" (with many heroes). [Source: Book on the *okka* by Dr.B.C.Uthaiah.]

Stories related to the *okka*:

- The Boverianda *okka* was the first to settle in Nariandada village. They came from Kabbe hill about 500 years ago, and have 1000 *bhattis* of wetland and

1000 acres of *bane* land here. [Source: Book on the Boverianda *okka* by Dr.B.C.Uthaiah.] They were a big *okka* and lived in a separate *ur guppe*.

- Once, in ancient times during a famine in Kerala, Payyavur Ishwara came to Kodagu, looking for rice for his temple, where worship had stopped because of lack of rice. He met the Boverianda *Karanava* who was stitching a *koundi* for his oxen at the time, and the *Karanava* promised to give rice every year to the Payyavur temple. As witness to the agreement, Ishwara placed his red silk kerchief and some money on the *koundi* that the ancestor was carrying. Since then, the Boverianda are the fore-most *thakka* at the Payyavur temple. They take rice on oxen (*akki eth por*) for the annual festival there in late February, walking the 30 to 40 kms route across the Kabbe hill and through forests on a journey that takes three nights and two days. The rice they take is the first to be offered at the temple. Even today when Korathacha, the temple representative from Payyavur, comes to Kodagu to inform and invite *okkas* for the temple festival, he comes to the Boverianda *ainmane* and rests for the night in the *nellakki*. Re-enacting the visit of Ishwara, he places his red silk kerchief on a *koundi* and keeps witness money on it. After going all around Kodagu for ten days, he comes to spend another night here on his way back to Payyavur. As *thakkas* of the temple, the Boveriandas have no *pole* (ritual pollution) in Payyavur and are allowed go to the temple even if there is a death in the *okka*.
- Once, when there was a drought and the rice crop in Kodagu failed, the Raja ordered that no paddy or rice should be taken to Kerala. But the Boverianda *okka* was committed to take rice to the Payyavur temple. So their ancestor asked the Raja for permission to do so. The Raja asked him to prove the truth of his god (Payyavur Ishwara) by causing it to rain. When the ancestor prayed to Payyavur Ishwara it suddenly started to pour. Convinced of the power of the god, the Raja gifted the Boverianda okka with 5000 acres of *male kad*, forest land on the western slopes of the Kabbe hill, up to Udumbe. Around 1950 the

okka lost half of that land, after one of its members unauthorisedly transferred it to his daughters.

- The Boveriandas used to be humiliated in the Arapattu Bhagavathi temple during the festival there. So they decided to build a Bhagavathi temple in Nariandada. Appayya *ajja* secretly arranged with a priest of the Arapattu temple to bring one of the three Bhagavathi *thadambs* (processional images) to Nariandada. During the temple festival, the priest, who was carrying one of the images, immersed it in the river for the ritual bath and then ran with it towards Nariandada. The villagers of Arapattu ran after him and shot him in his leg. When the priest fell, Appayya *ajja* carried the image and ran with it, after planting his turban on a stake to dupe the villagers. After installing the image in the newly constructed Bhagavathi temple in Nariandada, the Boverianda *okka* became the *ur thakka*. The tomb of Appayya *ajja* and a stone in honour of the priest who was shot are in the temple precincts.
- When a Boverianda man sent a marriage offer to a girl from the Bollachettira *okka*, her father declined the offer, saying that the lane to the Boverianda *ainmane* was not stone-paved and it would be difficult for his daughter to walk on it when it became slushy in the rainy season. It is said that the *okka* got the lane paved over-night and the girl married the Boverianda man!
- Once, when all the Boverianda men were away at war, since the ritual of *akki eth por* to Payyavur had to be continued, the women in the *okka* loaded an ox with rice sacks and let it go from the back of the house, praying to God to guide it. The ox went all by itself, fought off a tiger that attacked it on the way, halted at the same three points en route (where pilgrims usually halt for the nights on their way to Payyavur from Nariandada) and returned with *prasada* from the temple. In memory of this event, to this day, *akki eth por* from the Boverianda *okka* starts from the back of the house. The hill where the ox fought the tiger is called Choma *kund* (Choma means ox and *kund* means hill) [Source: Cheerammana Appumayya].

NADIKERIANDA-1

Community: Kodava.

Date visited: 5 Nov 2003, 23 Feb 2005.

Location – village: Karada.

Type of *ainmane*: Large *mund mane*, with two roofs. A stone-paved narrow lane leads up a steep slope from the road below to the *kaimada* to the left and then, up rough stone steps, to the arched *bakka pore* entrance and the large stone-paved yard in front of the *ainmane*. The *ale pore* extends on both sides of the *bakka pore* entrance. The part to the left (which used to be a stable in the past) has rooms downstairs and a hall upstairs, built in the memory of Dr.Subbiah who died young in a hunting accident in 1935, shot by his friend. (It cost Rs.1200, according to the minutes of the General Body meeting of that year). In the past, the part to the right of the *bakka pore* was a cow-shed with a *pathaya* upstairs, with wooden slatted walls. When renovated in 2002, the cow-shed was converted into a dining hall and the *pathaya* was replaced by a large meeting hall. There are *thombe kann* on all the four outer walls of the *ainmane*. Two small wooden boxes (*gud-potti*) with shutters are embedded in the western wall of the verandah. (They are empty now - no-one knows what they were used for.) Some of the old pillars in the *mund* that were rotting were replaced with newly carved ones in 1996. The *nellakki* has a beautiful old, simple hanging lamp near the north-west corner of the *mund*, and a wooden *bhasma kutt* near the south-east corner. ['Silent Sentinels' – The Traditional Architecture of Coorg', The HECAR Foundation, 2005, has architectural drawings and details of the *ainmane*.]

Direction facing: East.

***Kall boti*:** Yes. A mask was tied to it during a recent *Karana there.*

Age: About 200 years old. It was renovated in 1996 and in 2002. (The house at the rear, built by Nanjappajja is about 150 years old).

Original *ainmane*: No, it is the second. The first one and the old *kaimada* were to the south-west of the present *ainmane*, at a higher level, even higher than the current *kala* and car park there.

Woodwork: There are two feet wide wooden *aimaras* on three sides of the verandah (all except the northern side) and around the *mund*. The verandah has solid pillars with beautiful carved capitols on its eastern side as well as along its inner (western) wall. The door-frame as well as the window-frame and wooden screen in the window of the verandah are carved with geometrical designs. The *mund* has fluted pillars except for the *kanni kamba* in the south-west corner, which has simple flowers etched on it. The *kanni kamba* is a new one, replacing the old carved pillar there that was rotting. All the pillars have carvings on their capitols. The doors to the kitchen and to some of the rooms around the *nellakki* also have carved door-frames.

Electricity in the *ainmane*: Yes.

Telephone in the *ainmane*: No.

***Kanni kamba*:** Pillar in the south-west corner of the *mund*.

***Kanni kombare*:** Narrow wood-panelled room in the south-west corner of the house, with the entrance door from the adjacent room to its east. There is a long shelf on its western wall to keep the sacred lamp and *meedi*.

Floor: Fully cemented in 1976.

Roof: Tiled long ago. No one remembers when.

Number of rooms: Ten (including the kitchen and *kanni kombare*).

Attic: Large hall around the *mund* with only wooden benches kept there. The staircase is from the *nellakki*.

Kaimada: The present one is the second *kaimada*, built at the same time as the *ainmane*. *Meedi* is kept here during *Karanang kodpa* and on other auspicious occasions. The *kaimada* faces east and is located in a small open yard close to the *bakka pore,* at a lower level. It has wide cement steps, a low wicket gate to the central *gudi*, and four carved pillars and *aimaras* in front, with beautiful lotuses carved on the capitols. The raised *gudi* is enclosed with wooden slatted walls and has a beautiful carved door in front. Inside the *gudi* are three images of ancestors embossed on metal. In an open walled enclosure to the south of the *kaimada* are three tombstones to famous people in the *okka*. (The foundation of the earlier *kaimada* can be seen high up, to the south-west of the house - a raised platform with stones along its border, and a tomb nearby with crumbling cement plaster. Offerings are made there during Puthari and *Karana there*.)

***Al rupa*:** No.

Temples/shrines nearby: Karada Bhagavathi temple (where the *Bolak namme* is held, mid April). Malethirike shrine to Male Thambiran up the hill nearby (where the *namme* is held on March 14).

Festivals celebrated in the *ainmane*: *Karana there* is held in April/May when all members of the *okka* get together (see *There/Kola* below). *Karanang kodpa* (a very simple ritual which only those near the *ainmane* attend). Puthari.

Number of members in the *okka*: About 250 (about 75 families), none of whom resides in the *ainmane*; one (a bachelor) lives in the house at the back. (A Nambiyappanda woman and her two children live in the *ale pore* now.)

Book on the *okka* and Family tree: No book - only the ballad of Nadikerianda Devayya in the Pattole Palame. The Family Tree was first drawn in 1918 by N.A.Chinnappa (author of the Pattole Palame), and updated in 1975 by his son, N.C.Subbayya. It was updated again in 2001 by Saroj and Appaji Nanjappa and Rana Nanjappa, and traces the *okka* back 11 generations to *Karanava* Ayyanna. (Nadikerianda-2, the Palangala *bhaga* that broke away, has a Family Tree for that *bhaga*, drawn in 2008.). (We have copies of the Family Trees for both the Nadikerianda *bhagas*).

Name of *Karanava*: Ayyanna who is believed to have lived in the 1600s. N.A.Chinnappa says that there is no evidence to show how much older Devayya, the hero of the ballad of Nadikerianda Devayya, was than Ayyanna.

Name of *Aruva okka:* Ithichanda (mutual)

Thakkame* rights of the *okka: *Ur thakka* for Karada and *Deva thakka* of the Malethirike shrine in Karada (the latter, along with the Chottalyammanda Amma *okka*).

***Pattedara*:** N.C. Poovaiah (in Siddapur).

President of the *okka*: N.S.Chinnappa (Bangalore). The General Body meets twice annually, at Puthari and during the *Bolak namme*. The Family fund is used for festival expenses, sports, education, maintenance of the *ainmane* etc.

***Mand* nearby:** The *ur mand* is Koliyare *mand* (nearby, across the road) and the *nad mand* is Beliyane *mand* (by the side of the main road).

***Ambala* nearby:** By the road-side near the Chottalyammanda house, on the way to the *Malethirike* shrine.

***Deva kaad* nearby:** Dedicated to Bhagavathi, near the temple (nine acres).

***Thutengala* of the *okka*:** It is across the road, in the forest in front of the *ainmane*. Note: There is another graveyard for the Nadikeriandas in Madikeri, where Bose Mandanna's parents are buried. This was set aside in land owned by Nadikerianda Appacha, son of Monnappa Ajja, who owned a lot of land in Madikeri. (Appacha also gifted land for graveyards to the families of his two sisters – Konganda and Codanda).

Year when last wedding held in the *ainmane*: 1985, when the weddings of two brothers N. K. Nanayya (Jappu) and N.K. Chengappa (Dilip) were held simultaneously.

***There*/*Kola* in the *ainmane*:** *Karana there* is an elaborate two-day affair, celebrated annually in April/May by one of the *kades* of the *okka* taking turns (*therige*) to conduct it. Seven *theres* are held through the night, the first four in the evening and the other three the next day, starting very early in the morning. They are held in the following order: Kuttichatha (a spirit-deity), Karajjappa (who killed a tiger), *Nari* (tiger who fights a young man and dies), Kuliya (spirit-deity who embraces one of the young men there and has a baby – a figure made of straw is used to depict it), Vishnu-murthi (Narasimha with a lion's mask), *eth* (ox killed by a tiger), and Ajjappa (*Karanava* – the last and longest *there*, when the one possessed by the *Karanava* answers questions put to him by members of the *okka* and advises them*)*. The *theres* are performed by Bannas.

Folksongs sung in the *ainmane*: Not since about 40 to 50 years ago (when members sang with villagers in the *mund*).

Singers of folk songs in the *okka*: N.P. Kalappa (Ravi).

Paintings/drawings on walls: Have not heard of it.

***Kadanga* nearby:** Only small ones between land belonging to this *okka* and to that of others in the village.

Stories related to *okka* name:

- Their ancestors might have first settled in the village called Nadikeri and then come to Karada. Hence the name. [Source: N.C. Subbayya].

- When the first Nair ancestor came here, he settled in a hamlet (*keri*) in the middle (*nadu*) of the village where there is an *ambala*. Hence they were called Nadukeriya, which became Nadikeriya. At that time there was another *ambala* at the top end of the village – Mekeri and one at the bottom of the village – Kikkeri. [Source: N.P.Thammani]

Stories related to the *okka*:

- It is said that the ancestors of the *okka* were Nairs who came from Malabar with their troops and with the Moplahs (Muslim traders from Malabar) whom they had defeated. They occupied land in Palangala (where they settled the Moplahs, who later went to Edapala in Nariyandada) and in Karada, where they themselves settled. That is why they are referred to as Nayamma (which means Nair) Nadikeriya in the village and in folk songs. There is a field in Palangala that is called Nayamma *nadu bail*. [Source: Notes written by N.A. Chinnappa, author of the Pattole Palame].
- The Nair ancestor of the *okka* came from Kerala 600/700 years ago and married a Kodava woman called Kummachi. The Patrapandas gave him land in Karada. [Source: Patrapanda Kalinga].
- Two Nair brothers from Kalyat in Kerala, belonging to a Nayaka (chieftain/warlord) family that controlled parts of both Kerala and Kodagu, came to Kodagu. One brother started the Nadikerianda *okka* and the other started the Kalyatanda *okka*. [Source: Kunji Raman, Kolakeri, Napoklu].
- The Nadikeriandas were invited by the Ithichanda *okka* to settle in Karada. [Source: Ithichanda *okka*].
- The Nadikerianda and Chottalyammanda *okkas* are joint *thakkas* of the Malethirike shrine. Nadikerianda Devayya, a famous ancestor of the *okka*, along with the Chottalyammanda *thakka* got a shelter built for the priest at the shrine, and invited a *thanthri* from Kerala to perform the purification rites. When the *thanthri* was late, the *thakkas* asked the priest at the shrine to do the rites

himself. Angered by this, the *thanthri* cursed the two *thakkas* – the Nadikeranda with leucoderma and the Chottalyammanda with lunacy. It was decreed that the curse would not affect the *okkas* if they held *Karana* there every year, along with other prescribed *theres*. That is why the Nadikerianda *okka* conducts Choundi, Vishnumurthi and Kuttichatha theres among others during their *Karana there*. The first *kaimada* of the *okka* was said to have been built where Devayya was buried (probably the crumbling tomb near the foundation of the old *kaimada*) [Source: Song of Nadikerianda Devayya in the Pattole Palame].

- The first *ainmane* was believed to be cursed because all the young men there died before they were 30 years old. So Nanjavva (Kanjithanda *thamane*), widow of Nadikerianda Deviah, got this *ainmane* constructed. She lived about six generations ago (Source: Family Tree),
- Dodda Veerarajendra wanted to build a palace where the current Nadikerianda *ainmane* stands, because of its commanding view. But the Nadikeriandas who had chosen this spot for their *ainmane* told the Raja that this place was easily accessible to enemies since it was close to the main road. So the Raja built his Nalnad palace in Yavakapadi and the Nadikeriandas built theirs here. (Note: The Nalnad palace was built in 1791-95 and therefore it is likely that the current Nadikerianda *ainmane* was built around then).
- During Puthari, Jamma Mapille *okkas* from Edapala (Erteyanda, Kupponda, Kikkare) used to spend three nights in Karumbayya *ajja's* house near the *ainmane*. They were welcomed in the *mand* with a mat spread out for them. They beat *dudis* and sang and danced with the Nadikeriandas, leading the dance in the *mand*. Among them were the ancestors of the Nadikeriandas who were captured and converted to Islam by Tippu and later escaped and returned to Kodagu. They were not taken back into the *okka* because there were no rituals that allowed them to do that. [Source: N.C.Subbayya; Bachamanda Changuammayya; Pandanda Mandappa].

- Subedar Monnappa was clever and acquired a lot of land in Karada, Palangala and Arapatt as well as in Madikeri and near Sunticoppa. It is believed that he went to Kerala and acquired Kuttichatha's *manthra* and gained power from that [Source: Nadikerianda Appaji].
- This okka has two *bhagas*: This one, Nadikerianda-1 in the original *ainmane* in Karada, and Nadikerianda-2 in Palangala. The latter, also called Palangala Nadikerianda broke off from Nadikerianda-1 around the 1800s because a widow in the *okka* refused to marry either of two brothers, her husband's cousins, since she did not like their ways. In anger the brothers tore a piece of cloth (*muri keethith*) and walked away from the *ainmane* declaring that just as the two torn pieces of cloth could never be made one again, they would never come back to the *okka*. They settled in Palangala, and Poovaiah *ajja* of Nadikerianda-2 built an *othe pore ainmane* in Kerane. Subedar Monnappa of Nadikerianda-1 was in Govt. service in Madikeri then, and needed a good house there. So he exchanged land that he had acquired in Palangala (wetland in Yakot, close to the Nadikerianda-2 *ainmane*), for 'King's wall', a bungalow in Madikeri that belonged to his first cousin Kuttappa, son of Poovaiah *ajja* of Nadikerianda-2. The Nadikerianda-2 *ainmane* has since fallen. Now they only have a newly rebuilt *kaimada*. Poovaiah *ajja*, the ancestor who built the Palangala *ainmane* had white patches on his skin. When he died, his corpse was not taken to the Nadikerianda *thutengala*, and was buried at a spot that became the *thutengala* for Nadikerianda-2. There is no connection between the two *bhagas* now – not even *pole-thale*. [Source: Machaiah and Theja Poovaiah of Nadikerianda-2].
- Nadikerianda A. Chinnappa is famous as the author of the 'Pattole Palame' (1924), a compilation of the traditions and folklore of Kodavas (the traditions and customs are written in Kannada, while the folksongs, proverbs and plays are in the Kodava language), and the 'Bhagavanthanda Pat' (1929), a translation

of the Bhagavad Gita into the Kodava language using the metre and style of *Balo paat* (Kodava folk songs).

- N.A.Chinnappa's son N.C.Subbayya started nine High Schools in Kodagu (after retiring as a teacher), at a time when there were only three in the district. The best known of these is the Nariyandada High School (1959), for which land was donated by the Boverianda and Battiyanda *okkas* and where he and his wife Ponnamma rendered voluntary service. He was also responsible for the creation of many Middle and Primary schools in Coorg.
- N.Medayya was a freedom fighter.
- Subedar N. Bheemiah was honoured with the Veera Chakra for his bravery.

(From among the photos in the website for these *ainmanes*, only a photo of each *ainmane* has been shown here.)

SELECT BIBLIOGRAPHY

Appachu, Chattakuttada P. *Moolanivasi Kodagu Kembatti Janaru* (Kannada). Self-published, 2003.

Appanna, Bacharaniyanda P. *Kodagil Ainmane* (Kodava) in 'Kodava Siri' (a collection of talks broadcast in the 'Kodava Siri' programme of All India Radio, Madikeri, 1996–2003), Madikeri: Karnataka Kodava Sahithya Academy, 2003.

Basham, A.L. *The Wonder that was India*. New York: Macmillan Co., 1954.

Belliappa, Cheppudira P. *Nuggets from Coorg History*. New Delhi: Rupa & Co., 2008.

Bhatt, Shankaranarayana Aedurkala. *Sri Cauvery Vaibhava* (Kannada). Bhagamandala: Sri Ramakrishna Prakashana, 1987.

Belliappa, Bythadka Janaki. *Akshaya - Kodagu Gowda Traditions and Customs* (Kannada and Are Bhashe). Madikeri: Kodagu Mahila Gowda Okkuta, 2009.

Cariappa, Maneyapanda P. and Ponnamma. *The Coorgs and their Origins*. Mysore: Geetha Book House, 1981.

Changappa, Paradanda G. *Kodagina Moolanivasiyara Purana Samskruthiya Parichaya* (Kannada). Self-published, 2003.

——— *Paradanda manethana mathu Kunjilageri Mukkatira Manethana* (Kannada), Self-published, 1990.

Chinnappa, Nadikerianda A. *Pattole Palame* (Kannada and Kodava). Self-published, 1924. English translation by Chinnappa, Boverianda M. and Nanjamma. New Delhi: Rupa & Co., 2003.

Claus, Peter and Korom Frank. *Folkloristics and Indian Folklore*. Udupi: Regional Resources Centre for Folk Performing Arts, 1991.

Cole, Robert. *Manual of Coorg Civil Law*, 1861.

Curgenven. A.J., trans. *Hukum Nama* (Kannada), of Rajah Linga Rajendra Wodeyar (Lingaraja II), 1811–1820. Coorg District Press, 1911.

Dhanu, Inanda M. *Kodagira Namme Nal* (Kodava) in Kodava Siri (a collection of talks broadcast in the 'Kodava Siri' programme of All India Radio, Madikeri, 1996–2003), Madikeri: Karnataka Kodava Sahithya Academy, 2003.

Encyclopaedia Britannica. 1911.

Ferishta/Farishta (c. 1560–1620). '*History of Dekkan from the First Mahummedan Conquests*' translated into English from the original Persian by Jonathan Scott, 1794.

Ganapathy, Bachamada D. *Kodavas, A comprehensive Study*. Self-published, Madikeri, 1980.

Hegde, Krishnananda, *History of Bunts: Medieval Age to Modern Times*. Mangalore: Bharatiya Vidya Bhavan, 2008.

Hunter, W.W, ed. *Imperial Gazetteer, vol. II*. London, 1881.

Kalam, M.A. '*Sacred Groves in Kodagu District of Karnataka (South India): A Socio-historical Study*,' Pondy Papers in Social Sciences. Institut Français de Pondicherry, 1996.

Kamath Suryanath U., ed. *Gazetteer of India, Karnataka State, Kodagu District*. Bangalore, 1993.

Kodava Bhashika Moola Nivasiya (Kodava). Madikeri: Karnataka Kodava Sahithya Academy, 2003.

Krishnaiah, D.N. *Kodagina Ithihasa* (Kannada). University of Mysore, 1974.

Kushalappa, Cheppudira G. and Uthappa, Kuttanda G. *Deva Kad* (Kodava). Madikeri: Kodava Thakk Elthkarada Koota, 2002.

Moegling, Rev. H. *Coorg Memoirs - An Account of Coorg*. Bangalore: Wesleyan Mission Press, 1855.

Muthanna, Iychettira M. *A Tiny Model State of South India*. Self-published, 1953.

Muthanna, Kotera P. *Jagathigonde Kodagu* (Kannada). Self-published, 1969.

Muthanna, Podanolanda B. *Paddathira Beerya* (Kodava). Madikeri: Kodava Thakk Elthkarada Koota, 2003.

Muthappa, Chendrimada G. *Ithihasa Palelinji* (Kodava). Madikeri: Karnataka Kodava Sahithya Academy, 2004.

Nagaraj, M.G. *Kodagina Kaimadagalu* (Kannada). Bangalore: Kannada Sahithya Parishat, 2004.

——— *Kodagina Ainmanegalu mathu Sankeerna* (Kannada), Ithihasa Darshana, vol. 6. Bangalore: Karnataka Ithihasa Academy, 2001.

——— *Kodagina Kall Botigalu* (Kannada), Ithihasa Darshana, vol. 8. Bangalore: Karnataka Ithihasa Academy, 1993.

——— *Kembatti Holeyara Samskriti* (Kannada). Bangalore: Karnataka Sahithya Academy, 1993.

Napier, John. 'Kodava Song and the Public Non-Assertion of Difference.' Global Media Journal, Australian Edition, vol 4:2, 2010.

Panikkar, K.M. *A Survey of Indian History*. Bombay: Asia Publishing House, 1947.

Pattanaik, Devdutt. *A Handbook of Hindu Mythology*. Penguin, 2006.

Ponnapa, Kaveri. *The Vanishing Kodavas*. Mumbai: Eminence Designs Pvt Ltd, 2013.

Ponnappa, Lt. Col. Kongetira C. *A study of the Origins of Coorgs*. Self-published, Bangalore, 1997.

Ramachandrachar, D.B. *Kudiyara Samskrithi* (Kannada). Bangalore: Karnataka Sahithya Academy, 1993.

Richter, Rev. G. *Manual of Coorg - A Gazetteer*. New Delhi: Low Price Publications Reprint, 1995. First published, 1870.

Somaya, Brinda. *Silent Sentinels, Traditional Architecture of Coorg*. Mumbai: The HECAR Foundation, 2005.

Spear, S.G., ed. *UPASI (United Planters' Association of South India) 1893–1953*. Coonoor, 1953.

Srinivas, M.N. *Religion and Society among the Coorgs of South India*. Oxford University Press, 1952.

Subbayya, Keekanamada K. *Archaeology of Coorg*. Mysore: Geetha Book House, 1978.

Uthappa, Iythichanda Ramesh. *Poomale Kudiya* (Kodava). Madikeri: Karnataka Kodava Sahithya Academy, 2002.

Uthappa, Kuttanda G. *Land Tenure, Land Holding, Tree Rights of Kodagu*. Ponnampet: Model Forest Trust, 2004.

Vansina, Jan. *Oral Tradition as History*. Madison: University of Wisconsin Press, 1985.

KEY TO TRANSLITERATION

In the glossary section, non-English words have been transliterated using the Roman alphabet. Diacritical (accent) marks are used in the transliteration to guide the reader on the correct pronunciation of these words, the majority of which are in the Kodava language.

In the key to the transliteration given below, the pronunciation indicated by each diacritical mark is illustrated by the underlined portion of an English word, whose pronunciation is closest to that shown by the mark.

Transliterated letters	*Pronounced approximately as in underlined portion of English word*	**Transliterated letters**	*Pronounced approximately as in underlined portion of English word*
Vowels		**Consonants**	
a	but	b	bat
ā	car	ch	chin
ă	bird	d	then
aº	hundred	ḍ	down
ai	like	g	get
e	merry	h	hat
ē	fate	j	jet
é	at once	k	cut
ḗ	cat	l	let
ĕ	bird	l	plant
ē̆	earth	m	met
ë	couldn't	n	net
i	pin	ñ	bench
ï	couldn't	ṇ	as in Krishna
o	obedience	p	pin
ō	old	r	rank
ò	pot	s	sit
ṑ	saw	sh	ship
oo	mood	t	met
ou	how	th	thank
u	put	v	very
ū	rude	y	yard
ü	couldn't		

GLOSSARY

[Of non-English words, mainly in the Kodava *thakk* (language). The language is specified if it is not Kodava *thakk*.]

A

āchāri carpenter; *mara airi*

āḍ goat/let it be so

aḍchi bāḍé passage-like attachment to the hall; *kunji bāḍé*; *muri bāḍé*

ādi mūla the primordial source of all being

aimara wooden bench-seat laid on top of a low mud parapet built between pillars

aimbad fifty

ain original, principal, genuine

ainmané ancestral home of the native communities of Koḍagu

airi community of carpenters, goldsmiths and blacksmiths; *thachāyiri*

ājini wild jack tree, *Artocarpus hirsutus*

ajjappă kall stone in memory of a dead elder; *kāraṇa kall*

akam inside (Tamil)

akki rice

akki ïḍuvă ritual sprinkling of rice

akki pathāya wooden box for storing rice; *akki potti*; *pitāri*

akki potti *akki pathāya*

āl person

āl rūpa small crude figurine representing a recently deceased adult, embossed on a beaten silver sheet or carved in wood

ālaya dwelling (Sanskrit)

ālé dwelling

ālé pòré outhouse (literally dwelling hut) built close to the *ainmané* for additional living space

aliya kattu matrilineal (Tulu)

ambala roofed structure on a raised platform where elders of the village meet to settle disputes

amrïtha nectar of immortality

anchi tile

āné elephant

ānéyāt dance by a man positioned inside an elephant-shaped hollow cane frame.

anuvāda words of guidance, commands and reprimands spoken by the person possessed by the spirit of an ancestor

aramané palace

Aré-bhāshé literally 'half language', a mix of Halegannaḍa (old form of Kannaḍa), Tulu and Koḍava *thakk*

ariyuvavå one who knows

ārōḍa *ārvāḍ*

ārūtam *ārvāḍ* (Malayālam)

aruva *aruva okka*

aruvă representative of the *aruva okka*

aruva okka a friendly, neighbouring *okka* which performs the mutually agreed role of assisting an *okka* in rituals and ceremonies

aruvāmé mutually agreed arrangement between two *okkas* to assist each other as *aruvas*

ārvāḍ the primary/original/oldest *ainmané* of an *okka*

atha cattle

atha kott cattle shed

atta attic

āyudha implements or weapons

āyudha pūjé ceremony during *kail polüd*, when agricultural implements and weapons are ritually worshipped

B

bakka	guarded passage
bakka poré	guard's lookout hut at the top of the lane leading to the *ainmané*
bāl	blessing, meaning 'live long'; *bālō*
bālé	banana
bālé bakka	clearing by the side of the path to the *ainmané* where banana stems are staked to the ground, for the *bāle birüdü* ceremony
bāle birüdü	ceremony during weddings where a representative of the person being honoured cuts the banana stems with an *oḍi kathi*
bālō	*bāl*
bālō pāt	traditional folk song in the Koḍava language
balya mané	large house where all the members of the *okka* lived together in the past; also used interchangeably for *ainmané*
banda kula	clan that came later and settled in the village
bāṇé	forest highland
baraṇi	earthenware jar
bāraṇi	ritual offerings of food and liquor to ancestors or spirit-deities during special occasions; *éḍé*
bāriké	low-lying pasture land
basava	bull (Kannaḍa)
batté	way or path
batté kall	flat stones placed in a line on the path across a yard, to walk on when the mud in the yard is slushy
batté pāt	Song for the Way—folk song that describes the *ainmané*
bédaké	two pairs of wooden battens hung from the ceiling, with aligned holes near their lower ends, through which are slid two bamboo poles—used to hang various items; *nēlé*
beeră	hero
beeră kall	carved hero stone; *veera kall*
bhāga	branch of an *okka*
bhanḍāra potti	box in which money offerings, jewels, processional images and other paraphernalia related to a deity are stored
bhanḍāra thakka	*okka* that is traditionally responsible for the safe-keeping of the *bhanḍāra potti* of a shrine
bhanḍāra thakkă	headman of the *okka* that is traditionally responsible for the safe-keeping of the *bhanḍāra potti* of a shrine
bhasma	sacred ash
bhasma kutt	carved wooden container for *bhasma*
bhatti	basket, unit of measurement of wetland in terms of expected yield of paddy
bhūmi	wetland for rice cultivation
bhūtha	spirit of a dead person; literally 'of the past'
bill	bow
billāt	dance by men holding bows as they dance
bindigé	bronze or copper pot to carry water
birüdü	honour
bishu	first day of the new year in the solar calendar
bōḍ	to beg
bōḍ nammé	unusual temple festival where men in different guises sing *bōḍ pāt* and dance the *bōḍāt*, begging and teasing those around for money
bōḍ pāt	songs sung by dancers during the *bōḍ nammé*, that poke fun at gods, masters and onlookers as they dance
bōḍāt	simple unstructured dance by men in different guises during *bōḍ nammé*
bolak	earthern lamps lit with wicks
bolak nammé	temple festival of lights, when the temple walls are decorated with many *bolak*
bolakāt	dance by men during the *bolak nammé* temple festival
bolcha	lamp
bollé maṇṇ	white mud

bothü	posts made from the branches of specific trees, that are traditionally planted during *Kāvēri Sankramaṇa* in paddy fields, and near wells and cattle sheds to reaffirm custody of the land
bōti	post
būṇakké	a kind of tree, *Garcinia xanthochymus*

C

chadara	square
chadara kamba	square pillar
chāṇḍālă	an outcaste
chanḍé	large drum
chāvu pāt	funeral song
cheeni	a wind instrument, a pipe
chḗlé	red, gold-embroidered silk sash tied around the waist to secure the *kupya* worn by a Koḍava man
chemb	small pot
chingāra	adornment
chipp	shell
chipp anchi	small, humped tiles; *chipp ōḍ*
chipp ōḍ	*chipp anchi*
chooléyāt	dance by men dressed as dancing girls, during *bōḍ nammé*
chouri	yak-tail whisk
chouriyāt	dance by men holding *chouris* as they dance

D

dabbe	bamboo split vertically to make a conduit for water (Kannaḍa)
dabbe hanchu	small, humped tiles (Kannaḍa)
danḍané kula	the second *okka* to settle in the village
dappu	percussion instrument
dappu āt	dance by Jamma Māpillé men beating the *dappu* as they dance
dāsa	singing mendicant
deekshé	abstinence restrictions during the mourning period following a death
deekshé uthuvă	ritual denoting the end of traditional *deekshé* restrictions
dēsha	a region; *seemé*
dēsha kĕtt pāt	song of how the land was administered
dēsha thakkă	headman of the *okka* with the traditional *thakkāmé* of a region (group of *nāds*); *seemé thakkă*
dḗva	god
dḗva kāḍ	sacred forest, dedicated to a deity
dḗva thakka	*okka* with the traditional *thakkāmé* of a shrine
dḗva thakkă	headman of the *okka* with the traditional *thakkāmé* of a shrine
dḗvaḍa kĕtt	traditional restrictions during a temple festival
dēvara guḍi	shrine to a deity (Kannaḍa)
dēvara kōṇe	*pūjé* room (Kannaḍa)
dēvaru	god or deity (Kannaḍa)
dḗvathé	deity
devva	a spirit (Kannaḍa)
devva kottaḍi	shrine to a spirit (Kannaḍa)
dhāre	important ritual in some Hindu wedding ceremonies when the bride is given away in marriage (Kannaḍa)
dhōl	large drum
diwān	highest official in a king's court; chief minister
doḍḍa	large (Kannaḍa)
doḍḍa mane	ancestral home with an inner courtyard (Kannaḍa)
dollu	large drum (Kannaḍa)
dollu kuṇitha	dance by Kuruba men, beating *dollus* as they dance (Kannaḍa)
dōsha	fault, blemish
duḍi	Koḍava drum
duḍi kott pāt	song sung to the beat of the *duḍi*
dumbchiḍüva	putting out the flame of the sacred lamp (literally, filling it up)

E

éḍé	*bāraṇi*
ĕl thalé kāraṇavå	ancestor from seven generations ago
ĕlakki putt	dish made for *Puthari* by kneading seven ingredients—rice flour, ripe

bananas, milk, honey, etc.

eriya — extension of the plinth outside the outer walls of the *ainmané; thethi*

eth pāt — songs sung when driving pack-oxen

eth pōr — rice loaded on the backs of pack-oxen and taken to markets or as offerings to temples

G

gaddigé — monumental tomb

gōde kamba — pillar sacred to the memory of the *kāraṇavå* of the *okka* (Aré-bhāshé)

gōpi — milkmaid

gōthra — lineage traced back to ancient sages

gūḍ — niche in a wall

guḍḍa — bathing shed

guḍḍé mané — cluster of thatched mud huts close to each other

guḍi — small shrine to a deity

gunḍa — *dēvara guḍi* or altar (Aré-bhāshé)

guppé — cluster

guru kāraṇă — *kāraṇavå* who is the guru

H

hadi — a prop (Kannaḍa); *padi*

halegannaḍa — old form of Kannaḍa (Kannaḍa)

hanchu — tile (Kannaḍa)

Hari sēve — worship of God Venkataramaṇa

hase — decorative pictures drawn by men on a blackened part of the wall of the *nellakki naḍu bāḍé* in the *ainmané*, as part of Gouḍa wedding rituals (Kannaḍa)

I

illu — house (Tulu)

irümb — iron

irümb-airi — blacksmith; *kollă*

ishta — desired

ishta dḗvathé — chosen deity

J

jāgir — wetland free of assessment gifted to an individual for exceptional services rendered to the king; *jahāgir*

jahāgir — *jāgir*

jamma — land tenure that gives an *okka* hereditary right over ancestral land that is jointly owned by all the members of the *okka* and is nominally taxed

jamma malé — *jamma* right to hills, with leaseholds free of assessment

janma — lifetime (Sanskrit)

jōyi — mendicant

jōyi pāt — songs of the mendicant (sung with the refrain *thāli lellēlā*); *thāli pāt*

K

kad — new/first ears of paddy

kāḍ — forest

kaḍanga — ancient defensive trenches, unique to Koḍagu

kaḍike — *thuliya* (Aré-bhāshé)

kail mūrtha — *kail polüd*

kail polüd — festival when agricultural implements and weapons are venerated; *kail mūrtha*

kaimaḍa — shrine to the ancestors of the *okka*, located near the *ainmané*

kala — threshing yard

kalanji — yam

kalasha — pot with water used in rituals

kall — stone

kall beppă — ritual placing of a stone in memory of a dead person

kall bōti — stone post

kall mané — stone house

kallōṇi — stone-paved lane

kamba — pillar

kaṇatharé — circular well

kaṇi pūjé — worship of Goddess Kāvēri and mother earth

kaṇiyă — astrologer

kaṇṇ — small hole

kanni — virgin/planet Virgo

kanni kamba — pillar sacred to the memory of the *kāraṇavå* of the *okka*

kanni kồmbaré	room sacred to ancestors; *kanni mūlé kồmbaré; meedi kồmbaré*
kanni mūlé	south-west corner of the *ainmané*
kanni mūlé kồmbaré	*kanni kồmbaré*
kappeyāt	dance by men hopping like frogs
kāraṇa	cause, origin
kāraṇă	*kāraṇavå*
kāraṇa kala	ancestor platform; *kāraṇa tharé*
kāraṇa kall	*ajjappă kall*
kāraṇa kồla	performance ritual in an *ainmané* in honour of the *kāraṇavå* of the *okka*; *kāraṇa théré*
kāraṇa pāt	song of ancestors
kāraṇa purushă	the original person
kāraṇa tharé	*kāraṇa kala*
kāraṇa théré	*kāraṇa kồla*
kāraṇachi	earliest-remembered female ancestor of the *okka*
kāraṇang koḍpă	ritual offerings to ancestors; *kāraṇang meedi beppă*
kāraṇang meedi beppă	*kāraṇang koḍpă*
kāraṇavå	founder or earliest-remembered male ancestor of the *okka*; *kāraṇă*
kāraṇavanḍa aimara	*aimara* for the *kāraṇavå*
kāryakāră	senior officer in the king's service; commanding officer in the army
kātakāyi	rebellion
kathiyāt	dance by men holding *oḍi kathis* as they dance
kāti	show
kattồlé	door frame
kāvēri sankramaṇa	celebration of the birth of river Kāvēri
kāvukāră thakkă	one who officiates as the priest only during a temple festival
kayyālé	verandah
kĕkola	burial ground of the *okka*
kembathi	hibiscus
kĕtt	structure (Malayālam)
kiḍāsa	worship of paddy by Gouḍas, after planting is completed (Aré-bhāshé)
kĭḍiké	window
koḍichi	dancing girl
koḍichi pāt	songs of the *koḍichi*
kōl	cane used in folk dances; *Puthari kōl* dance
kồla	performance ritual in honour of an ancestor or a spirit-deity; *théré*
kōlāt	folk dance where the dancers hold sticks and strike them as they dance
kollă	*irümb-airi*
kolli	water-logged area
kolli ồté	wild reed that grows in water-logged areas
komb	long-curved musical horn/area up to which the sound of a *komb* is heard/a group of adjoining *nāḍs*/horn of a stag
komba meesé	mutton-chop moustache
kồmbaré	room
kombāt	dance by men holding *komb* (stag horns) as they dance
kommé	large pot-shaped container for grain
koppa	hamlet
koppath mané	house in a hamlet
koravukāră	one who takes responsibility
kồté	fort
kott	shed
kottaḍi	shrine (Kannaḍa)
koundi	quilt placed on the back of a pack-ox
koundi kott	shed where *koundis* are stored
kōyimé	customary right to perform prescribed duties/dances, etc., related to a shrine
kuḍa(m)	west (Tamil)
kūḍa	along with
kuḍi	family/*okka*
kuḍi beeră	spirit of a hero of the *okka* who died a violent death
kudré	horse
kudréyāt	dance by a man positioned inside a hollow horse-shaped cane frame
kuḍumalénāḍ	land of steep hills (Tamil)
kula	*okka*/race
kula dēvaru	deity of the *okka* (Kannaḍa)
kula dḗvathé	deity of the *okka*
kulur māvü	machilus tree
kundă	dancing boy

kunji/kuñña infant
kunji/kuñña bāḍé *aḍchi bāḍé*
kūpodi cooked rice and curds along with pickle, etc., packed in banana leaves
kupp slat
kupya traditional attire of Koḍava men—a wrap-around collarless black or white coat that reaches below the knees and is secured with a sash
kuthi hollow container made of bamboo or copper
kutt block of wood
kuttaḍa the *kuḍi* (family) to which the *okka* belongs
kutumba founding family of Gouḍas (Aré-bhāshé)
kūvalé a kind of creeper, *Schumannianthus virgatus*
kuyya rice rice cooked on open hearths near a temple during the temple festival

L

lō palamé hearsay

M

machi ceiling of wooden planks
machi mané house with a wooden ceiling and attic
māda ceremony that ends the period of ritual mourning for a dead person
maḍak fold or bend
maḍak mané L-shaped house
makka parajé tradition where a man marries an unmarried girl or a widow from an *okka* that faces extinction, and his children from this marriage carry the *mané péda* of the *okka* that is facing extinction
malé hill
malla large (Tulu)
malla illu ancestral home of Tulunāḍ
mambathāya *pathāya* made of mud
mammarïnjă one who climbed up or crossed over
mand open space set apart for sports, dances and social gatherings
mandiyāt a type of dance by Yerava women
mane house (Kannaḍa)
mané house
mané dḗvathé deity of the house
mané pāt song of the *okka* that relates the history of the *okka*
mané péda house or *okka* name
mangala auspicious ceremony, like a wedding
mangala pāt wedding song
maṇṇ mud
maṇṇ mané thāngnavå one who built the mud-house as a shelter for the *okka*
mantapa ornamental pavilion
manthra magical incantation
mara wood or tree
mara airi *āchāri*
marathra bōti wooden post
marathra kupp wooden slat tiles
masaṇa cemetery (Kannaḍa)
masi black soot from burnt hay
masṇi cemetery where a married daughter of the *okka* is buried/cremated if she dies in her natal home
masṇi kāḍ forest where the *masṇi* is located
matha monastery
māvå maternal uncle
meedi daily or periodic ritual offering of food to the *kāraṇavå*
meedi kòmbaré *kanni kòmbaré*
mēypa kott shed where paddy is pounded and dehusked manually to make rice; *ora kott*
mlēcha foreigner (Kannaḍa)
mòga sacred mask of a deity used during ritual performances
mooḍu seeme eastern region (Kannaḍa)
moond three
muchă Nilgiri langur, a native species of black monkey with a long tail
muḍi tall headdress made with a framework of cane, worn by the person possessed by a deity

muḍipu cloth bundle in which money promised to God Venkataramaṇa in fulfilment of vows is kept (Kannaḍa)
mūḍiya girls
mukkāli low, three-legged wooden stool
mūla nivāsi earliest inhabitant
mūlé corner
mūlé anchi corner tiles
mummaḍakanḍōṇi lane with three bends
mund sunken inner courtyard open to the sky
mund mané house with sunken inner courtyard open to the sky; *nāl kĕtt mané*
munḍé a kind of wild plant, *Pandanus odaratissimus*
munn ahead
muri bāḍé *aḍchi bāḍé*
muri keethuvă tearing a piece of cloth
mūrtha important ritual during a *mangala*, when the bride/groom/person being honoured is blessed by all those assembled
mūrthi spirit-deity

N

nāḍ administrative unit which consists of a group of villages
nāḍ kōl *kōl* dance performed at the *nāḍ* level
nāḍ mand open space set apart for sports, dances and social gatherings at the *nāḍ* level
nāḍé kākuvă traditional recitation of humorous stories during *Puthari*
nāga sthāna platform on which a stone symbolising the snake god is embedded
nāl four
nāl kĕtt mané *mund mané*
nālkāli four-legged high wooden stool
nara bali human sacrifice
nari mangala ceremony to honour one who has killed a tiger
nāt vaidya native medicinal practice
nāti pāt songs sung when transplanting paddy; *uyya pāt*
nāyakă administrative chief
nélé sacred platform dedicated to a deity; *sthāna*
nḗlé *bédaké*
nellakki bolcha sacred lamp in the central hall
nellakki naḍu bāḍé central hall
néré three kinds of leaves rolled together and tied with a length of a creeper—for a *Puthari* ritual
nérké bamboo slats
ninda kula clans who settled in the village
nishāni kaḍanga *kaḍanga* demarcating the boundary of a village

O

ōḍ tile
oḍi kathi broad-bladed Koḍava war-knife
ōja red silk scarf used to decorate the gun of a man who shot and killed a tiger; and in the case of a woman, to decorate the coils of her hair
ok one, one bond, unanimity, harmony
okka exogamous patrilineal clan whose members claim descent from a common ancestor
okka parajé tradition where a man marries an unmarried girl or a widow from an *okka* that faces extinction, and carries the *mané péda* of that *okka*
okkaṇe recital of the names of the ten *kutumbas* and eighteen *gothras* of the Gouḍa community
ola inner
ola kayyālé inner verandah
olé hearth
ōṇam harvest festival in Malabār
ondané kula the first *okka* to settle in the village
ōṇi lane
ora kott *mēypa kott*
ṏté reed
othé single
othé poré one-winged house, with a single roof
otti flat unleavened rice bread

P

pāché paṇi	barter of labour
paḍé	war
paḍé beeră	war hero
padi	*hadi*
padi kamba	half column embedded in a wall
paisāri	wasteland
palachi	jackfruit tree
paleya	low wooden stool
pāleyagāră	local chieftain
pāmbāt	dance by men swaying like snakes
pandal	structure with roof supported by pillars, erected in front of a house for a special occasion
pandalāt	dance under a *pandal* by Yerava boys and girls, during death ceremonies
pānḍava paré	megalithic tombs found in Koḍagu
pānḍava slab	rough granite slab
panji	pig or boar (Tulu)
paré	large drum
pariya kali	stylised mock fight during *Puthari* between a pair of men holding shields and canes in their hands, as they dance
pāt	song
pathālōdi	the ten days following the *Kāvēri Sankramaṇa* festival
pathānḍa kūtk pannand	uniting the eleventh (spirit of the recently dead) with the ten (spirits of ancestors who had died earlier)
pathāya	large wooden structure for storing harvested paddy
pāthi	conduit for water
pāthi anchi	small, humped tiles; *pāthi ōḍ*
pāthi ōḍ	*pāthi anchi*
patté	title deed
pattédāră	headman of an *okka*, in whose name the *patté* for the *jamma* land of the *okka* is recorded
pattédārthi	female head of an *okka*
patti	yard in front of the *ainmané*
pāyasa	rice cooked with milk and sugar
peeché kathi	traditional dagger in an ornate scabbard, that is tucked into a Koḍava man's sash
peeli	peacock feathers
peeliyāt	dance by men holding peacock feathers as they dance
peepal	a tree, *Ficus religiosa*
pitāri	*akki pathāya*
poli	shower
polichi pāt	song in praise of the dead
polüd kuthi	container made from hollow bamboo, used during *Puthari*
ponn-airi	goldsmith; *thattă*
pora mané	outhouse
poré	hut or thatched roof
pott kaḍanga	small *kaḍanga*
potti	box
potti mara	wooden shelf fixed to the wall
prasāda	offerings to a deity in a temple
pūjé	ritual worship
puthari	harvest festival
puthari kalanji	a special kind of yam eaten during *Puthari*
puthari kōl	traditional folk dance by men holding canes, performed in the *mand* during *Puthari*
puthari pāt	*Puthari* song

R

rāgi	a cereal, *Eleusine coracana*
rāja	king (refers to the kings of the Hālēri dynasty who ruled Koḍagu c. 1600 to 1834)
rūpa	image

S

sāgu	land for cultivation
samādhi	tomb
sanad	title deed
sankramaṇa	first day of a month in the traditional calendar in Koḍagu, when the sun passes from one zodiac sign to the next one
sanyāsi	ascetic; religious mendicant

sathya pramāṇa	swearing to the truth of a statement
seemé	*dēsha*
seemé thakkă	*dēsha thakkă*
seer	unit of volumetric measurement
shivarāthri	Hindu festival in honour of God Shiva
smashāna	cemetery
sōbāne	songs sung during Gouḍa wedding rituals (Kannaḍa)
sthāna	*nélé*
subrahmaṇya shashti	Hindu festival dedicated to God Subrahmaṇya
suggi kuṇitha	harvest dance by Yeravas and Kurubas (Kannaḍa)

T

thachāyiri	*airi*
thaḍamb	processional image of a deity
thadbhava	form of a word derived from Sanskrit or any other language
thakk	language
thakka	*okka* with a *thakkāmé*
thakkă	headman of the *okka* with a *thakkāmé*
thakkāmé	hereditary leadership role over an *ūr*, *nāḍ* or shrine held by an *okka*, with specific responsibilities and ceremonial duties; literally 'the right to speak for'
thāli	pendant worn by Hindu women, symbolising their married status
thāli pāt	*jōyi pāt*
thaliya	plate
thaliyathakki bolcha	oil lamp lit with wicks, placed on top of rice spread on a bell-metal plate
thaliyathāt	dance by women holding bell-metal plates with lit oil lamps placed on them
thāmané	a girl's natal *okka*
thāmané mūḍiya	daughters of the *okka* who are married out
thambuttŭ	dish made by kneading roasted rice flour and ripe bananas
thanḍ	staff
thāngi ninda kula	clans who settled in the village
thanthra	mystic rites for the worship of God Shiva
thanthri	one versed in mystic rites for the worship of God Shiva
tharavāḍ	ancestral home of Nāirs and Namboodris in Kērala (Malayālam)
thattă	*ponn-airi*
thāyi mané	original house (literally, mother house)
thāyi théré	performance ritual in honour of a female ancestor
theertha	sacred water
therang	slide
therangĭḍiké	window with a sliding shutter
théré	*kȍla*
therigé	tribute; a family's turn to conduct a ceremony or festival in an *okka*
thethi	*eriya*
thiri thōk	flintlock gun lit with wicks
thoḍang	clasp for the war-knife
thōk	gun
thōk mara	*nḗlé* used to hang guns
thombakké	bud of a banana plant
thombé	heart
thombé kaṇṇ	hole in the outer wall of an *ainmané*
thȍra	a kind of plant, *Polygonum chinense*
thott	cradle
thotti	trough (Kannaḍa)
thotti mane	ancestral home with a sunken inner courtyard (Kannaḍa)
thrishūla	trident
thūḍ	flammable torch
thūk	hang
thūk bolcha	ornate brass hanging lamp
thulā sankramaṇa	first day of Libra
thuliya	large, standing, open, cylindrical structure of cane and reed, used for storing paddy; *thuyya*
thūtĕngala	cremation ground of the *okka*
thuyya	*thuliya*

U

ubba	gate consisting of a pair of stone posts, and bamboo poles that slide through matching holes in the posts
uḍumb	iguana

umbala kṑmbaré	dining room/kitchen; *umbala mané*
umbala mané	*umbala kṑmbaré*
umbali	non-transferable wetland given to an individual for valuable services rendered to the king, assessed at a fraction of the regular rate
ummathāt	graceful dance by women, striking cymbals as they dance
upp	salt
upp pathāya	large wooden container for storing salt
ūr	village
ūr guppé	village settlement
ur kutt	rounded piece of wood; *urït kutt*
ūr mand	open space in the village set apart for sports, dances and social gatherings
ūr thakkă	village headman
urït kutt	*ur kutt*
ūrormé	get-together of villagers for a feast in the *ūr mand*
uthuvă	untying
uyya pāt	*nāti pāt*
V	
vāhana	mount
vāra	lease of agricultural land for a share of the produce in lieu of rent
vasāra	extension to a house
vasthra	long veil worn around the forehead by Koḍava women and tied back at the nape of the neck
veera	hero (Kannaḍa)
veera kall	*beeră kall*
vṑlaga	music with horns, pipes and drums played by a band
vṑlagathāt	freestyle dance to *vṓlaga* music
Y	
yāla malé	hills on the slopes of which cardamom is grown
yeravāt	dance by Yerava men and women swaying to the beat of *duḍis*
yugādi	new year's day according to the Hindu lunar calendar

COMMUNITY NAMES:

Airi
Amma
Balegāra/Telugu Baṇajiga
Baṇṇa
Bāṇya/Gāṇiga
Betta Kuruba
Brahmin
Buṇé Patta/Beene Patta/Cheeni Patta
Bunt
Christian
Dēvānga
Golla/Aimbokka
Gouḍa
Hajāma/Nāyinda
Hālu Kuruba
Heggaḍé
Jāgir Thurka
Jaina
Jamma Māpillé
Jamma Marāthi
Jēnu Kuruba
Kaṇiya
Kāpala
Kembatti
Koḍava
Koḍava Nāir
Kōleya
Kōmati
Kȍyava
Kuḍiya
Kumbāra
Lingāyath (Veerashaiva)
Madivāla
Maléya
Mārangi
Mḗda
Mòplah/Māpillé
Okkaliga Gouḍa
Pāléya
Paṇika
Poomalé Kuḍiya
Shivachāliya
Thēmalé Kuḍiya
Yerava

ACKNOWLEDGEMENTS

First and foremost, our sincere thanks to the men and women in the *ainmanes* for their warm welcome, and for giving us their time during our fieldwork. Without their co-operation, this project would have remained unfulfilled.

Our affectionate gratitude to

Nadikerianda Ganga and Chinnappa for their cottage in Karada, our hub during the fieldwork; Boverianda Chondu and Cariappa whose house in Virajpet was our home during many field trips; and friends and relatives, who invited us to their homes during our fieldwork—Nadikerianda Swathi and Mandanna (Suntikoppa), Ajjamada Seetha and Nachappa (Guyya), Mookachanda Devaki Aiyappa (Mayamudi), Biddanda Juby and Chinnappa (Kargunda), Cheppudira Veena and Appaiah (Kutta), and Dr Iychettira Saraswathy Subbiah (Madikeri).

Boverianda Maya and Muddaiya who joined us on our early field trips.

Kambiranda Kaveri Ponnapa, Geetha Krishnan Kutty, Bacharaniyanda Appanna, Codanda Somiah and Nadikerianda Rana Nanjappa, for their valuable suggestions on the manuscript.

Nadikerianda Ponnappa, for the beautiful cover illustration.

Our sincere thanks to

Ganesh, Satish, Ashraf, Naufal, Nazdeer and Kasim, who drove us on roads, good, bad and non-existent.

Bacharaniyanda Annaiya for his delightful folk paintings, which allowed us to imagine the pictures once painted on the *ainmane* walls.

Mukkatira Belliappa who collected *okka* names at the Kodava Hockey Festival, Napoklu, 2003.

We are deeply indebted to

The Coorg Foundation and its former director, Kakamada Changappa, for funding the fieldwork.

Kalyatanda Nanjappa, Chinshai Technologies, Gonikoppa, for designing and setting up the user-friendly website.

Jayapriya Vasudevan and Priya Doraswamy, Jacaranda Press, for their enthusiasm and help in getting the book published.

Niyogi Books for publishing this book and Sucharita Ghosh for her insightful editing.

INDEX